THE WAR
OF THE
WHITE ROSES

Yorkshire Cricket's Civil War
1968–1986

Stuart Rayner

First published by Pitch Publishing, 2016
Paperback edition, 2018

Pitch Publishing
A2 Yeoman Gate
Yeoman Way
Worthing
Sussex
BN13 3QZ
www.pitchpublishing.co.uk

A CIP catalogue record is available for this book
from the British Library.

ISBN 978-1-78531-407-0

Typesetting and origination by Pitch Publishing

Printed in India by Replika Press

Nominated for the Cricket Writers' Club Book of the Year award

"Chronicles the county's fall from grace after winning seven County Championships between 1959 and 1968 – and the bitter divisions it caused. The book interviews former players, committeemen, supporters and opponents including Boycott and Durham bowling coach Alan Walker, who ran him out during his final innings, in 1986." – **GazetteLive.co.uk**

"The story of a 'civil war' at one of England's most illustrious cricketing counties has been told in a regional daily journalist's new book. Many of the former players, supporters and committeemen Stuart approached for interviews were reluctant, not wanting to rake up the past. Fortunately some, including Boycott himself, were more willing." – **HoldTheFrontPage.co.uk**

"The story of how Yorkshire ripped itself apart between 1968 and 1986. The book ends in 1986 because so did Geoffrey Boycott's career – with a run-out at the Scarborough Cricket Festival that left him eight short of 1,000 First-Class runs for a 24th consecutive season. Whether he liked it or not, Boycott was invariably at the centre of Yorkshire cricket's civil war." – **TheNorthernEcho.co.uk**

"For a glimpse of Yorkshire's old methods of breaking in a player, it's worth looking at Stuart Rayner's excellent new book *The War of the White Roses*." – **Simon Briggs, Sunday Telegraph**

"Fifteen from '16 – the best cricket books of the year. Yorkshire were a shambles in the 1980s, more of a debating society than a cricket club, as an enraged captain of that era, David Bairstow, once observed. An objective and authoritative account of the politicking in Yorkshire's civil war that will serve as a reference for years to come." – **David Hopps, ESPNcricinfo.com**

"Admirably comprehensive and even-handed account of Yorkshire's years of strife. Rayner persuaded enough of those involved in the period to contribute to give his book extra substance, and his assiduous use of source material is apparent on every page." – **ESPNcricinfo.com**

"Rayner has done his homework – this is not just a Boycott-blaming exercise. He follows in depth the travails of a club run by blunt-speaking but finger-worrying men, who made terrible mistakes. 4 stars." – **The Cricketer**

"I read this book with the phrase 'exactly what it says on the tin' ringing in my mind. If the thought of re-visiting the battles that raged around Yorkshire dressing and committee rooms from the final years of Brian Close's captaincy to the retirement of Geoffrey Boycott has the slightest appeal, this book that must be compulsory reading." – **The Cricket Statistician**

Contents

In memory of Mike Bore,
2 June 1947–2 May 2017

Introduction and Acknowledgements

THE *War of the White Roses* had only been published a couple of days, and already it looked like a new chapter might have to be written.

In March 2016, the members of Yorkshire County Cricket Club received a letter from chairman Steve Denison asking them to oppose Geoffrey Boycott's re-election to a board he served between 2007 and 2012. 'Great publicity for your book,' more than one friend told me; but it smacked of an unwelcome re-run of some of the most depressing times in the history of a great cricket club.

If it is not already, the battle between one of Yorkshire County Cricket Club's greatest players and his supporters and the men who ran it will be very familiar to you by the time you have read this book. Sometimes the committee won, sometimes Boycott did, but invariably Yorkshire lost. Too often between 1968 and 1986 politics took precedence over cricket and the club which to this day has won more County Championships than any other rarely seriously competed for another, let alone won any.

Finally that had changed. Yorkshire won back-to-back titles in 2014 and 2015. But as I observe in chapter seven, the club has always had 'an uncanny knack of shooting itself in the foot when things are going well'. The widely-expected hat-trick of Championships eluded them. But in avoiding another draining and damaging bout of civil war, the club showed itself to be a more mature one than the insular, conservative institution described in these pages.

When the postal votes were counted, 758 members heeded Denison's plea to opt for those with the financial experience he felt heavily-indebted Yorkshire needed rather than the vast cricketing expertise Boycott had, but was promising not to bring to bear on a team that was operating rather nicely without it. Only 602 voted for Boycott.

Not only did he accept the decision graciously, so did his supporters. 'The last thing I want is any trouble,' Boycott told the *Yorkshire Post* before the vote. 'I'm 75 years of age. I need trouble like a hole in the head.'

He was just as conciliatory after the club's annual general meeting at Headingley. 'I'm disappointed but nothing's changed,' he said. 'I'll be here for the first match of the season.'

As a Yorkshireman, it was a relief. As the author of *The War of the White Roses* it was vindication.

The introduction to the first edition of this book described 2016 as a 'safe vantage point… from which to look back at the darkest period in [Yorkshire's] history'. Many of the former players, supporters and committeemen I approached for interviews declined because they did not want to rake over the past when things were finally going so well again. Although I totally understood and respected their attitude, I was confident the club could withstand and would benefit from the analysis. One of the most pleasing responses to the book came from the high-ranking club official who told me it had given him a better understanding of the club's history ahead of that 2016 AGM.

Those who do not learn from history are doomed to repeat it, and Yorkshire's habit of self-harm in the good times makes the lessons of *The War of the White Roses* even more important during them. The story told in this book starts in 1968 because the seeds of the discord which ripped a proud club apart were sown in the complacency and hubris inadvertently created by what many believe was its greatest team. Yorkshire are now strong enough and the events distant enough to look back on them objectively.

The War of the White Roses is an attempt to explain what happened in the bad times between 1968 and 1986 which were almost as important in framing the identity of the club as the many glory years preceding them. Other counties could have avoided much of the bitter in-fighting of the 1970s and 80s and settled into a gentle, humdrum existence but quietly making up the numbers is not what Yorkshire cricket stands for.

My aim is not to apportion blame, because I firmly believe almost everything those involved did during this period was in the belief it was the right thing for Yorkshire – even if to others at the time and those of us with the benefit of hindsight it is clear that was not always the case.

My interest in this period was really piqued in December 2013 by a book that had been gathering dust on my shelves for some time. My passion for Yorkshire cricket comes from my mum, but it was my dad who unwittingly set me on the path towards writing *The War of the White Roses* when he bought me a second-hand copy of David Bairstow's diary of Yorkshire's 1984 season.

Finally getting around to reading it made me interested to know more about the political upheaval Bairstow and his team-mates had to contend with.

It soon became apparent there was no definitive book on that period of Yorkshire's history written from a neutral perspective. There were some good ones from the viewpoint of those who, like Bairstow, were heavily (and in his case reluctantly) involved, and wider histories of the club or the game, or biographies of Boycott, which mentioned it. Perhaps it was hubris of my own, but I decided to write that book myself.

Now living outside the county, and having been born in it halfway through the period, gives me a certain distance which I hope makes for a fair account of a divisive period in the club's history. I have been touched by how many people have described it as such.

I would like to thank all those who have helped or encouraged me along the way, from my dad thinking of me when he came across Bairstow's diary in a second-hand bookstall to those who have spoken or written kindly of it after reading it, and too many in between to mention them all. If you were not already, just by reading you have become one of those people.

Special thanks must go to David Warner, widely regarded as the fairest journalist covering Yorkshire at that time, and now a vice-president of the club. The fascinating collection of cuttings he lent me was of great help and I hope to see them again one day in the club museum. The advice offered by David and the *Yorkshire Post*'s excellent cricket correspondent Chris Waters, who wrote the foreword, and many others whose knowledge of Yorkshire County Cricket Club is far greater than mine will ever be has been gratefully received.

Thanks also to Paul Cunningham, Richard Neale and Rachel Wearmouth for reading drafts from their different perspectives and suggesting improvements, Mick Pope of Adelphi Archive and Penny Coleman of *The Gazette* in Middlesbrough for their help in obtaining photographs, and the team at Pitch Publishing for transforming it all into the book you are reading now. I am indebted to my employers, ncjMedia, for allowing me time to finish writing the book, and the staff at the British Library (the Boston Spa and London branches) and those in Leeds, Harrogate, Northallerton and Scarborough who helped as I ploughed through microfilm, microfiche and old newspapers in my research.

While others were understandably reticent, Jack Bond, Geoffrey Boycott, Matthew Caswell, Geoff Cook, Andrew

Dalton, Sidney Fielden, David Hall, George Hepworth, Richard Hutton, Ashley Metcalfe, Martyn Moxon, Chris Old, Kevin Sharp, Jack Simmons, Bryan Stott, Julian Vallance, Alan Walker, Neil Whitaker, Mike Bore, Russell Devy and Ted Lester were kind enough to share their very different experiences of what, for many of them, was a difficult time. I hope I have represented their views fairly. Russell and Ted sadly died during the writing and since publication of the first edition, Mike – a warm and welcoming man who served the club on and off the field for many years – has also passed away. This paperback edition is dedicated to his memory.

I hope you enjoy reading this book as much as I enjoyed writing it.

Foreword by
Chris Waters

THE question I am asked most often in my position as *Yorkshire Post* cricket correspondent is, 'What do you do in the winter?' If I had a pound for every time I'd been asked that by a Yorkshire supporter since joining the paper in 2004, I'd be writing these words from a villa in Barbados. I exaggerate, but the question is pertinent, for what does a *Yorkshire Post* cricket correspondent write about in the winter months? Fortunately, there is plenty of international cricket to monitor, while I am sometimes asked to help out with the football.

Between 1968 and 1986, however, the period covered in *The War of the White Roses*, there would have been no need to pose such a question. What did the *Yorkshire Post* cricket correspondent do in the winter? Why, he simply wrote daily about Yorkshire cricket, just as he did in the summer. Back then, covering Yorkshire was a year-round affair with a football-esque merry-go-round of controversies to chronicle. Thankfully, I was born while the hostilities were in progress, and it was on my predecessors that the often onerous task of trying to keep pace with the madcap developments fell. Not that I have escaped the aftershocks of in-fighting and intrigue. They still rumble to this day with age-old enmities occasionally resurfacing.

It is no secret that the civil war's central figure was Geoffrey Boycott, and that you were either for or against one of the game's greatest and most contentious figures. Many of the club's supporters were for him, and many of his team-mates against, although opinion was – and still is – split.

An example of how deep the wounds are – and how relevant the period remains – was brought home to me in the closing weeks of 2011 when I received a phonecall from an old Yorkshire player. 'Have you heard?' he said in a horrified voice. 'The club has nominated Boycott to be its next president.' I knew all right, for I had already received a handful of similar calls from ex-players, and this chap wasted no time in cutting to the chase. 'What can you do to stop it happening?' he demanded. 'What can you write about Boycott in the *Yorkshire Post*?' I replied that as a non-Yorkshireman with no experience of the troubles, I had nothing against Boycott, who had always been very helpful to me, and that if anyone wanted to express concerns about him becoming president they would have to articulate them on the record, after which I would then give Boycott the right of reply. Predictably, the caller did not want to put his head above the parapet and seemed angry that I would not fire his bullets for him. For the record, Boycott was appointed president – supported by an overwhelming majority of the club's members – and his two-year term was a palpable success.

Like many, I can see that there is good and bad in the former opening batsman, and indeed in many who were prominent during the period in question. But after that phonecall in 2011, I remember reflecting that most of these disagreements pre-date the Falklands War, and that it might be a good idea for everyone to move on – not least for their own sake. Alas, some will never do that, to the extent that the aftershocks will only ever truly die out when the various malcontents also die.

One person who did move on, however, was Fred Trueman, who shattered two decades of silence between himself and

Boycott when the latter was diagnosed with throat cancer. The reconciliation was genuine and inadvertently led to one of the most remarkable days of my journalistic life when Trueman, Boycott, and two other prominent figures in the civil war, Brian Close and Raymond Illingworth, came together for a reunion at a Yorkshire pub in 2005 at Trueman's behest. After reading Stuart Rayner's magnificent book, brimming with integrity and fair dealing, you may find it difficult to believe that such a reunion could have taken place. I sometimes wonder myself if it really happened, and my overriding memory is of thinking it such a shame that these four giants of the game could not have been so cordial with each other all their lives.

Sadness, in fact, is the emotion that perhaps most strongly emerges from these pages. Ultimately, it is a tragic tale of how a great club tore itself apart and sank to the very bottom of English cricket in the process, a tragedy that too often ventures into the realms of macabre comedy due to a cast list of characters disinclined to call a spade a shovel. It has taken a long time for Yorkshire to recapture past glories, but the club is now threatening a period of dominance not seen since the calamitous chain of managerial decisions that triggered the civil war in the first place. The club has ridden some stormy seas since 1968, and although it will always be a hotbed of passionate debate, it has lately got back to doing what it once did best – winning County Championships. Everyone who loves Yorkshire County Cricket Club will at least agree that is a good thing.

1

An Era Ends,
An Error Begins

YORKSHIRE'S third straight County Championship title had not yet been confirmed and already their secretary, John Nash, was getting big ideas. 'I hope that the team now equal or beat Surrey's feat in winning the Championship in seven successive seasons,' he told the *Yorkshire Post*.

Four days earlier the White Rose County had finished their 1968 campaign by beating the team of the 1950s, Surrey, live on Yorkshire Television with five minutes to spare. While they wound their season down at the Scarborough Cricket Festival, Kent and Glamorgan still had two matches each to try to overhaul them; the last against one another. They needed more bonus points from each than any county had won all season. The headline above Nash's quotes said it all, 'All over bar the shouting'. Yorkshire won the title by 14 points.

Never mind four Championships in the next four seasons, Yorkshire would have to wait until the following millennium to get their hands on English domestic cricket's most prestigious trophy again. In 1968 such a barren spell would have been unthinkable but the county's complacency was one of many contributing factors. Nothing summed it up better than the dismissive response of cricket chairman Brian Sellers when Raymond Illingworth asked for the same treatment other counties gave their players, 'Let him go then, and he can take any other bugger who feels the same way.' The modern-day Yorkshire County Cricket Club, poles apart from the dysfunctional committee-run institution described in this book, is finally returning to its former glories but the sadness is it has taken nearly half a century and so much wasted talent. The civil war whose roots lie in the glory of 1968 ripped the club apart for decades.

The county's passion for its 'national' sport can be a strength and a weakness, making the highs higher and the lows lower. Between 1968 and 1986 it too often brought the worst out of the club, its players and supporters. 'It was like a serial war,' admits Bryan Stott, who opened the batting for Yorkshire from 1952 to 1963 and served on the committee between 1982 and 1993. '[It was] very, very upsetting when you knew how good it could be for the players. I feel really sorry for the lads that had to play cricket for us at that time. You need all the support you can get when you play for Yorkshire because you've got some super-critical spectators. If they think you're an idiot, they tell you you're an idiot. It was such a disappointing time because the outcome could have been so different.'

Cricketers who had spent their lives dreaming of playing for or captaining Yorkshire would end up wishing they never had. Promising careers ended prematurely, huge amounts of potential went unfulfilled. What ought to have been a game played for fun turned into a job that made lives a misery, and not only for those directly involved. Wives and children were abused and friendships broken off; team-mates became enemies and fans turned on one another. Tens of thousands of pounds that could have been spent on cricket were frittered away in an attempt to settle old scores but all it did was widen divisions and enrich lawyers. If it was a war – and at times that word was not as far-fetched as it ought to have been – it was often war by proxies. Many of the flashpoints were laughably childish, some illegal, from colleagues refusing to speak to one another or sabotaging their team's chances of winning to secretly-taped conversations and obscene phonecalls. A committee loaded with experience of playing first-class cricket was swept aside by a group of supporters with none, only for some of the key figures to switch sides and launch a counter-revolution. One player rose above it with a metronomic consistency that at its best was world-class, yet Geoffrey Boycott was as passionately hated by some who were supposed to be on his side as he was loved by others. It was a period so extraordinary it could probably never be repeated, but however uncomfortable they can be at times, its stories need to be told to ensure it is not.

Even in the good times in-fighting was part of Yorkshire cricketing life but in 1968 so was winning trophies. The 1968 title was their sixth of the 1960s, taking them to 29 outright (plus one shared with Middlesex in 1949). Nearly 50 years on, Surrey's 18 is the closest any rival has got. It was not just the other counties they bested, even the Australians were beaten – by an innings and 69 runs. England needed five attempts to defeat the tourists in the 1968 Ashes, and the Australians came to Bramall Lane in July 1-0 up after two Tests. 'Yorkshire, in the field, looked an infinitely better team than the England Test one,' *Wisden* opined. 'From 1963 onwards they were probably the strongest collective unit the Championship has had,' Stott argues.

'Individually the team of the 1960s wasn't as good as the team of the 1950s, nor probably the 1920s or the 1930s, but it had that special all-for-one-one-for-all approach that probably set it apart,' explains Richard Hutton, who made his debut in 1962, following in the footsteps of his father Len, who played from 1934–55. At first glance, Nash's optimism that

Yorkshire's dominance could extend into the 1970s seemed well founded. For the first time in the club's history they had done a Championship double – Bob Platt's second XI winning the Minor Counties title without losing a game. 'We were far superior,' argued left-arm seamer Mike Bore, who took 39 wickets in 11 matches that season.

Not everyone, though, saw as rosy a picture. As the *Yorkshire Post*'s cricket correspondent since 1934, Jim Kilburn placed the bar high when judging the county's cricket team. 'Jim used to set his standard on Leonard [Hutton] as a batsman and Bill Bowes as a bowler,' explains Stott. 'If you didn't come up to that standard, you might just get a mention that you were in that team. If you came above that standard, you would get a mention because Jim thought you were good enough. It was accepted because Jim had seen the Yorkshire team play at that level. It was a wonderful yardstick.' Kilburn was unimpressed by what he saw in 1968. 'When the definitive history of Yorkshire cricket comes to be written the season of 1968 is not likely to form an outstanding chapter,' began his review of the campaign. 'The overall impression will be of a year without exceptional satisfaction.' He added, witheringly, 'In day-by-day, week-in, week-out performances they suggested competence, adequacy for general purposes rather than greatness.' This was essentially the team rebuilt in the late 1950s reaching the end of its natural cycle. Its average age was nearly 32 and the public, as well as the committee, were eager for fresh faces.

What Kilburn also recognised, and Nash possibly did not, was that in 1968 even the staid world of cricket was changing. In true Yorkshire style, the county's cricket club stubbornly refused to change with it. Bore recalled Fred Trueman leading 'a bit of a revolt' when the club brought in athletics coach Alan Whitehead to work on the players' sprinting skills. In 1968 bonus points were introduced for batting and bowling in an ongoing crusade to promote 'brighter cricket' and give something to play for when the British weather made draws inevitable. Even though they had earned them the 1968 pennant – second-placed Kent won one more game – Yorkshire nevertheless looked down their noses at bonus points, seemingly regarding the very idea of trying to gain them as undignified. Limited-overs cricket, another modern development many in the county disparaged, was starting to take hold and in 1970 pitches were covered, tipping the balance from bowlers to batsmen and changing the skills both required.

Most significantly for Yorkshire, 1968 was the first year counties were allowed to employ overseas professionals. Not only did they stand alone in refusing to, it would be another 23 years before they even permitted anyone born outside their borders to represent them. It was Yorkshire officialdom to a tee – unashamed pride and a stubborn refusal to move with the times mixed with an arrogant belief that those spawned within their boundaries made up some sort of cricketing master race. Expectant mothers would often not be allowed out of the county without some contingency to rush them back if they went into labour early. To those from further afield or not interested in cricket it might have seemed faintly ridiculous, but to the parents denying their son his birthright would have been more ludicrous.

Until the policy was relaxed in 1991, only 29 exceptions were made. Geoffrey Keighley – born in the south of France but, like his surname, of West Riding stock – was the only one after World War Two, and one of only four to play more than 20 games. Ironically, Yorkshire cricket's most dominant figure, Lord Martin Hawke, had been born prematurely in Willingham by Stow in Lincolnshire rather than the baronial seat at Wighill Park near Tadcaster. He, his 1911 successor as captain, Tiverton-born Everard Radcliffe, Capt. Ronald Stanyforth and William Harbord were given special dispensation because they were amateurs. Ces Parkin was making his debut in 1906 when it was discovered he was born 20 yards outside Yorkshire, in Eaglescliffe, County Durham.

He never played for the county again. He was unlucky. It took 30 years until William Blackburn was found to have been born not in Sawley, but Clitheroe. In 1964, legendary West Indian all-rounder Garfield Sobers played for Yorkshire on the Bermuda leg of a post-season tour which also took in Canada and the United States of America but there was no question of the county budging when it came to competitive cricket, so in 1968 he joined Nottinghamshire. While Yorkshire were not prepared to look 20 yards away, their 16 first-class rivals could go anywhere on the globe in search of talent. In 1971, 43 overseas professionals played county cricket.

Fortunately for Yorkshire, in the 1960s they had world-class players of their own, not least 't'greatest fast bowler who ever lived' as Trueman liked to call himself. By 1968, however, he was having to face up to being simply t'greatest bowler who ever lived. *Wisden*'s report of his debut at Cambridge University in 1949 would go on to be a standing joke. The bible of cricket described him as 'an off-spinner' despite taking his maiden wicket with a bouncer fended to short leg. Trueman's pace was as much a matter of personal pride as his wicket tally, but by 1968 time was catching up with him. Perhaps but perhaps not tongue in cheek, Brian Close suggested it was the bowler's doing that towards the end of his career *Wisden* incorrectly recorded Trueman as being born in 1932, not 1931. He was still as skilful as ever but increasingly more reliant on his force of personality and sharp cricketing brain than the even sharper pace of years gone by.

One thing that never left Trueman was his charisma. Chris Old encountered it as soon as he walked into a Yorkshire changing room, at Bramall Lane in 1966. 'There was nobody there,' Old, Yorkshire's 12th man that day, recalls. 'All the pegs were filled. There was a newspaper in the corner with a pair of feet coming out of the bottom and the odd puff of smoke coming from it. I put my bag down quite loudly and Fred Trueman lowered the paper and said, "Who the bloody hell are you?"

When I explained he said, "They're all over at the nets. There's a bloke called Boycott there, you go bowl at him because I'm not!" That was my introduction to a Yorkshire dressing room.'

At Middlesbrough in May 1968, Yorkshire dropped Trueman. His brushes with authority and habit for cutting it fine or even turning up late for matches had cost him his place before, but it was the first time since his junior days he had been left out for cricketing reasons. The 37-year-old's place was taken by Old, a fraction over half his age. 'Fred was getting tired,' explains Stott. Richard Hutton, a team-mate and lifelong admirer, puts it more bluntly, 'I think he realised with his bowling he was a busted flush.' Trueman was only seventh in Yorkshire's 1968 bowling averages, 32nd nationally. What hurt him most about being dropped was that it was the opposition captain, Warwickshire's Alan Smith, not Close who broke the news to him. Throughout his life Trueman's relationship with authority was rarely comfortable. It is the main reason why, despite being the first bowler to 300 Test wickets, he only played in 67 of the 120 matches between his England debut and final appearance. The chips he had on either shoulder sat as uneasily with the men from Marylebone Cricket Club who ran the game as his willingness to speak his mind, and they were small-minded enough let it to influence their team selections.

Yorkshire had been just as good at making Trueman feel under-appreciated. In 1951 he was only awarded his county cap, a symbol he was now a *bona fide* first-team player with a pay rise to boot, the Monday after asking captain Norman Yardley for it in light of interest from Lancashire, Sussex and Surrey. When Yorkshire, the only first-class county not to send him a congratulatory telegram after taking 250 Test wickets, presented him with a silver tea service to mark his 300th – then unprecedented – he asked them to take it back and inscribe it. These things rankled with Trueman. In 1967 the county aggravated him further.

After 20 years' service the bowler had qualified for a second benefit year, reward for his loyalty which would help set him up for retirement. Yorkshire had annoyed Trueman by delaying his first by a couple of years because others were ahead of him in the queue, and he missed out on a second when Ken Taylor was chosen instead for 1968. Close's suggestion of a £1,000 thank-you – a fraction of what Trueman would have earned in a benefit – was also rejected. Being left out at Acklam Park and having to face up to life as 'only' a fast-medium bowler pushed him to the edge. Trueman wanted to bow out in style before he was cynically pushed aside like so many past Yorkshire heroes. 'I do not want to play as a second-rater and would rather go now than remain on sufferance,' he wrote when announcing his retirement. First, though, he had to magic up a high to bow out on.

'I've always said the win over Australia was Fred's greatest moment in the whole of his illustrious career,' says Hutton. 'He led us to not only a win, but a win by an innings. I took the new ball with Fred and in my first over of the second innings I yorked Bill Lawry, which caused Fred a huge amount of joy because Lawry had scored [58] runs in the first. Fred, I think, saw him as a thorn in our side and he didn't particularly like bowling at left-handers, so his relief and joy when I got rid of him in the first over was unbounded. Some 25 years later I was somewhat galled to see the *Daily Telegraph*, who were doing flashbacks to great sporting moments. Fred was quoted *ad infinitum*. At one point he said, "I knew as soon as I got rid of Bill Lawry, we were through 'em." I very hastily put pen and paper together. It was typical of Fred to grab the credit!'

Trueman called the win, only Yorkshire's second against the Australians, 'One of the greatest days of my life,' demonstrating inspirational leadership, brilliant fielding and shrewd captaincy deputising for the injured Close. Trueman pressed for a declaration half an hour before lunch, then took six wickets in the match (Hutton claimed four and Illingworth eight) and some brilliant catches including a one-handed effort to remove Doug Walters as the Australians were bowled out twice. He even ran Ian Chappell out from extra cover. It just highlighted to Trueman what he had known all along – he was cut out for this captaincy lark. Yorkshire won four and drew the other three matches he took charge of in 1968. In all he led his county 31 times, winning 16 and losing four.

Having ended the season a champion, in November Trueman informed Yorkshire's president Sir William Worsley he was retiring. Worsley tried to talk him out of it, arguing Trueman had plenty of good years left in him – two, the player reckoned – adding, 'We're holding a meeting next week and there's every likelihood you will be offered the captaincy.' It was the first Trueman had heard of it. As far as he was concerned, 'It is more coveted than the captaincy of England!'

The offer had come too late. Trueman wrote a column for the *Sunday People*, and not for the last time it would be a fly in Yorkshire's ointment. As Trueman spoke to Worsley that Saturday, the early editions were coming off the presses bearing exclusive news of his retirement.

The committee decided to give the club's greatest fast bowler a farewell present of his choosing. Trueman picked a Charles II silver cruet set and Yorkshire bought it for £220, but informed him they had only set aside £100, and he would have to pay the difference. 'There was no ceremony,' Trueman recalled in his autobiography. 'No drinks in the committee room prior to being officially presented with the gift. A committeeman simply handed it over to me one day when I was at Headingley. When I got home and took the cruet set out of the box, I discovered they'd not had it inscribed.'

Yorkshire had seen countless outstanding players retire only for someone to emerge in their place. In 1968 they were confident it would happen again. 'I was the new Fred Trueman!' exclaims Old, approaching his 20th birthday when the news broke. 'He was 5ft 10in, as wide as he was tall, and there was me 6ft 3in and like a pencil, so we looked exactly alike! Fred's was always regarded as a superb bowling action, mine was always regarded as a good bowling action, so it was a natural thing that I was exactly like Fred but I was totally different. One of Fred's comments was that I was the only person who had to run around in the shower to get wet. I think I was 12 stone wet through. Towards the best years of my career I'd be two-and-a-half to three stone heavier because the muscles had grown, the strength was there.

'In my first couple of games I was seen as a batsman who bowled but I could see that Fred was going to retire and I looked around at who the opposition were as quicker bowlers to take his place. That seemed to be the area in which I could get into the side quickly and the batting would help. But I couldn't bowl the overs Fred had. I bowled well for a certain length of time, but towards the end of the day it was a struggle. I hate to admit it in a way but before I started playing I was more a fan of [Lancashire's] Brian Statham than Fred Trueman. I didn't see the point of running up 25, 30 yards every ball and watching the batsman pick the bat up and watch it go past, whereas with Statham they had to play every ball. That was the type of bowler I wanted to be.'

Had Trueman been the only departure, Old and Co. might well have muddled through. Ken Taylor, a talented artist and former professional footballer, also retired at the end of the season, aged 33. 'It was Ken's time,' says Stott. Only three Championship centuries in the previous seven seasons made Taylor's runs replaceable but with three Test caps and 12,864 runs for Yorkshire his departure further diluted the pool of dressing-room experience. By far the biggest loss was Ray Illingworth's, and again Yorkshire intransigence was to blame for one of the most disastrous mistakes in the club's 150-plus years.

By 1968 Yorkshire were the only first-class county who refused to give their players contracts, only match fees under an annual gentleman's agreement which, bizarrely, ended during the season, on 31 July. Not only did their players lack security, their pay did not reflect the fact they played for the country's best team even at a time when wages across the sport were low. The committee which ran the club regarded playing for Yorkshire as a privilege and exploited the fact most players saw it the same way. In 1968, Illingworth was hoping for a little better. Converted from a medium-pacer to an off-spinner by former Yorkshire bowler Bill Bowes, Illingworth turned himself into a very good batsman, bowler and fielder, but it was as a thinker on the game that he was one of the all-time greats. He had always been aware of his value, Yorkshire forever complacent about it. Like Trueman, Illingworth had only got his cap by threatening to leave – in his case in 1955 – and by 1968, aged 36 with 30 England caps, and a wife and two daughters to think of, it was security more than money he was seeking. The trouble was, he was up against the man he called the 'King of Yorkshire Cricket'.

The uncompromising Brian Sellers became Yorkshire's vice-captain for 1932 but thanks to Frank Greenwood's business commitments he led the side in 29 matches that year. Yorkshire did not lose any. It was no surprise when the cricket committee headed by his father, former player Arthur Sellers Snr, gave him the top job for the following season. Sellers oversaw six Championship titles between 1933 and 1948, joining the club's general committee in 1946. In 1959 he became chairman of the cricket sub-committee, cautioning it would take three years to overturn Surrey's dominance and win back the title. They did it that season. Ted Lester played for Yorkshire from 1945 to 1956 and had a spell as second-team captain before becoming scorer in 1962 until 1988. 'The side just before the war was very dependent on Brian Sellers, who was not a great cricketer but a magnificent leader of men,' he told me when I spoke to him before his death in 2015. 'When Sellers captained the side there was only one person in charge

– "You do what I say!" If you didn't, you were on your bike. It was a hard game playing under Brian Sellers, but he got the best out of everybody.'

In whatever role he held, Sellers was always passionately devoted to bringing Yorkshire success, and there was no let-up in the sergeant major approach when he swapped the dressing room for the committee room. 'Sellers wasn't called "Crackerjack" for nothing,' points out Richard Hutton. 'He could be very crude. When I was having a particularly bad spell he hauled me up and I remember him saying to me, "You call yourself a quick bowler? A quick bowler needs three things – length, pace and direction. You've got bugger all!" That didn't leave my soul with much hope.

'In a [1964] match at Portsmouth in which I got five wickets in one innings and we won the match, the heel fell off my boot as I was bowling and I finished the job in borrowed boots. When we got back to Headingley the next day Sellers hauled me into the office and said, "I hear you had to borrow a pair of boots? As a quick bowler you should always be travelling with two pairs of boots." I found it hard to afford one! Not a word of congratulation about the wickets and winning the match, but a bollocking for not having a back-up pair of boots! That's how it was. There was a fear element. If you were in the field and Sellers suddenly appeared on the ground the word would go round and we went up a couple of notches, licking the palms of our hands, to show how keen we were.'

In 1963 with Close, Trueman and Phil Sharpe playing for England against West Indies, Illingworth captained Yorkshire four times, winning two matches comprehensively and drawing one. So far down the pecking order and in demand with England himself, five years on he had not taken charge again. The idea of challenging himself as captain was tempting, and he was aware other counties were prepared to offer that opportunity as well as a contract. Perhaps as a result of Sellers's brutally autocratic style, Illingworth was also surprisingly insecure.

'Geoff Cope was Illingworth's replacement when he was away with England and in that season Geoff finished at the top of the national [bowling] averages,' Hutton explains. 'From the bowling point of view it felt as if we'd never been without Illingworth. I think Illingworth felt as if his future might be in jeopardy, which was a strange thing for him to feel because he was almost a regular in the England side and a vital part of Yorkshire's machinery. But he insisted on a contract and was told by the committee, "We don't give contracts and you can either take it or leave it." So he left it. Presumably Yorkshire wanted to keep the situation as flexible as possible to get rid of players who weren't pulling their weight because there would be such a queue of other players waiting to get into the team. There were so many cricketers being produced by Yorkshire at the time that they could virtually populate the whole of the Leicestershire team! The future crops weren't quite as effective, as it turned out.'

As the starting point of a negotiation he hoped would end in a two-year contract, Illingworth asked for three. He was confident he could perform for that long but, having done some coaching alongside Arthur Mitchell, reasoned if he lost his place he could contribute off the field for the remainder. 'He thought he'd got several of the other players to agree with him but when it came to it nobody backed him up!' says Old. There were no negotiations. Sellers refused to yield to what a club statement laughably referred to as 'a pistol at the head'. At Bradford Park Avenue in August Illingworth handed in his letter of resignation and waited to hear what the committee would make of it at their next meeting. He had good reason to believe they might be sympathetic, but the matter never got that far thanks to Sellers. Illingworth reckoned it was a quarter of an hour after he handed in the letter that Bill Bowes, covering the team for the *Yorkshire Evening Post,* informed the spinner he had been asked to speak to him on behalf of the press about his departure. Illingworth's sympathetic team-mates, led by their captain Close, tried to persuade him not to go. He had hoped it would not come to this but was no more willing to back down than Sellers. Illingworth joined Leicestershire as captain and doubled his wages.

The man earmarked as Illingworth's successor was not the safe bet Yorkshire hoped. Cope would play 267 times in all competitions but in difficult circumstance he was unable to meet the lofty standards of the man he replaced. The off-spinner won three England Test caps (and two in one-day internationals) in 1977/78 but in terms of his bowling average, 1967 (when he finished second nationally) and 1968 would be the best seasons of his first-class career. Even before Illingworth left, rumours were circulating that Cope illegally bent his arm when sending down his quicker delivery. The accusation would blight and, when it re-emerged after bans in 1972 and 1978, end his career. While Cope floundered slightly, Illingworth flourished. Less than 12 months after being fourth in line for the Yorkshire captaincy, he was England skipper. In 1970/71 he led the first England side to regain the Ashes in Australia for nearly 40 years. In 1972 he guided Leicestershire to their first major silverware, in 1975 their maiden Championship. In his ten seasons as captain Leicestershire, a county with no history to speak of when it came to winning trophies, claimed five. Illingworth's personal success mirrored Yorkshire's decline – and for what? By the time he picked up his first silverware with Leicestershire, Yorkshire players were on contracts anyway.

'Illy was such a great mentor,' says Hutton ruefully. 'With hindsight the situation could have been so easily avoided and that would have made a tremendous difference. Without that there would not have been all this nonsense that followed.' Even the club's official history called the decision, 'A total catastrophe, a move that cost Yorkshire more dearly then almost any other.' Sellers's intransigence had sown the seeds for decades of decline.

2

'You've Had A Good Innings'

A S Yorkshire closed in on a third County Championship in as many years, Brian Close gave his team a speech so extraordinary that Richard Hutton can still remember it nearly half a century on. 'We were having an exceptional run and it happened to coincide with a period of injury for Brian Close,' the former all-rounder recalls. 'Fred [Trueman] took over the captaincy and we had a remarkable run of success. Fred seemed to get a new lease of life. I think he was touting to become the official captain for the following season. It got to such a pitch that I remember Brian Close, still injured, coming into the dressing room at Park Avenue, Bradford. He sat us down and felt compelled to inform us that he was still the captain of Yorkshire.'

If the third most successful captain in the county's history came across as a little paranoid in 1968, he had good cause to be. Trueman had started his seven-match run as Close's understudy with 5-45 in an innings-and-56-run hammering of Yorkshire's great rivals Lancashire at Headingley, then followed it with 6-20 as Leicestershire were crushed by 143 runs. The White Rose County claimed four big wins and two draws, and the deputy skipper led the way with 27 wickets at an average of 14.74.

As Trueman's end-of-season discussions with president Sir William Worsley and cricket chairman Brian Sellers would show, it had not gone unnoticed at a time when the knives were out for Close on the committee. After telling Worsley of his retirement plans in November, Trueman's next port of call was the cricket chairman. According to Trueman, Sellers told him he had helped the Yorkshire committee out of a difficult situation.

Like Trueman, Close was no stranger to controversy. He thought he detected his vice-captain's hand when dragged into yet another argument earlier that year. Each season Yorkshire supporter Betty O'Neill sent £5 to the ground hosting their opening match to buy everyone a drink. In 1968 the cheque did not arrive in Harrogate until after Yorkshire decamped. Many detours later it eventually reached Close's home on 19 June. That day the cricket committee had called Close in to tell him the senior players were unhappy with his captaincy and believed he was too wrapped up in his love of horse racing.

Mike Bore was just starting his professional career when he first came across his captain's other great love. 'Closey introduced me to the players then gave me a £10 note,' he told me when I spoke to him before his death in May 2017. 'He said, "I understand you're 12th man today." I said, "Yes I am, captain." He said, "Have you ever backed a horse?" I said, "Never," so he said, "Here's your first time to practise. I want you to put this £10 on this horse, then come back to the ground and if they've accepted it [the bet], just stand on the balcony and put your thumb up." At lunchtime he said, "The horse runs at half past two, so at three o'clock, go back and see if it's won and if it has put your thumb up."

'It won at 50-1. He said, "You know, I might be using you a bit more as 12th man!" He gave me £20 – a month's wages –

and told me not to tell anybody. He said if anybody asks where you've been just say you were doing a job for the captain, and I'll deal with it.'

Taking the 12th man away from his duties to run an errand at the bookies seems a legitimate example of Close's passion for horse racing conflicting with his job but as far as Bore was concerned, it was only a problem when he was behind the wheel of a car. 'I've seen it with Clive Rice at Notts,' explained the former bowler, who moved to Trent Bridge in 1979. 'He used to bat at number four, [Derek] Randall at three. Randall, it was like he was on a hot tin roof. He'd be up, down, "Oh look at that! Oh God, look how fast he is, he's just bowled an enormous bouncer!" Rice would be leaning back on the changing room bench reading this thick Wilbur Smith book, turning the pages and looking up at the cricket every now and then but never interested in what Derek was saying, then he'd bat as though he was as fresh as anything.

'With Closey it was the racing that took the pressure off him. But you were told by the other players if Closey asked you to drive him, don't. He'd always end up wanting to drive and he was the worst driver in the world. He'd be sat at the wheel reading a *Racing Post* with a flask and a fag on. When he came to roundabouts he wouldn't go around, he went across! When the end of the game came you rushed to get ready because if you were last you'd be caught with him.'

As far as Close was concerned, any complaints about his leadership could only have come from his vice-captain and he became convinced Trueman was plotting against him. Most Yorkshire players tried their best to avoid committeemen wherever possible but Close's injury brought the fast bowler into regular contact with them.

More damaging than any concerns about horses or captaincy was the accusation he 'misappropriated' Mrs O'Neill's money. When an angry Close took the cheque, still in its oft-redirected envelope, out of his pocket and threw it at the committeemen his story was accepted, but without apology. Relations had become so strained Close told Sellers either he or his star bowler would have to leave. Trueman's retirement settled that, but Close was on borrowed time.

In June 1968 Close was in his sixth season as captain, and had already won three titles and a Gillette Cup with one more of each to come. His aggressive, sometimes unfathomable tactics were as legendary as his bravery. 'You'd look at his field placings and think, "What the hell has he put him there for?"' Bore told me. A gregarious character who liked a smoke, a round of golf (left- or right-handed, it did not matter he was so talented) and a gamble – whether on the horses or to try and conjure a wicket – he managed to be as strong a leader as many of his predecessors yet far more popular with his team-mates.

Close batted, bowled spin and seam, and was often found fielding in positions that were downright dangerous in an era of no helmets and rolled-up newspapers as shin pads, so anything he asked his players to do was nothing he would not. 'Within the team there were often little arguments but there was never any problem with Brian's captaincy, however hot-headed he might have been at times,' says Hutton. 'Whatever was said to him by players, he never bore any malice against them.' His stock in the committee rooms – even Yorkshire's – had long been much lower.

'In November of 1959 Brian Sellers invited Ronnie Burnet [then Yorkshire's captain] out to lunch,' recalls Close's former team-mate Bryan Stott. 'Brian Sellers said to Ronnie, "You've got to retire." Ronnie said he didn't want to. He'd won the Championship! Brian Sellers said, "Vic [Wilson] is finishing and if we let Vic go, Brian Close will have to skipper the side," and Brian Sellers did not want Close to skipper the side. Brian Sellers thought he wasn't ready and we all thought he was. I don't know why but Brian Sellers had got a blockage on Closey.'

Wilson could no longer get into Yorkshire's first-choice team and was on the verge of retirement when he was made captain for 1960, holding Close back for another three years. He had practically been a back-seat leader under Burnet, but Wilson froze him out until he eventually took over in 1963 and won the title in his first season. Close always had been a fast starter.

Close was 18 when he became first the youngest player capped by England (on making his debut), and only after that Yorkshire (on merit). He had been the youngest to the double of 1,000 runs and 100 first-class wickets in a season, and the only player to do it in his debut campaign. Close blamed his ghost-writer for describing it in his autobiography as 'an albatross round my neck', but it raised expectations that were never met. A groin injury on the 1950/51 tour of Australia put his England career on hold for five years and he repeated the double only once, in 1952. He did not make a Championship century until 1955 and never scored one in a Test match, or a first-class double-hundred. His time in charge of England summed up his brilliant yet still slightly unfulfilled career, winning six of seven Tests before being savagely cut short after another brush with controversy. His crime was gamesmanship in a Championship match.

In August 1967 Close had set Warwickshire 142 to win in one hour and 40 minutes. In that time Yorkshire only bowled 24 overs, including two in the final 15 minutes, interrupted by a very brief shower. 'That was probably the first instance where Sellers began to have thoughts about Closey's captaincy because it didn't show Yorkshire in a good light,' comments Richard Hutton, who played that day. 'Sellers I think came under a good deal of disdain from his fellow county chairmen.

'My role has been inaccurately portrayed because when we got back on the field after having been off for rain, only for a short time, there were two or three overs remaining. Fred was bowling deliberate no-balls so there wouldn't be the time to get in further overs. It was a while before the umpire cottoned on to what was going on and stopped calling the no-balls. I was fielding at deep long-on to Fred and Closey called me up to bowl what would have been the second-last over. I trotted up from deep long-on. I remember a fielder saying to me, "Slow down! Slow down! Walk, don't run!" Being young and impressionable I stopped trotting. I hadn't bowled from that end previously in the match, so Closey told me to mark out my run and have a practice. In those days it was habitual for a bowler bowling newly from an end to have a practice run-up. That virtually ensured there wouldn't be another over – and certainly not after my first ball was a straight full toss, which Alan Smith missed. The accusation that I was directly guilty of deliberate time-wasting is not correct.'

Not that Hutton is pretending everything Yorkshire did that day was whiter than white. The rain caused them to sprint off the field in the final hour, but by the time umpires Charlie Elliott and Laurie Gray reached the boundary, it had already stopped. 'We were a long time coming back out,' Hutton admits. 'Closey couldn't be found. I don't know whether he'd gone to the loo or he was hiding somewhere. It took some while for everyone to get assembled. It was not a good performance all round.'

The game finished in a draw, Warwickshire nine runs short of their victory target, Yorkshire taking only five of the ten wickets needed to replace Kent at the top of the Championship. After the match scorer Ted Lester went into Warwickshire's dressing room and apologised to their captain, M.J.K. Smith. Highly-respected cricket writer Neville Cardus accused Close of 'tactics which went to the laws' extremes'. Jim Kilburn commented that, 'Yorkshiremen expect matches to be saved by cricketing skills rather than tactics open to question.' *Wisden* editor Norman Preston complained, 'The image of cricket was besmirched.' The umpires agreed, reporting Yorkshire to Lord's. It was a landmark moment, prompting a rule decreeing a minimum 20 overs be bowled in the final hour of future Championship games.

It had not even been Close's only moment of controversy that day. As he went in for lunch he confronted a spectator who apparently called him a 'bald-headed bastard.'

'Excuse me, was it you that said that?' he claimed to have asked Doug Nicholls, putting his hand on the shoulder of the man from Walsall Wood, only to be told he had got the wrong person. Two days later the *Sunday People* ran a far more sensational version, but it was Close's rather genteel story Nicholls backed up.

Close spoke to Warwickshire secretary Leslie Deakins about the incident at the close of play before heading for a drink with Nicholls and was told not to worry about it. On the advice of England chairman of selectors Doug Insole, Close did not respond to the *People*'s story, which claimed its columnist Trueman, whose car had been damaged at the ground, later came back to apologise only to discover Nicholls had gone. Sellers, however, did respond – in writing – giving the story legs.

Close claimed that a month earlier the *Daily Express*'s Crawford White had told him, 'For God's sake, Brian, keep your nose clean because they are just waiting at Lord's for a chance to prevent you leading the [England] side in the West Indies.' Now 'they' had it. On 23 August 1967, the day before he was due to captain England at The Oval, Close was called before a panel of Marylebone Cricket Club president Arthur Gilligan, Hampshire's Cecil Paris, David Clark of Kent and Derbyshire president Edward Gothard. Close had recently criticised Clark's plans for the future of county cricket, and earlier in the season clashed with Gothard over Derbyshire's defensive tactics. Yorkshire were found guilty of time-wasting and Close held responsible. MCC's executive committee rejected his version of events despite not asking opposite number Smith or the umpires, or apparently receiving any contradictory evidence beyond the newspaper report. The England selectors stood by Close, nominating him as captain for the Caribbean tour but an emergency meeting of the full MCC committee voted 14-4 against the selectors, choosing Colin Cowdrey instead. Close did tour West Indies that winter, but only as a journalist.

Having lost Trueman and Ray Illingworth, it was hardly surprising 1969 was a difficult season for Yorkshire. At one point it got so tough Trueman offered to return 'if required and when available'. The club called it a 'fine gesture' but they would rather give young players a chance. Tony Nicholson broke a finger, a calf injury restricted Close to 18 Championship appearances, and Geoff Boycott, John Hampshire and Phil Sharpe saved their best for international cricket, scoring more centuries for England than Yorkshire.

With 11 uncapped players used, including debutants Bore, Andrew Dalton, Colin Johnson and Rodney Smith, Yorkshire's 13th-place finish in the Championship was the lowest in the history of a club which had only finished outside the top four on four occasions in the first half of the 20th century. Their end-of-year report actually claimed 12th, but only three wins determined Yorkshire finished below Worcestershire, who also had 142 points.

Ironically, in view of what was to follow, limited-overs cricket offered Close's salvation. Big wins over Norfolk, Lancashire, Surrey and Nottinghamshire set up a Gillette Cup Final against Derbyshire only for two opening batsmen to pick up injuries at Hove days earlier. John Snow damaged Boycott's hand, while Barrie Leadbeater hurt a finger attempting a catch. Both had broken bones but only Boycott's was diagnosed at the time, so Leadbeater, his heavily-strapped left hand so swollen he could not take his glove off at lunch, had to play. His 76 in a 69-run win earned him the man of the match award, and Close a final trophy as Yorkshire captain.

At the end of the season Jimmy Binks joined the exodus. The wicketkeeper had long been a valued lieutenant of Close, but Trueman and Illingworth's departures saw him promoted to vice-captain and he responded well enough to be named one of *Wisden*'s cricketers of the year. In mid-May he was hauled in front of the cricket committee over an off-the-cuff remark while in Norwich for the first-round win. With the game stretched into a second day by rain, Binks and Hampshire bumped into two Yorkshire committeemen while out for a drink. During their conversation, Binks said he and his team-mates felt the committee sometimes seemed to be working against them. He was only saying what most of the dressing room were thinking. Binks thought no more about it until he returned home and was summoned to explain his remarks. Disillusioned, and with a promotion available in his winter job with industrial manufacturer J.H. Fenner and Co., he hung up his gloves at the end of the season, aged 33.

Although they finished 14th in the Sunday League, Yorkshire's 1970 Championship form suggested they had weathered the storm. They challenged again for the title and although eventually fourth, Yorkshire were only five points off second. The loss of senior players 'put greater focus of responsibility on those remaining', Richard Hutton explains. It was a mixed testimonial year for the captain. Close injured his shoulder diving for his ground while batting in his first Sunday League game of the summer, against Glamorgan at Bradford Park Avenue. Even with cortisone injections he missed over a month with torn ligaments. Close being Close, he saw his team flagging without him, at one point dropping to third-bottom in the Championship, and rushed back early. Although unable to bowl or grip the bat properly in his right hand, his presence had a revitalising effect. Boycott, Yorkshire's star batsman, had been struggling, with 353 runs from his opening 15 first-class matches but finished the season with more than 2,000, including what was then a career-best 260 not out against Essex.

If Close could still inspire his players, he remained equally adept at attracting controversy. In August Yorkshire were the visitors on the day Lancashire retained the Sunday League title with victory off the penultimate ball. 'We were at Old Trafford in front of a very big crowd who got at Closey, who obviously felt under pressure on the field,' Hutton recalls. 'They started up a chant of "Keep your hair on Brian Close!" which of course aggravated him even more.'

Yorkshire's bald captain was in no mood to receive an uninvited post-match visit from who, unbeknown to him, was Lancashire's president, Lionel Lister. 'Lister gloated over Closey at a very importune time and Closey let rip with a stream of abuse, I think, which immediately got reported to Brian Sellers,' Hutton continues. 'That was probably the nail in his coffin.'

At that time the Yorkshire and Lancashire committees used to move *en bloc* to each other's venues for the Roses matches for one gargantuan party and they would be sensitive to what others might be saying about them. I think they felt a great need to keep the peace off the field whatever the competitiveness might be on it.'

Once Sellers pointed out to Close who the dressing-room intruder was, the captain went home to write a letter of apology to Lister, but the ammunition had already been served to those on Yorkshire's committee who were tiring of him. Although secretary John Nash had a copy, his written apology was never mentioned when the incident came back to bite Close.

Other factors added to the hierarchy's antipathy. In a time of transition, Close's reluctance to blood youngsters concerned them. 'Brian would always look to a senior player rather than push a younger player forward,' explains Bryan Stott. 'It sounds worse than it is. Brian skippered to a certain extent on the seat of his pants. He would make a decision and work on it. Having played with him so long everybody knew when things were going to happen. You were keeping your eyes on Brian all the time. He knew everyone would react immediately and didn't want to wonder about a youngster who might be wandering a bit. The better the team, the better captain he was because he had experienced players following him.'

At times it caused problems, as former Harrogate Cricket Club president Julian Vallance recalls. 'Peter Kippax was 12th man for three Championship matches and that was his holiday gone,' he says. 'He was asked to do it at Harrogate and he told John Nash, "I will do it if I'm playing, but I will not be 12th man." When he got there, Closey put the side up and Kip was 12th man, so he left and went to work. That was Closey disobeying what he was supposed to do. He wouldn't play an uncapped player ahead of a capped player. You can't run a side like that.' Sir William Worsley would later claim there were at least three other examples. 'Brian was very loyal to his tried-and-tested,' comments Hutton. 'I think the committee came to the view that he could be obstructive in giving the younger players in the second XI opportunities.'

In Close's defence, Hutton, Boycott, Hampshire, Leadbeater, Chris Old and Geoff Cope established themselves under his captaincy. At the end of the 1962 season outgoing captain Vic Wilson had written to the committee suggesting they release Boycott because he was neither a good enough player nor the right character for Yorkshire. Close, recognising the 22-year-old's incredible powers of concentration, urged the committee to reconsider and saw him develop into one of the world's best batsmen. Close handed debuts to Richard Lumb, Dennis Schofield, Neil Smith and future captains David Bairstow and Phil Carrick in 1970.

Another bugbear was Close's disdain for limited-overs cricket. The first-class game's biggest problem as a spectator sport has always been that matches take too long for those in full-time employment to watch. Even when Championship matches were squeezed into three days it was impossible for them not to take in weekdays, depriving most workers of the ability to see either the start or finish. In the early post-war years, the sport rode the challenge out, with Roses clashes between Yorkshire and Lancashire played to crowds which today defy comprehension.

By the 1960s, with so many more ways for people to spend their leisure time, attendances were in decline. In 1963, MCC created the Gillette Cup, a competition which (in theory) compressed a whole match into a day, and removed the gripe of many a non-cricket fan – the draw. For all the new skills it brought, many traditionalists felt the purity of the sport was lost. From MCC members' benches at Lord's to the dilapidated seating at cash-strapped county out-grounds, there was no shortage of cricketing snobs looking down their noses at one-day cricket. One just happened to be captain of Yorkshire.

'Throw down some sawdust, everybody put on top hats and red noses, and you've got the John Player League,' Close famously said of the Sunday competition which followed the Gillette Cup into existence in 1969. At just 40 overs per side, it neatly fitted into the afternoon schedules of the recently-launched BBC2 and provided a platform for cigarette companies banned from advertising on television since 1965. Close's feeling that limited-overs cricket bred bad habits into his players was a populist view, not only in his own dressing room and among the rank and file whose hard-earned money was struggling to keep Yorkshire cricket in the manner to which it had become accustomed, but even the committee room. The *Yorkshire Post* noted the club joined the new league 'without enthusiasm'.

While the ordinary traditionalist supporter could, and often would, grumble to his heart's content about the damaging effect of the new-fangled one-day game, those running Yorkshire County Cricket Club had little choice but to enter into the spirit of it. Whether he liked it or not, Close was one of them.

The disdain for 40-over cricket was at least good for team bonding. 'We used to have what was called the Saturday Night Club when we were away,' Bore explained. 'You'd have a few beers, not to the extent of getting drunk, and they'd conduct a board meeting. There was a set routine about how you addressed people. If you didn't do it properly you'd be fined – only 10p, but you had to drink your beer off, so you had to be careful what you said and who you said it to. There'd be 25 eggs on a tray. You'd hold your hand out and they'd scrape an egg into your hand. You had to drink your half, then when the chairman said you may eat your egg, if you spilt any or it squirted out you got fined double. There were three toasts you had to get in the right order. Because you were playing one-day cricket the next day you could get up at ten o'clock-ish for some breakfast, then make your way to the ground. It was like a party night, but it wasn't. There were no outsiders allowed in, just the players, the scorer and sometimes we might have a physio with us. Geoffrey [Boycott] would be there but he was the only one allowed not to drink beer or lager. It used to be absolutely hilarious at times.'

The introduction of overseas players had made it more difficult for Yorkshire to win Championships, increasing the importance of the shorter competitions on the field as well as the balance sheet. After losing £8,109, the committee regarded 1970 as a financial disaster. Half of that was attributed to revenue lost because of the first-round Gillette Cup defeat to Surrey at snowy Harrogate. The Sunday League was more lucrative still and guaranteed games in a way the knockout competition could not. A total of 23,724 spectators paid to watch Yorkshire in the 1970 competition compared to 38,007 in the Championship, but player antipathy was hardly likely to sustain, never mind grow, the crowds. 'The committee decided that they could not have one captain for weekdays and another for Sundays,' John Nash explained.

Different skippers for different formats is commonplace in the 21st century, but in 1970 it was far too radical for Yorkshire. It would be 2015 before they belatedly adopted the idea. Even by then, Close was still the only captain to have led the county to success in more than one limited-overs competition. His two Gillette Cups sat alongside three trophies for every other captain combined – not bad for someone who did not like one-day cricket. Viewed from a modern perspective, making Illingworth Yorkshire's limited-overs captain for 1969 and keeping Close in charge of the three-day side could have avoided decades of conflict, but at the time it was not an option.

By September 1970 there were rumblings Close's shoulder might cause him to retire, but they proved unfounded and by then he had survived what the players darkly called the annual 'sacking meeting'. Sellers is supposed to have told Ted Lester, 'I wanted to get rid of him but the committee are so weak.' So when Close was called to Headingley on 25 November, he thought it was just for a routine meeting to plan for 1971. When he arrived, only Sellers and Nash were there. The Lister incident was brought up, along with Close's disdain for one-day cricket. 'Well, Brian, you've had a good innings. I'm going to give you the option of resigning or getting the sack,' said Sellers, presenting him with two prepared statements, one for each scenario. Close opted for resignation.

The hard man of English cricket found the decision too much to take. He lived only 25 minutes away in Tong Park, but was unable to complete the drive home without having to stop, his vision misted, to be sick by the roadside. It was, he said, 'The worst day of my life… The bottom had suddenly dropped out of my world.' Close was home before noon, though his wife was not, picking their daughter Lyn up from playschool. When Vivien returned she persuaded him to ring Jack Mewies, a solicitor friend, and Roy Parsons, the Justice of the Peace who organised his benefit. When both told him not to resign, Close rang Nash to say he had changed his mind. It took around 20 to 30 minutes to get through and by the time he did, at 12.45pm, he was told the resignation statement had already been made public ahead of the agreed 2pm time.

'After long and careful consideration your committee decided not to reappoint D.B. Close as captain for 1971 and

44

in view of that decision it was also decided that he should no longer be a playing member of the team,' it read.

In the 19th century it was common for ex-Yorkshire captains to return to the ranks, but no one had yet done so in a competitive game in the 20th. Close's 'often stated dislike of one-day cricket, a form of the game which becomes increasingly important as the years go by' was mentioned, and concerns over the 39-year-old's increasing vulnerability to injury were also cited. Close's 22-season Yorkshire career was over, although the failure to come to a decision before July's 'sacking meeting' cost more than a year's wages as he was paid up until 31 March 1972.

Many saw Illingworth's departure as key to the downfall of the best man at his wedding. Trueman might have been Close's official vice-captain until his retirement, but Illingworth had his ear. 'Close and Illingworth did disagree quite a lot but I always feel if the captain has people giving him other ideas, if what he's doing doesn't work he can go on to something else,' says Chris Old. Yorkshire supporter George Hepworth's take on it is, 'Brian was the kind of man who'd say, "Come on lads, follow me," and run through a brick wall. The attitude of Raymond would be, "Hold on lads, there's a door here, let's see where this leads us."' Illingworth was seen as a steadying influence, jumping in when the cry of 't'rudder's gone' came from Binks behind the stumps, and at times steering Close away from trouble off the field too.

There was outrage among the members at the decision to sack a Yorkshireman for speaking his mind. *The Cricketer* magazine called Close 'a martyr'. 'The White Rose of Yorkshire is looking tarnished and wilted. One can hear the rumbling of great Yorkshiremen of the past turning in their graves,' Jean McRae of Hull dramatically wrote to the *Yorkshire Post*. 'Until today I have been proud that I am a Yorkshirewoman; now I am ashamed,' declared F.W. McQuiggan from Liverpool. G.R. Frost of Ilkley was one of many to give up his membership in protest. On 3 December the newspaper printed what it said was the only letter it received defending the decision, from Norman K. Hoyle of Lancaster.

A group known as the Action Group was formed in protest with Mewies – whose firm of solicitors, now run by his son, still sponsors the Craven League – as chairman, Lord Masham its president. Although both were friends of Close, his sacking was merely the breaking point for supporters disenchanted with the running of the club. The Action Group demanded contracts for capped players, the preservation of three-day cricket and a smaller general committee. The county was divided into 16 districts, each with representatives elected by its members every three years – but only in person, and only by men. Bradford and Leeds had three each, Sheffield six. Vice-presidents automatically served on the committee – there were nine in 1971 – as did the treasurer, while further members could be elected. At the time of the 1971 annual general meeting there were 37 men on Yorkshire's ruling body. There were only 17 people in the Cabinet which ran the country.

Yorkshire's 1970 annual general meeting was attended by 130 people; over 1,000 were in Leeds Town Hall on 30 January 1971, including members from Newcastle, Blackpool, Beckenham and Bath. Despite demonstrably having the committee's support, Sellers was accused of 'dictatorial behaviour', the club of 'kangaroo justice' for not asking Close's side of the Lister incident. In a show of defiance, members rejected adoption of the committee report and the statement of accounts by 570 votes to 507. A show was all it was. Mewies's attempted vote of no confidence was ruled out of order because the club had not had 14 days' written notice, and calls for the committee to resign met with little support. Despite being a magnet for the dissent, Sellers was re-elected, along with every other vice-president, the president, and treasurer Michael Crawford. Close, who was not at the meeting, challenged Sellers to go head-to-head with him on television, but he refused. 'All that the rejection [of the accounts] means is that the Action Group have won five bonus points on the first innings. Now it is our turn to bat,' he said dismissively.

The Action Group met in Leeds in February to demand a special general meeting (SGM), and afterwards Mewies claimed he had 'far more' than the 260 signatures needed to force one. He actually had pledges of support rather than the autographs required, and a 47-day postal strike made obtaining them difficult. John Warner, an oil company director from Adel, stood against journalist Ron Yeomans, the Leeds representative since 1957, in the general committee elections. Sales manager Roy Wilkinson opposed Raymond Clegg, elected 12 months earlier, in Bradford. Both elections drew record turnouts despite snowy weather, but Warner lost by 247 votes to 130, Wilkinson 284-253.

The process of out-manoeuvring the dissidents was already under way. A sub-committee was appointed to review the constitution, and the general committee called its own SGM to discuss the findings. Nash's resignation months earlier as only the club's fourth secretary was finally made public. Sellers was re-elected as cricket chairman, although he soon resigned.

Despite this act of provocation, the Action Group recognised the need for conciliation. A day-long meeting with the committee produced proposals to put to the SGM: contracts of one to three years for capped and uncapped players from April 1972, and all members except juniors to be given the vote at general and district meetings. The number of Sheffield representatives would be reduced to three, slightly offset by creating a Rotherham district. Vice-presidents were no longer to be automatic committee members but up to six could be nominated for three-year terms at each AGM. In return the committee got proxy votes at general meetings and postal votes at district meetings. The position of Yorkshire chairman was created, and given to Arthur Connell, a Sheffield solicitor on the general committee since 1954. The national fight against a reduction in three-day cricket was lost, with the number of Championship matches cut from 24 to 20 for the 1972 season (it had been 28 until 1968).

By the time these changes had been made, Close had joined Somerset. Like Illingworth, he flourished in a new environment. At the first opportunity, at Taunton in June 1971, Close became the fourth player to score first-class hundreds for and against Yorkshire, and all four seasons where he had a first-class batting average of more than 40 – the benchmark for a quality batsman – came with Somerset. In 1974 he recorded his lowest bowling average since 1950. Close took over as captain in his second season and helped mould exciting young talents Ian Botham and Viv Richards into legends of the game. England saw the error of their ways, in 1972 making the arch-critic (his opposition never softened) England's first skipper in a home one-day international series. He even played three Tests versus West Indies in 1976, aged 45. Eventually even Sellers apologised for sacking him.

Even when it comes to their finest servants, Yorkshire have too often struggled with happy endings. 'I don't think the way the club have managed people at times over the years has been a great example, that is for sure,' says Kevin Sharp, who left as a player in 1992, then again as a batting coach in 2011. 'The exit route has often been quite ugly. When I got released as a player I got a day's notice. I'm sure it's improved of late but they were never good at managing people, certainly from an exit route. It's left a lot of people a bit sour.'

Yorkshire's members may have shown themselves not yet ready for revolution but a genie had been let out of the bottle and for the next 15 years the committee struggled in vain to put the top back on. When Close found himself sat with committee members Ted Umbers and Capt. Desmond Bailey at a dinner after his sacking, he told them, 'In the next ten years you will realise your mistake.' It took a lot less than ten years, but this book is the story of how right he was.

3

The Chosen One

YORKSHIRE wasted no time picking Brian Close's replacement, selecting Geoffrey Boycott the same day. It would be one of the most controversial decisions in the club's history, shaping events beyond the next decade and a half that he played on for – rarely for the better though that was not always his fault. Boycott had been chosen by the slimmest possible margin – the cricket chairman's casting vote – yet wielded great power as captain, and even more after losing the job.

Captaining Yorkshire had long been Boycott's dream but now he admits taking the job was his biggest mistake in cricket. 'I hear people occasionally say, "I wouldn't have changed anything in my life,"' he told an official club DVD. 'I think, "Well either you're a liar or an idiot."' He is by no means alone in regretting he said yes. It caused divisions that remain to this day.

There were plenty of candidates to be the club's 20th full-time captain, but no outstanding ones. Yorkshire not only lost Close, Jimmy Binks, Ray Illingworth and Fred Trueman's ability in the space of two years, but a wealth of leadership. Phil Sharpe, Doug Padgett, Richard Hutton and Don Wilson all had support inside and outside the dressing room as captain. After Binks's departure in 1969, Sharpe had been made Yorkshire's first official vice-captain since Brian Sellers, news Padgett – the senior player – found out from a man in the street. Sharpe led the side in six matches in 1970, winning three and losing two.

Others favoured Hutton, whose father Sir Leonard captained England rather than Yorkshire, but was one of the county's all-time greats. 'I don't think I considered myself a candidate,' Richard reflects. 'They'd appointed Philip vice-captain to Closey and it was a big shock for him to be overtaken, because that was the expectation – that Philip would succeed Brian. It was a severe nose out of joint for him. Presumably they hadn't been too impressed with the way he'd handled the side when Brian happened to be absent, although I can't remember any specific instances. Philip and Douggie were not people that pushed themselves forward. In many ways they were probably a bit too nice. I can remember Brian Sellers mentioning the captaincy to me in an off-hand way at Lord's in about 1967, 1968. I think he said to me, "Do you think you could do it?" I don't think I gave a very positive response.

'I'd only really had ambitions to play for Yorkshire and to play for England. I hadn't had any personal ambitions such as wanting a captaincy or to score this number of runs or take that number of wickets. Largely I was in it for the companionship of one's fellow players, being part of a team, and I made a lot of friendships as a result. That's how I look back at it.' Hutton's reluctance was not untypical. Mike Bore said he 'got the impression the others didn't want the job'.

Yorkshire's committee chose between Wilson and Boycott. Wilson was popular with his team-mates – 'full of energy, full of fun, a good player and a brilliant fielder' says Bryan Stott – his rival more focused on attainment than entertainment. Boycott was Close's choice, though not for 1971. At the end of the 1970 campaign he had told the committee he wanted to play on for a couple more seasons, then have one more under his leadership. Boycott has always been a student of the game and in his early days as a bespectacled civil servant looked the part too. His curiosity about Close's methods, often asking questions, was not lost on the captain. Boycott shares the view it would have done him good to have continued learning under arguably Yorkshire's greatest skipper, but other opinions are split. 'It might have helped if Closey had been able to groom him. I'm not trying to push blame on Boycs but I think his inexperience as captain probably had a detrimental effect,' said Bore, then a junior player. Ted Lester, Boycott's second-team captain and later a trusted confidant, felt it was doomed to failure. 'They would never, ever get on,' he told me. 'It was a great pity.'

Very few Yorkshire players got on with Boycott in 1971. Being unpopular is not necessarily a barrier to being a good captain, but Richard Hutton believes a lack of personal skills made him a bad man-manager. 'Boycott was so self-centred and had such a bad way with people that you could never expect him to handle people properly or reasonably,' he argues. 'I also had the suspicion at times that although we might be playing badly as a team, as long as he was getting plenty of runs it was all power to his elbow and strengthened his position as captain. It seemed he was always looking over his shoulder but by and large he played for himself. His personal achievements were put far ahead of the team's. There were times when I felt he actually undermined the confidence of the younger batsmen who needed to be boosted. For a player who was achieving so much as an individual to treat others so poorly, it was not something I expected of a cricketer who was an automatic choice for England and supposedly respected. I didn't like the way he treated other people, particularly younger players. I thought his manner with them was destructive. I just didn't see him capable of building any morale among the team.'

It was particularly difficult for those on the fringes, according to Bore. 'A lot of us in the second team would assemble for a match, particularly home matches, not knowing if we were playing or not,' he revealed. 'It was never divulged until just before the game who was 12th man and who could go home or play club cricket on the Saturday. We used to turn up to practise before home matches and you'd get back in the changing room to go out and say, "Do I put my bowling boots on or my fielding boots?" He'd say, "What's it to you?" and he'd walk down the stairs leaving you not knowing who was 12th man. I think John Hampshire in the end started to try and suggest to Geoffrey that the lads need a little bit of encouragement and to let them know early enough.'

He also had a short fuse when things were not going well for him. 'Against Gloucestershire at Middlesbrough [in 1972] Mike Procter was drumming in,' Bore recalled. 'He bowled a short ball and Boycott hit him out of the ground for six. It started a bit of [signals 'chatter' with his hand] during the last hour of the day. One of the Gloucestershire players broke a finger and in them days the 12th man was provided by the home team so the away team could send players back to play for the second XI. I was 12th man. Procter kept bowling these short-pitched balls and Boycs kept hitting them for four or six. We're all wondering what's going off here, because it's not like Boycs – he normally just wanted to be there for the next morning.

'About two balls before the end of the day's play he hooks this one and mishits it to me at fine leg. I caught it and got the most awful looks given to man. By the time I got off the pitch all my kit and my civvies were floating in the communal bath. He took me outside the changing room and had a go at me, he said I should have dropped it. I said, "I'm sorry, I don't agree with you on that." I didn't play again for a month. I found it difficult to please the man.'

Boycott had long had a reputation for selfishness within the club. When he initially broke into the second team an unnamed colleague is said to have commented, 'We don't want that so-and-so in our side. We have a happy side here.' His maiden Roses hundred came at the first opportunity in a 249-run stand with Bryan Stott at Bramall Lane in 1963. Stott was out shortly before tea, Boycott just after. 'Geoff came back into the dressing room, put his hand on my shoulder and said, "I beat you!"' recalls Stott, who made 143 to Boycott's 145. 'I thought, if that's all you can say after what's gone on today, I'm lost for you.' At times his single-minded determination to excel was a real strength, but at others a major weakness. Boycott was, and still is, notorious for running-out batting partners. Ken Taylor fell victim in only the youngster's second game, Sharpe later that season. 'The trouble with The Master,' Martin Searby commented in the *Scarborough Mercury* more than two decades later, 'is that he seems to want to be the judge of a run at both ends.' The committee's hope was presumably that giving Boycott extra responsibility would force him to think more about others.

What further exacerbated the disconnect between Boycott and his team-mates was a reluctance to socialise with them. While most Yorkshire players found the bar an enjoyable place to unwind after a day's cricket – especially if it had a piano – as a very occasional drinker dedicated to his fitness Boycott preferred to keep his own company and get the good night's sleep which gave him the best chance of producing his top form the next day. Unable to show the better sides of his complex personality, being out of earshot gave his team-mates free rein to grumble about the less attractive ones. 'The whole conversation was on their dressing room and the internal politics,' explains Geoff Cook, who played for Northamptonshire from 1971 to 1990. 'Boycott invariably wouldn't be there so you saw opinions in their true light.'

The intense opener felt talking cricket in the evening would make him more uptight about the following day's play. But while his absence at the bar and self-absorption in the dressing room helped him score more runs, they were a great loss to his team-mates. 'Geoffrey would usually go straight home. Sometimes he wouldn't even change into his civvies,' according to Bore.

'Players don't really drink now, they go back to the hotel and have a swim,' bemoans Alan Walker, who played under Cook in the 1980s and is now Durham's bowling coach. 'It sounds like, "Ah, you're just having a pint," but you were like a sponge trying to soak up information. Especially when you're starting off, you would circle these guys who you'd seen on TV and if suddenly you were involved in the conversation, you fed off the slightest thing. If I was in company with Malcolm Marshall and he said something about my bowling, my God, that was a massive thing. It was like an injection of self-belief.'

Although Huddersfield-born Walker was never part of Yorkshire's dressing room he thinks the idea Boycott's reluctance to socialise was held against him – a view shared by the man himself – is overplayed. 'I imagine he was hard work, but I expect it was more selfishness than not socialising which counted against him,' he suggests. 'Peter Willey was an absolutely brilliant professional at Northants. He'd maybe have a pint and a half but he'd be in bed by ten o'clock on every night of every game, the model professional I thought. It wasn't frowned upon, it was almost admired because he could do it and no one else could.'

The sharing of ideas was, he says, one of the great strengths of the Yorkshire team Chris Old first came into in the late 1960s. 'There are not many people get the opportunity of starting a career with a side that had more internationals than non-internationals in it,' he points out. 'It was an opportunity to learn from these people – not necessarily on the field but off it, just talking to them. Discussions in the dressing room as we were batting were usually about how people bowled or fielded, and how they would bowl at people. As a 16-, 17-year-old you were being given advice by the likes of Fred Trueman and Brian Close immediately you walked through the door.

You would be foolish if you didn't learn from it. I tended to go in and listen or ask the odd question.

'Unfortunately once these people had left the dressing room there weren't the international players around to actually pass on that knowledge and I think some of the attitudes of the people coming in weren't as professional. I hadn't got the confidence to carry on what they did because there were still some senior players in the side but the youngsters who came in didn't seem to be asking the cricketing questions. They were more interested in what was going on outside of the game. We perhaps should have been talking more about the game but if people are not wanting to listen and learn from it, it's very difficult to continue what you were doing.'

There was still plenty a young player could learn from Boycott, but as Martyn Moxon discovered when he came into the side in the 1980s, it was best done by watching. 'Most senior players offer advice, really,' says the man who went on to be Yorkshire's captain, then director of cricket. 'Geoffrey had a different attitude. You never knew from one day to the next how he was going to react to you. One day he could be really friendly and accommodating, the next day he could be really grumpy and ignore you. I learnt to take it as it was. If it was one of the bad days, don't be overly bothered by it, if it was one of the good days, great.

'Geoffrey was very focused on his own game, particularly when he was batting, so there was very little if any advice passed on while we were batting together but I learnt a lot from being up the other end to him – how he played different types of bowling, how he went about his batting, his preparation, the way he looked after himself. Geoffrey was probably ahead of his time with the training he did fitness-wise off his own bat. He had an unbelievable work ethic as far as practice was concerned. It was only latterly in his career that I kind of learnt his philosophy was that the onus was on the player to come and ask him for advice. I was happy that I was learning from him by being at the other end, so it didn't bother me too much.'

Kevin Sharp, who was handed his debut by him in 1976, did most of his learning from the driving seat of Boycott's car. 'You didn't see him socially that much but if you had an open mind you could get an awful lot from the snippets – they might only be one-liners,' explains Sharp, another who later served on Yorkshire's coaching staff. 'But I did travel with him. I used to drive his BMW and coming from the streets of Leeds having hardly ever had a car in my family, that was great. I remember the first time I drove it with its power steering, I nearly went straight into a field! I was in my early 20s, I'm driving a BMW, I'm thinking it's Christmas! So we'd talk. I'd like to think he had a bit of care for this cheeky curly-haired kid.'

Just turned 30, Boycott had never captained before 1971 – neither had Wilson, but he was three years older and had played in all seven of Yorkshire's County Championship-winning sides of the 1960s – yet of all the many criticisms thrown his way over the next 15 years, a lack of tactical acumen could not be one. Throughout the first half of the 20th century Yorkshire had shown being the best player was no requirement for captaincy – far from it at times – yet cricket's decision-makers are often drawn towards choosing the most talented player to head a team rather than the best leader; and Boycott was the club's one world-class player. His total of 1,425 first-class runs for Yorkshire in 1970 was nearly 350 more than the next best from fewer games. He was in Brisbane preparing for the 1970/71 Ashes when secretary John Nash telephoned to offer the captaincy. When he was injured before its final match Boycott was 19 short of Don Bradman's record for the most runs in an Australia–England series. They had come at 93.85 per dismissal; only Wally Hammond with 113.12 in 1928/29 had a higher Test average in Australia.

Even in 1970, however, Boycott divided opinion within Yorkshire. The vote for Close's replacement was tied, six cricket committee members choosing him, six the less intense Wilson. The casting vote was chairman Brian Sellers's. He opted for Boycott, then asked his colleagues to vote again to give the result the sheen he wanted. So the opener was 'unanimously' selected by a sub-committee containing many downright hostile to the thought of him as captain. 'What duplicity and farce!' he chortled later but the ongoing reservations of some committee members were no laughing matter. 'Brian Sellers did a lot of the things Boycott did and got away with it,' Ted Lester pointed out. 'Brian Sellers had the committee behind him but Closey never had and it was the same for Boycott.'

'You're joking!' was Boycott's immediate response to being offered the captaincy at around 8.30pm Brisbane time on 25 November. He had left for Australia confident the job would not be available any time soon. Perturbed by rumours about Close's future, and unenthusiastic about playing under Phil Sharpe, before setting off for Australia Boycott made a first visit to his captain's home in search of reassurances Close was not about to retire – and got them. His mind was put at rest when Nash told him Close had resigned, which at that stage was true. Only at the following day's press conference was an embarrassed Boycott told he had been sacked, and later still he discovered how lukewarm his 'unanimous' selection was. Wilson was also with England but out of the hotel when Nash rang, so it was left to Boycott to break the news to the left-arm spinner that he was to be Yorkshire's new vice-captain. Shortly before his death Sellers apologised to Wilson for not handing him the job instead. 'I buggered Yorkshire cricket up,' he admitted.

The new captain was not the only one caught off guard. 'I was out on a limb,' Old explains. 'I was the only one from the Middlesbrough area going down to Leeds for nets. Most of them were from the Leeds/Bradford area so they'd been brought up together. They knew much more about each other and had that camaraderie more so than the people who came from outside. It was a shock for me when I heard that Brian was going – well, had gone. It was probably an equally big surprise that Geoffrey got it. I couldn't say I had anybody else in mind, but I didn't think of Geoffrey as the one to take over. The best players don't necessarily make the best captains and I hadn't seen him in a captaincy light.' Lester had. 'I think he was destined to be captain,' he told me. 'I knew most of the team fairly well and I couldn't have picked anybody else.' In selecting Boycott over the more senior Wilson or Sharpe (Hutton was younger), Yorkshire were thinking long term. Despite ferocious, sustained opposition, he captained for the next eight seasons.

Having in the minds of some supporters usurped a popular leader was always going to make Boycott's life uncomfortable, and he blotted his copybook in Australia. Walter Metcalfe of Market Weighton wrote to the *Yorkshire Post* in January 1971 demanding the appointment be cancelled before it had begun after Boycott threw a strop, and his bat, in the sixth Test at the Adelaide Oval. England did not have a single lbw appeal upheld in that winter's Ashes, and tensions came to the surface in the previous Test, in Melbourne, when captain Illingworth criticised Australian umpire Max O'Connell. Run out for 58 by Ian Chappell on the opening day of the next game, Boycott flung his bat to the ground in a show of dissent, put his hands on his hips and stared at O'Connell, who was again standing, before being booed back to the pavilion. More practical objections were also raised.

Yorkshire president Sir William Worsley had defended the decision to sack Close by arguing he might miss a number of games through 'unfitness'. Chairman Arthur Connell claimed two orthopaedic surgeons were unable to guarantee Close's fitness for the 1971 season, even though the man himself said he had been passed fit. The two viewpoints were not mutually exclusive. There was no reason for any such concerns about Boycott, but as an integral member of the England team he would certainly miss Yorkshire matches on international duty – which is why it was necessary to appoint a deputy.

Sod's law dictated that while Close was a County Championship ever-present for Somerset in 1971, Boycott quickly picked up an injury. In a one-day game against Western Australia in February, a ball from Graham McKenzie broke his left forearm three to four inches above the wrist. The initial prognosis was that he would be out for eight to ten weeks. Yorkshire were due back for pre-season training in nine. 'It certainly seems he will miss the opening few matches,' the *Scarborough Evening News* reported. In fact, Boycott returned ahead of schedule, so it was a major surprise when he declared himself unfit for what should have been his first official match as captain, against county champions Kent.

'We were on a Bunsen burner at Bradford and Underwood bowled us out twice in just over two days,' Richard Hutton recalls. 'That was a wonderful start to his reign! It could hardly have been worse.' A 'Bunsen burner' is cricket slang for a turner, the type of pitch ideally suited to 'Deadly' Derek Underwood, the country's leading left-arm spinner. Underwood took 7-28 in the first innings and nine wickets in the match. Boycott returned for the next match, in more benign conditions against Warwickshire at Middlesbrough, and scored 61 and 110.

'He played the next game?' says Hutton. 'Well there you are. He never played unless he was 120 per cent fit. I think eventually we ceased to be surprised at his unavailability. You can't run a team with a captain like that. We were playing with ailment after ailment but we carried on. I used to suffer with sore shins and it was agony at times.' It reminded Hutton of a tale from Boycott's youth. 'Peter Chadwick, who used to play for Harrogate in the Yorkshire League and was a Yorkshire second team player tells the story of when Harrogate were playing at Barnsley,' he says. 'They arrived to see Boycott batting out on the pitch against his own bowlers and subsequently finding it not to his liking, he declared himself unavailable to play for

Barnsley.' His reluctance to play when less than fully fit would be a frustration throughout his Yorkshire career.

In 1975 David Warner wrote in the *Bradford Telegraph and Argus*, 'What he should realise… is that a half-fit Boycott is still a much better prospect than most county players, let alone raw colts, and that if his presence in the side boosts morale he should be there.' Bradford Park Avenue in 1971, his first game as captain, was surely even more of a case in point. By not playing, Boycott, who had stayed on to help his England team-mates through the Sydney Test and spoken enthusiastically about how missing the subsequent New Zealand tour would allow him to focus on his new job at Yorkshire, cemented his reputation for selfishness. That he scored runs as soon as he returned only underlined it. In June Sharpe was on course for his first century of a benefit year where he was sponsored for each (as well as half-centuries) when Boycott hit a ball straight to Keith Boyce, Essex's best fielder, called for a single, and saw his partner run out by a direct hit on 92.

If Boycott's critics could not shake their reservations, he managed. 'The emotional pull of leading Yorkshire, plus the fact that I really felt I could do the job, blinded me to practically any other consideration,' he admitted. 'I did not realise until much later in my life that it might not have been the most important thing in the world; perhaps I would have been happier simply trying to be the best player and fulfilling myself rather than the hopes of others.' Taking the job and clinging on to it for so long would cause him, and his county, years of heartache.

4

'A Giant Among Pygmies'

IT was more than a decade later that Peter Briggs described Geoffrey Boycott as 'a giant playing among pygmies', but the gulf in class between the opener and his Yorkshire team-mates was evident right from the start of his captaincy. Few if any cricketers on the planet, and certainly none within Yorkshire, could come close to matching Boycott in 1971.

'There was a period when he never played and missed at a ball for two weeks,' team-mate Mike Bore claimed. 'Every ball he either left it or he scored off it. This was the talent of the bloke, the concentration. Phil Sharpe would pipe up and say, "You've got to watch this bloke, he's phenomenal. You've got to think he's on our side, not the opposition's."' That Sharpe had to add that rider shows Boycott's brilliance was not always appreciated by his team-mates. At times it worked against him.

A remarkable 1970/71 Ashes tour was just the start. To break his arm before the final Test and miss the subsequent trip to New Zealand could easily have taken the wind out of Boycott's sails. However, when his domestic season belatedly got under way against Warwickshire he continued where he left off three months earlier, top-scoring with a 100-minute century to lead Yorkshire's successful chase of 267 in 52 overs. It was the positive innings of a man on top of his game.

'My instructions from previous captains have been to give the innings a start,' he explained. 'Now I feel I have to give an example to the rest of the lads. If they see me poking about they might think it is difficult.' His fourth match, against Middlesex at Headingley, ended in another run chase. Again Boycott led the way, making 112 not out from 213 as Yorkshire won with five overs and eight wickets to spare. Such carefree innings would be the exception, not the rule.

Even though he missed seven of their 24 matches, Boycott still scored a quarter of Yorkshire's runs in the 1971 County Championship. Eleven of his 13 centuries that summer came in the competition, plus two against Pakistan in a three-Test series in which he averaged 116. As Jack Bond, then Lancashire's captain, puts it, 'If you were choosing anybody at that time to play for your life he was always the person you would want. When you got him out it was like getting three or four players out. Mind, you could leave him in on occasions and he would run two or three of his team-mates out!'

Bond's Lancashire colleague, spinner Jack Simmons says, 'When I bowled him at Headingley [in a 1971 Sunday League game] I was over the moon. He would always quote scores and things at you, particularly Peter Lever [Lancashire's Yorkshire-born bowler]. Lever would say, "I got you out at such a time," but Geoffrey would say, "Ah, but I scored this many runs against you in that game," and he didn't need to exaggerate. He was normally spot on.' Captaincy brought the best out of Boycott as a batsman, averaging 70.2 in first-class cricket when he led Yorkshire, as opposed to 52.99 when not.

The quality of his performances actually heaped pressure on to the miner's son, who compared leading from the front to 'batting with a sack of coal on my back'. First introduced to Boycott when he was a few days old, Yorkshire supporter

George Hepworth can genuinely claim to be a lifelong friend and he explains, 'He always valued his wicket highly because quite honestly, if he'd have got out Yorkshire would not have been where they were. I'm not going to criticise any other players because I was never good enough to be in their shoes but Geoffrey, I don't think, got the support he deserved.'

During Boycott's eight years as skipper, only Richard Lumb and John Hampshire averaged more than 30 in Championship cricket. Their figures combined came to only a run more than Boycott's. In the Sunday League he scored at 46.24 per dismissal (again much lower back in the ranks), and Hampshire, with 38.83, was the only other to average above 30. In its preview of the county's final match of 1971, the *Harrogate Herald* summed up Boycott's dominance in a one-word headline, 'Boycottshire?' The word would reappear plenty of times over the next 15 years, though not always in reference to his batting.

It was not just in the scorebook Boycott's team-mates were overshadowed. 'He was the only figure the press took any notice of,' says Richard Hutton, editorial director of *The Cricketer* magazine after playing for Yorkshire. 'The other ten in the team were relegated to insignificance. I suppose initially it was the quantity of runs, then his outspokenness and his lack of social grace that would make him a figure from which the press felt they could get mileage. It would probably subconsciously be another demoralising factor, rather than something that we resented.' What did cause grudges, according to Mike Bore, was the way Boycott lorded his superiority. 'He thought people had come to watch him play, and not Yorkshire,' he tpld me. 'He would tell you that in the team talk in the morning.'

Boycott's global standing even shaped the way Yorkshire games were played, explains Ashley Metcalfe, an opening partner when their careers overlapped. 'The opposition always wanted to get Boycs out,' he explains. 'So if you were opening with him the opposition would try particularly hard to get wickets early on. Boycs was good enough to get one off the first ball of the over and sit and watch at the other end while I was having to duck and weave, and face some pretty tricky times. I didn't quite have that talent to get one off the second ball and pass it back. It made life pretty tough. I always remember the first time I faced Michael Holding at Chesterfield [in 1985]. Boycs opened with me and Michael said, "I'm going to try 100 per cent until I get Boycs out. After that, I'll relax a bit." I thought, "Oh good!" He only just got his run-up in! He ran from the edge of the outfield every delivery, steamed in, until about an hour later he got Boycs out. I remember thinking from my point of view it was a torrid, torrid hour and you're just there to survive. But it was a huge learning curve, it was brilliant to play in. That's how the opposition tended to be. They wanted to get him out, they saw him as the danger man and rightly so.'

Boycott started his captaincy full of optimism and was not shy in expressing it in public but he had inherited a team – and a club – gutted of experience. His bold words about challenging on all fronts raised unrealistic expectations among an unforgiving public. *Yorkshire Evening Post* cricket correspondent John Callaghan claimed the side which opened the 1971 season without Boycott at Bradford Park Avenue was possibly the worst the county had fielded. It contained four current and four future England internationals! 'We'd won three Championships and the Gillette Cup and it was expected that we would be up fighting for them for the next few years,' says Chris Old. 'As we lost the senior players the expectations were still that we'd win something but we didn't have the depth of players coming through to keep pushing for it.

'Before, when you got into a situation we always had somebody who would come off and perform. We hadn't got the batsmen coming up or the strength of bowlers. We got the odd one but not the two or three we needed.'

Yorkshire's second XI again won the Minor Counties Championship in 1971, but there was no longer the first-team experience to buy talented youngsters time while teaching them to make the most of their abilities.

Between them, Fred Trueman, Ray Illingworth, Jimmy Binks and Brian Close had made almost 2,000 first-class appearances for Yorkshire, including Binks's incredible unbroken run of 412 Championship games between June 1955 and September 1969. Doubts about his batting limited Binks to two England caps (even though he opened once for them), but his wicketkeeping claimed 1,109 dismissals for Yorkshire. In 1960 he became only the seventh gloveman to take 100 in a season. 'The team had always prided itself on the strength of its fielding and Binks was a vital part in that because of his ability to tidy things up,' Hutton says, but his contribution went way beyond that.

'Jimmy had this sixth sense,' says former team-mate Bryan Stott. Old adds, 'I remember the first over I bowled in one game, I was running to fine leg to field and he was running to say, 'You're just doing so-and-so wrong,' and immediately you can do something about it. After he retired I remember saying to David Bairstow one day, "If you see something happening in my action, let me know so I can put it right." David's comment was, "I've got enough on seeing the ball coming, let alone seeing what's happening to you!" Not that I hold it against David, because he was a young lad just starting in his career, but it was something you missed a little bit.'

Binks helped Bore on and off the field. The pair were both from Hull and worked for J.H. Fenner, whose managing director Sidney Hainsworth was on Yorkshire's committee. 'Coming from Hull, which in theory was in a non-cricketing area, it was hard to break into the West Riding group,' Bore explained. 'Understanding the language was difficult! I was pleased I played a season with Jimmy because I learnt a lot from him. I was a medium-pace bowler and he stood up to the wickets as if I was a spinner. He was a big help to me. As the wicketkeeper you're the central figure of the team. He can tell if you're bowling properly. He would talk to you about where you're trying to bowl and what you're trying to do with this batsman. He would make suggestions with field placings. It was all part of the learning curve.'

In between England call-ups, Illingworth contributed 234 wickets and 1,695 runs to Yorkshire's hat-trick of titles between 1966 and 1968, Trueman was the all-time leading wicket-taker in Test cricket, and when he was sacked Close was the club's eighth-highest run-scorer. Like Binks, they doubled as dressing-room enforcers, fiercely guarding Yorkshire standards and quite happy to upbraid anyone who let them slip, be they debutant, star player or captain. 'When you've got so many talented players you do have lots of disagreements about lots of things to do with cricket but once we left the dressing room, everybody fought for one another,' Old explains. 'There were lots of characters in there and big egos that didn't see eye-to-eye but once they got on to the field or went out in public, all they were interested in was Yorkshire winning.'

An infamous incident of the time highlights the point. Bore recalled, 'In one of the last few games at Bramall Lane, Tony Nicholson and Boycs were having an argument on the field about tactics and Boycs kept having a go at him in the dressing room. Closey had enough so he went over to Boycs, picked him up by the scruff of his neck and hung him on the pegs with his feet dangling down.' Such arguments were never far from the surface in the 1960s. 'Brian was keeping a lid on a lot of things,' argues Stott. 'The safety valve blew when he left.' No team could expect to lose so much experience – not to mention talent – in such a short period of time and simply shrug it off.

The brain drain went beyond four greats of Yorkshire cricket. Doug Padgett – a veteran of seven title-winning sides – was 13 months older than fellow batsman Ken Taylor, who retired in 1968. Padgett played in 21 of 24 Championship games in 1971, though he missed the 1,000-run first-class benchmark for only the second time since 1958. Boycott thought the straight-talking Bradfordian still had a role in the first team in 1972 and beyond but Yorkshire saw him as a replacement for legendary coach Arthur Mitchell, who was retiring through ill health. Padgett was happy to do both but the committee felt he could give more while playing for the second team, where Bob Platt had stood down as captain. It was the norm then for county coaches to work closest with the second string. 'I think if Doug had been senior professional to Geoffrey [beyond 1971] – or even if Doug had been appointed captain and Geoff served a couple of years under Doug to learn the ropes – possibly things could have been different,' comments George Hepworth.

Defeated on that, Boycott asked for scorer Ted Lester to be given a more prominent role as team manager, relieving the captain of some of his more onerous off-field responsibilities to focus on matters in the middle. Again he was denied. 'I think I could have helped him a lot,' Lester told me. 'We talked about it. I was fortunate or maybe unfortunate to have brought him up in the second team. I got on well with Geoff but he was his own worst enemy. He would always come and ask me what he should do but it was very difficult. He knew what he wanted to do, so I couldn't say, "Oh, you silly bugger, don't go doing that!"' Without Lester as manager and with Padgett in the second team Yorkshire had no continuity during Boycott's frequent international absences, and few brave or influential enough to put him in his place when he was leading his county. 'It's rather easier to deal with an individual when he is not in any position of authority than if he is captain,' points out batsman Andrew Dalton, who felt Padgett could have been a very effective interim captain once the decision had been made to sack Close.

That dismissal had fatally wounded Brian Sellers as cricket committee chairman and to Boycott's great regret the 1971 season was the last of his 13-year reign, replaced by John

Temple. In February 1971 John Nash retired as secretary after 40 years, handing over to Joe Lister. During a period when squabbling players needed to be firmly dealt with, Temple and Lister were settling into new roles and certainly in the case of the new cricket committee chairman, were far less inclined to stamp their authority. Even the masseur of 19 years, George Alcock, retired and in December 1973 Sir William Worsley, a former Yorkshire captain and MCC president, died of pneumonia after 12 years as Yorkshire's president.

While the loss of so much experience left Boycott short of guidance, the removal of such huge on-field talent influenced how he batted. All too often when playing for Yorkshire, he had little choice but to bat defensively to save a game rather than set up victory. Realising it was so important not to give his wicket away soon encouraged Boycott to cut out dashing innings like those against Warwickshire and Middlesex. Of his 40 Championship centuries as Yorkshire captain, half came in draws, 15 in victories. Cricket is an unusual sport, an 11-a-side contest boiled down into one-on-one duels between batsmen and bowlers – 'Basically an individual's sport disguised as a team game,' Boycott called it. 'It was very much about him in my opinion,' says future team-mate Martyn Moxon. 'He was solely concerned with making sure he got his runs so he couldn't get criticism, and to hell with anything else really.'

More often than not, Boycott rationalised that as easily Yorkshire's leading batsman, his best interests were automatically those of the team. If he did well, Yorkshire would. As his and his county's fortunes went in opposite directions in the 1970s the facts did not bear that out, but it is difficult to escape the conclusion the White Rose would have fared far worse had it not been for Boycott's consistent brilliance. They might not have won enough Championship games when he was around in 1971, but they did not win any when he was not. The bowling, too, was badly damaged, as one of those left to fill the void explains. 'Illingworth, Trueman and Nicholson were more or less taking 100 wickets each,' says Old. 'Two or three years down the line it was people taking 80s, 70s, 60s – it was a big difference. The senior players might be performing as well as they had but because there wasn't the pressure from other people they didn't take the wickets they had in the past.' Bore added, 'Coming in after all these good players had left, you thought, "We can't replace them just yet."'

Tough situations in the middle generally brought the best out of Boycott but sometimes encouraged his worst character traits. When batting, caution was his natural response to pressure – from good bowling, high expectations, testing conditions, poor form or reduced fitness. Where some would take the mentally softer but often effective option of counter-attacking to try and break the shackles, he would simply work harder. It was an approach he encouraged youngsters to follow in his 1982 coaching manual *Master Class*. 'A batsman should obey his own instincts regardless of criticism,' he wrote. 'If it's not in your nature to hit out and score fast, don't do it. You'll only throw your wicket away.' He also suggested, 'Just as you don't drive your car in first gear all the time, when batting you must think about moving into a higher gear.' Of those two pieces of advice he preached, it was the first he practised more vigorously.

In the 1970s, grafting to knock the shine off the ball and give those coming in later the opportunity to play shots was seen as a more important part of the opener's job, but even judged by the standards of the day Boycott had an unwanted reputation for overdoing it. In 1967 England dropped him for a Test match after grinding his way out of a trough of bad form with 246 not out in nearly 10 hours. It set up a win over India at Headingley but there were claims – which he denied – that he ignored orders from captain Brian Close at tea on day one to speed up. The charge of selfishly slow scoring even followed Boycott at times into the Yorkshire League when he dropped down a level in search of match practice. In his

1987 autobiography, he told a story which perhaps gives an insight into why he often seemed so risk-averse at the crease. Making his debut for Yorkshire Schoolboys against Derbyshire at Chesterfield in 1955, he was sent out at the fall of the third wicket with instructions to score as quickly as possible so the side could declare. He did, making 13 before getting out. His reward was to lose his place for the next match. More than 30 years on, he still felt burnt by the 'injustice'.

Moxon did not become Boycott's opening partner until the early 1980s but his comments apply equally to any of the right-hander's 25 seasons as a professional cricketer when he says, 'He could be an attacking batsman when he wanted to be but his general philosophy of batting was to eradicate risk, so if anybody bowled a good ball at him, he would treat it with respect and defend it but if you got it slightly wrong, he would put it away for four.'

Ashley Metcalfe agrees it was down to mindset rather than ability. 'Boycs's driving force was scoring huge numbers of runs,' he says. 'If that meant avoiding any risk he would do so. He had an enormous amount of natural ability but he just restricted the risk so he had less chance of getting out. My personal view of the game is you're more there to entertain. We're actors to a certain degree on a stage. He'd worked out the style that was going to be most successful for him. He could have hooked and pulled any bowler in the country. How many times did I see him play that shot? Not many, because he felt it was too risky. He was at one end of a scale and lots of others were further towards the other.' Often Boycott would show what he was capable of in the innings or match after being criticised for slow scoring. He followed up his India double-hundred with a match-winning 98 not out against Gloucester, just missing the season's fastest century because a nine-wicket victory had been wrapped up.

Boycott reckoned his 'honeymoon period' as Yorkshire captain lasted half a season, by which time the county were out of the Gillette Cup, having lost their opening game to Kent. Boycott top-scored with 46 but his team was hopelessly short of runs, losing by six wickets with more than 17 overs to spare. His own form seemed immune to their struggles. Few matches highlighted the gulf between Boycott and the rest more starkly than July's return Championship game against Middlesex at Lord's, where he carried his bat for 182 carefully compiled runs off 112.5 overs. Yorkshire's next highest first-innings scorer was Phil Sharpe with 36. Even when it was in Yorkshire's best interests, his caution added to the suspicion he was more concerned with his own success than the team's. In terms of his batting average, he would only have one better season than 1971, but it reflected badly on him as captain because Yorkshire finished 13th in the Championship, then their lowest placing, and one-from-bottom in the Sunday League. According to the club's official report, 'The season of 1971 was, without doubt, the worst in the history of the club, both from a playing and financial point of view.'

The speed of Yorkshire's – and therefore particularly Boycott's – scoring was a factor in their three-day struggles. Bonus points were accrued for every 25 runs scored over 150 in the opening 85 overs of each first innings. Solid foundations were a feature of their batting in 1971, making more than 300 in nine first innings, yet the speed at which the runs came meant only Northamptonshire, Essex and Worcestershire claimed fewer than their 47 batting points. Yorkshire had never really taken bonus points seriously, something the annual report demanded must change, so put into historical context the total was not that shabby – only two below the previous summer's and ahead of 1968 and 1969.

All that really mattered to Yorkshire was winning which was fine except in 1971, handicapped when leading wicket-taker Richard Hutton was called up for five of England's six Tests, they rarely did. In 12 Championship draws (nine under Boycott) they were unable to capitalise on nine first-innings leads. Unsurprisingly, it was worse when the captain was on England duty, stand-ins Don Wilson and Doug Padgett's teams only contributing three batting points from seven winless games. Nevertheless, the failing added to the narrative: on and off the field, Boycott was reckoned to be bad for Yorkshire.

His all-too-often one-paced batting caused problems for those coming in later, even more so between 1974 and 1980 when Championship first innings were restricted to 100 overs. 'He scored huge quantities of runs but it's quite often forgotten the context in which they were scored, often at a fairly slow pace which could put other batsmen under pressure to make up for that by hastening things along,' points out Hutton, whose hate-hate relationship with Boycott continues to this day. 'I felt particularly infuriated when we might be on an absolute shirt-front of a pitch, where he would monopolise the strike and the opposition would realise it was to their advantage to keep him on strike. Frequently mid-on and mid-off were pushed back for balls five and six of an over and he'd end up scrambling a suicidal single without much concern for the ability of the non-striker to make his ground. The resulting run-outs were such a demoralising factor. I've seen him push back half-volleys! Consequently we would frequently be scoring at not much more than one an over. This is coming from your captain.

'His presence in the dressing room was definitely a dampener because if he hadn't got runs he was as miserable as sin. If he was getting runs – or at least occupying the crease – he wouldn't be in the dressing room. When he was out cheaply he withdrew completely from games, showing little interest in what was happening on the field because he was so bottled up within himself. [Future Yorkshire chairman] Michael Crawford told a story of when he was captain of Leeds and Boycott played. With Leeds batting second and Boycott out early, he got ready and was about to leave the ground before the match was over. Michael Crawford had to inform him that it was not the way one conducted oneself. He was far better when he'd got some runs. If he hadn't, he just went into a mind block. I remember saying to him once as I came in to bat, "What's it doing out there, Geoff?" which I suppose was a pretty naïve sort of question but it's normally what you ask as an incoming batter. He said to me, "You'll find out!" That's really unhelpful – "I don't want to be bothered with you."'

Some sportsmen are so gifted they find it hard to empathise with those of less ability. Many of Boycott's Yorkshire team-mates did not have it in them to match him, not just in terms of performance but even his fanatically disciplined approach – 'Dedication is too mild a word,' Bill Bowes once wrote – and he struggled to come to terms with that. 'I felt sorry for the bowlers when he was captain because he did not have a lot of patience with them,' Kevin Sharp admits. 'There was one game where somebody had bowled two or three poorish deliveries and he almost turned his back on them muttering, "I don't get any half-volleys and full tosses when I'm batting!" I remember thinking, "Bloody hell, I'm glad I'm not bowling when he's stood there!" It wasn't an arm around the shoulder saying, "Come on mate, you can do this," it was turning his back on them and, "Get it right next time." His concentration, work ethic and standards were so high he probably found it hard to accept that somebody in his team wasn't performing as he wanted him to do.

'I remember Boycs giving me a bollocking against Derbyshire at Harrogate in 1984. I'd made 100 by mid-afternoon, it was nice for batting on that pitch, everything was there for the taking and I got out to a soft shot [caught by Kim Barnett for 104]. He really got stuck into me and told me if you make 100 you make 200, you don't give it away because the time will come when you can't score a run. I never forgot that and whenever I got to 100 again I would always start again. Things like that were good advice.'

Mike Bore experienced how unforgiving it was to bowl for Boycott. 'Geoffrey was not an easy man to please,' he says.

'I wouldn't say Geoffrey's a bad man but he would lambast people with his tongue. He wanted success, that was very important to him. He wanted the best out of everybody but he didn't find it easy to draw that. I was playing at Trent Bridge once when he was having a go at Phil Carrick, arguing on and off the field about tactics. In the end, Boycs said, "Give me the ball, I'll bowl and you go and field over there." They came out after lunch and they were having another ding-dong and Boycs just stood on the edge of the boundary and I'm sure he said to Phil, "You take over. You seem to know what you want, do it!"'

Young cricketers, even those who would go on to be superstars, had always been made to know their place at Yorkshire. 'Early in my career I used to travel on the train to matches because I couldn't afford a car,' Bore said. 'Then the sponsored cars started appearing. The names – Geoffrey, Hamps [John Hampshire], Sharpey – they'd all get a sponsored car. You'd think, "What about us?" We'd get, "Fuck you," thrown back at us, "you've got to earn it." It was only when I got to Notts that there were cars for all the players.'

For someone who could often come across as brash and cocky, many of Boycott's team-mates regarded him as surprisingly insecure. At times, the outstanding batsman of his generation looked to younger and/or less talented colleagues for reassurance when it ought to have been coming in the opposite direction. 'He was a phenomenal player with a phenomenal record but he was totally committed to how he could get the best out of his own performance,' comments Metcalfe. 'If he played and missed at a couple of deliveries in an over he might come down the wicket and ask what the ball had done. He wasn't coming down the wicket to ask how you were feeling or if everything was all right at your end, it was more about the experiences he was going through.'

Yorkshire's final game of 1971, against Northamptonshire at Harrogate, underlined Boycott's mastery of batting, but also in the minds of some critics how he put himself before his county. They arrived in the spa town in the worst run in their history, 17 first-class matches without a victory. He may not have been the manager as Boycott hoped, but the game was an example of the role Ted Lester was still able to play as an adviser. 'I found him so helpful as a new captain and even when I'd done the job a few years,' Boycott tells me. 'He was like a father figure to me. When I became captain he was a former player I could turn to for advice. I liked him and I liked his ideas. He was very knowledgeable and gave me good advice. Years later once I got my feet under the table we got win money from the club and talent money. If we played one-day matches and you got the man of the match award you got a cheque with it. It all used to go into a pot and get shared among all the players. I made sure all 11 players got a share and Ted and the 12th man got a half-share each. I helped Ted out because he helped me so much.

'"Northants are ready for home," he was saying to me. "Put them in and we'll bowl them out." It was the last game of the season and they didn't really have the stomach for it. Once we got ahead of them with my innings there was no way they were going to fight back and win. Professional cricketers were always looking for a day off, especially in the last game of the season. We had the chance to wrap the win up quickly, so that's what I did.'

Northamptonshire proved Lester right, dismissed for just 61 after Boycott won the toss and Hutton took 4-6 in 12 overs. Their Middlesbrough-born opener Geoff Cook was making the first of 56 appearances against his home county. Until number 11 Peter Lee's late flourish in his final Northamptonshire game, Cook's 12 was their first-innings top score. 'We came off a win at Sussex in the previous game, so it made us okay in the league,' he recalls. 'We were a little bit demob happy and we went to Yorkshire and just played really poorly. It had been a long, hard season and they just caught us at the right time because we had a poor team.'

Yorkshire's response was to make 266/2 and, with a big total looming, declare. Boycott was 124 not out when he called Hampshire into the dressing room, nudging his average for the season into three figures. It was nearly twice that of the country's next best, which belonged to Essex's Keith Fletcher. Phil Sharpe was Boycott's nearest Yorkshire challenger with only 34.29. Only two batsmen had previously averaged more than 100 in an English season and both were Australian. Don Bradman is almost universally acknowledged as the greatest to play the game, while Bill Johnston only made 102 runs in 1953, but was not out in 16 of 17 innings.

'It was only afterwards we realised the reason for the declaration,' Cook says. 'The players were absolutely aghast at the whole thing. That was really my introduction into Yorkshire cricket. It just seemed a bizarre, selfish decision. It was insulting in many ways to the opposition, to the game of cricket, to the spectators. Boycott wasn't to know that we would play abysmally and that Nicholson [in conjunction with Geoff Cope, who also took three wickets] would bowl us out in the second innings unless he'd read our mentality very astutely. It just devalued the whole game. I'd been a Yorkshire follower as a young lad but it was my first year in professional cricket and you just thought, "What's going on here?" It was quite amusing really and if we hadn't played so badly I would have loved to have been able to capitalise on that situation and play well enough to expose it. But they were too good for us.'

Northamptonshire were bowled out for 106 second time around, ending Yorkshire's winless streak with an innings-and-99-run victory which meant Boycott did not have to bat again and endanger his 100.12 average. He made centuries in all four of Yorkshire's Championship wins that season, and on the two occasions he batted twice, passed 50 in his first innings too.

Watched by approximately 5,000 spectators, Yorkshire's final three-day game of 1971 finished before tea on day two. Harrogate Cricket Club secretary Reg Dickins told the local newspaper, 'We could have done with another day's play,' but there was no mention of the timing of the declaration in the *Herald*'s report. Cook's anger at Boycott's decision was not shared by Hutton who, 44 years on, did not remember it. 'Probably at the time we didn't reckon that he was so Machiavellian,' he says. Hampshire, who succeeded Boycott as Yorkshire captain, admitted had he been in the same position, he probably would have been tempted to do likewise. Ultimately, Boycott had an inarguable defence. 'I don't think I did owt wrong,' he responds when I ask about his declaration. 'I made runs and we won the game in two days! If you're a cricketer playing all summer the last thing you want to do is play for three days in the final game of the season when you could win it in two.'

Whatever the misgivings about his captaincy, there was no disputing Boycott's ability or his importance to Yorkshire. 'He was an amazing man and an amazing cricketer,' says Cook. 'He was very difficult to warm to but easy to admire. Apart from the odd one-off where his selfishness came to the fore, more times than not he was a terrific contributor who set fantastic examples from a mental and technical point of view.' His critics may not have liked it, but in 1971 Boycott was indispensable to Yorkshire.

5

Club Before Country

BY the end of its first season Geoffrey Boycott's captaincy was under threat from within. In the words of Don Mosey, his initial summer in charge had made Boycott 'a hero with the public and cordially detested by his colleagues'. At the end of it, the latter tried to do something about it.

Two players' meetings were called to address the dissatisfaction which had been building over the last six months – one by the committee, another just for squad members at the Leeds home of Yorkshire supporter Sam Wildblood. When the time came to pull the trigger, few dared do it in front of the listening captain and the speaking was largely left to Richard Hutton.

Intelligent, well-spoken and more critical of Boycott than most, Hutton was the natural spokesman for the malcontents. Just not in 1971. The all-rounder won all five of his England caps that summer so, like the captain, Yorkshire did not command his full attention. 'I was wrapped up in playing for England and I don't think I was too concerned at the time, although I must have been aware the rest of the team were unhappy,' he says. 'The relationship between the players, other than one, remained good. I don't think a selfishness had developed by that stage. I think there was a good commitment to the team among virtually all the players. There was probably a desire not to rock the boat too much because most of them might feel that their positions could be under threat. We didn't have that feeling during Brian Close's captaincy because he stood by his tried and tested. Quite a lot were happy to sit on the fence.'

If the players were wary of trying to remove Boycott because of what might happen if they failed, the club had to be conscious of what could follow if attempts to remove him succeeded. At that time the end of a Yorkshire captaincy meant the end of a Yorkshire career, and Boycott was still by far and away the county's best player. The problems were swept under the carpet, and he was reappointed for 1972.

The 1971 season had its inevitable Boycott controversy in May, after he was run out against Lancashire at Old Trafford for his first single-figure score of it. At the close of play he voiced his frustration at what he felt was negative bowling from Peter Lever and Ken Shuttleworth. What Boycott thought were off-the-record comments were widely reported in the Sunday newspapers. It caused a diplomatic storm but was no sacking offence. Of more concern to his team-mates was his behaviour after Lancashire chairman Cedric Rhoades demanded an apology, withdrawing mentally as well as physically from the contest as his side successfully fought to save the game. 'He spent the remainder of the match in the physio's room with his head wrapped in towels complaining of nervous exhaustion, leaving us without our prime batsman,' recalls Hutton. It was not the only such occasion of his captaincy.

Boycott lamented that he 'just did not have the brains to pack it in' at the end of the 1971 season. Too proud to walk away, he looked for areas to improve. The club's new secretary Joe Lister was one of those who offered advice. Lister, nephew of great Yorkshire off-spinner George Macaulay, had twice played for the county in 1954 before moving to Worcestershire – first as a batsman, then secretary. He advised Boycott to stamp his authority on the team and push the committee into action but the captain's willingness to think beyond the boundary at times meant straying into other people's territory.

In 1971 Yorkshire's first team was picked by the 12-man cricket committee but in Boycott's second season in charge it was left to a selection committee of John Temple, Brian Sellers, Billy Sutcliffe and Frank Ambler, plus coach Doug Padgett and the captain. It was a sign of his influence that Boycott was able to push such changes through, as well as conducting negotiations on the first Yorkshire contracts – three years too late to keep Ray Illingworth. 'I used to do the pay negotiations for Lancashire's players because the captain stayed out of that,' explains Jack Simmons. 'We'd have a meeting with David Lloyd and myself, or David Hughes or Paul Allott. I got on well with Geoffrey, probably more so as time went on. Occasionally he asked me how much our capped players were on and I would tell him. He would say, "I should definitely get that because I'm better than your lot!"'

Perhaps partly because of his stature as a player, the new captain seemed to carry more authority off the field than predecessor Brian Close, who was usually summoned during matches to make recommendations to the cricket committee, then sent back on to the field while the teams for the next few games were picked. At the end of the 1972 season Boycott and Padgett would even be co-opted on to the cricket committee, restoring a right withheld since 1959, albeit it took another year for them to actually be invited to a meeting.

Boycott's analysis in the winter of 1971/72 was not all about picking faults with others, however. Before the new season started he made notes on the back of an envelope outlining how he needed to develop as a leader. Highlights included, 'Give the players more freedom to bat and bowl as they wish... do not tell them how to bat, bowl or field... advise them only if they want advice... encourage them and give them confidence all the time... tell them they're great.' How did he measure up? 'Some of the time, yes,' says Chris Old, Yorkshire's captain from 1981–82. 'But there again I think we can all say that. There are certain circumstances when you do or say things that were inappropriate at the time.'

Hutton is less forgiving. 'Not very well,' is his verdict. 'I could never say he encouraged and gave confidence. I thought he undermined confidence with his often brusque and cruel comments. I detected a menacing and bullying aspect to his captaincy. He would use threats against you. He was going to write all about it in his book and bring it to public notice, which of course he does but only when it's his side of it to be told. It was just the manner in which he spoke. He never spoke with you, he spoke at you. At one time or another he could fall out with everyone.'

Boycott needed a good start to the 1972 season, not in terms of his own form but Yorkshire's. He got it. By early June they were top of the County Championship with 51 points from eight matches, only for Geoff Cope to be suspended for throwing in a game against Warwickshire at the end of the month. The off-spinner tried in August to persuade the Test and County Cricket Board he had remedied the problem but it would be late July 1973 before he was allowed to return to first-team cricket.

The Warwickshire match on which Yorkshire's season really turned, though, came on 5 July when Boycott was struck on the middle finger of his right hand by a Bob Willis delivery in a Gillette Cup tie at Headingley. It removed the top of his finger, leaving the bone exposed and the flesh needing ten stitches. Initial reports were that he would be out for 'at least two weeks'. Yorkshire had reached the inaugural final of England's third limited-overs competition, the Benson and Hedges Cup, and were due to play Illingworth's Leicestershire at Lord's in 17 days. At the time of his injury, Boycott was still in prime form, averaging 86.43 in the Championship, and making a match-winning 75 not out against Gloucestershire to book Yorkshire's place in the 55-over final. They lost three of their next four Championship games, two by an innings.

Boycott was given metal protection for the bone but once doctors told him he risked amputation of the finger by playing in the final, there was only one logical course of action. It was Yorkshire's second consecutive Lord's final he had missed after John Snow's bouncer broke his hand in the run-up to the 1969 Gillette Cup game. The 1965 final, widely regarded as one of Boycott's greatest performances, was destined to be his only Lord's showpiece with Yorkshire, though he did score a problematically slow half-century there for England in the 1979 World Cup. 'If he'd played that might have made all the difference because Leicestershire were just an up-and-coming side,' admitted Mike Bore, Yorkshire's 12th man on the day.

As if being without their star batsman was not enough, the two senior candidates to replace Boycott were badly out of form. The question was whether they dared cause more ructions by addressing the matter. They half did. Vice-captain Don Wilson went down with flu in the run-up, giving Yorkshire a way out of that selection dilemma. Phil Sharpe was next in line but suffering enough with the bat that the selection committee suggested he drop into the second team the week before the final in search of runs. He declined. Tony Nicholson, who would later be the fourth player to captain Yorkshire in 1972, had a fitness test on his hamstring on the morning of the game, while Hutton had one on his heel. Both played in a side led by Sharpe.

As in 1969, Barrie Leadbeater had to play through the pain in a final Boycott missed with injury, although this time he picked up the problem during the match, retiring hurt after being struck on the wrist. He returned to top-score with 32 in Yorkshire's inadequate 136/9, which Leicestershire passed with seven overs and five wickets to spare.

The man of the match was Huddersfield-born Chris Balderstone on his last weekend of cricket that summer before heading off to captain Carlisle United. Yorkshire had released the slow left-armer in 1969, only for Illingworth to reinvent him as a batsman at Leicestershire, where he impressed sufficiently to win two England Test caps in 1976. Balderstone top-scored with 41 not out as Illingworth claimed his first major trophy as captain.

A side's maiden success is always a crucial moment, and the victory kick-started the Foxes' emergence. One wonders how the course of Yorkshire history might have changed had they lifted the trophy but it was a fillip they never experienced under Boycott. He is philosophical about it. 'It would have silenced a lot of those people if we had but it's one of those things,' he says when I put it to him. 'I wasn't able to play, so I couldn't do anything about it.'

As soon as Boycott returned two and a half weeks later against Surrey at Scarborough he was at the centre of another row. England captain Illingworth made plans for him to play in the decisive fifth Ashes Test at The Oval but Boycott did not consider himself ready for such an important game after only three days' county cricket and 23 runs, so stayed with Yorkshire and made 204 not out – against Illingworth's Leicestershire. In the wake of their series-levelling defeat England's supporters, Illingworth included, criticised Boycott for putting club before country, Yorkshire's for not scoring quickly enough to take them to a bigger score than 310/7 declared in the Championship match. It caused a tit-for-tat, Boycott complaining to the national selectors when Illingworth dropped out of the subsequent one-day series with a leg strain, then declared himself fit to play for Leicestershire against Yorkshire in a game his county needed to win as they chased the Sunday League title.

Illingworth was forced to miss the match, which Yorkshire won by three runs. Kent took the title. Bad blood between

Boycott and Illingworth would have a big bearing on both men's later careers.

Once more Boycott spent his winter soul-searching about the Yorkshire captaincy, to the point where his mother, Jane, told him to stop 'brooding' over it. Matters were not helped by the contracts he had been negotiating since April 1972 still not having been agreed. When he returned from a coaching holiday in South Africa in 1973, Boycott claimed cricket chairman John Temple told him 'the committee felt I was acting "like George Best!"' Nevertheless, Temple rejected his offer to stand down, and team-mate Tony Nicholson also told him not to resign, then went with him to speak to the committee about the problems he was encountering. Medium-pacer Nicholson, Yorkshire's leading wicket-taker in 1972, had just been released from hospital after a life-threatening thrombosis in his leg. Again, it seems, Boycott was seeking encouragement from someone who needed it more than he did.

Boycott's contract was the last to be agreed, on 13 April 1973. At a time when Ted Heath's government was looking to control inflation, the committee were not prepared to accept his request for £3,000 a year so he asked instead for £1 a run in all competitions. Given that, Boycott was only prepared to sign a one-year deal, causing Yorkshire's committee to warn that the benefit he had been awarded for 1974 could not be guaranteed if he was not prepared to commit to it. It was almost a reverse of the situation he faced ten years later.

Given everything he achieved on a personal level while playing for Yorkshire, it was extraordinary to hear Ted Lester say of Boycott, 'I'm sure he'd have got more runs if he hadn't had that burden on his shoulders.' The then-scorer adds, 'I'm sure he felt a lot of pressure but he took it well. He was in an impossible position. I felt sorry for him, I must admit. There wasn't really anybody he could trust. He was very much a loner.'

It hardly helped Boycott's cause that he again trampled on committee toes at an end-of-season question-and-answer session. There he explored his ideas about the overall running of the club, which included concentrating matches on one main ground, giving the captain more power and appointing a managing director. The slap on the wrist chairman Arthur Connell gave him for pronouncing on club policy – without, as Boycott pointed out, ever explaining to him what it was – did not stop him doing so again in an interview with Ted Dexter in the *Sunday Mirror* in July 1973. 'It is still considered right and proper if the players get on with playing their game while someone else makes the important decisions,' he told the former England captain. 'I hope the opportunity may come to make a change.'

Doubly annoyed because Boycott's comments came days after the committee came to his defence following a scathing Fred Trueman *Sunday People* column about his captaincy, Connell wrote to him, 'Mutual trust and mutual loyalty between the committee and the captain of the club are essential, and the committee cannot tolerate public criticism of the committee or its policies by its captain. You are free to make whatever criticisms you wish to the committee direct, but not through the media.' Loyalty would be a much-used word in Boycott's many run-ins with the committee.

Yorkshire's system of district representatives – slimmed down in 1993, then ended in 2002 – made changing the policy of taking matches around the county almost impossible to drop, and Boycott's ideas appeared to be all about reducing their powers and increasing his. They were never likely to win him much-needed friends in the committee room. John Callaghan, relatively new in his job as the *Yorkshire Evening Post*'s cricket correspondent in 1973, claimed, 'It was suggested to me by the secretary, Joe Lister, that if I wanted to ingratiate myself with the inner sanctum, then I should write stuff to help him get rid of Boycott.'

The players' concerns were growing too. After Boycott's contract was finally agreed his solicitor, Duncan Mutch, worded a statement with Connell which included the line, 'Geoffrey Boycott feels that he will be leading a team of enthusiastic players who have the opportunity to lay the foundation for the re-establishment of Yorkshire cricket.' When the final press release was sent out, 'enthusiastic' had been removed. In spite of results and his personal unpopularity, Boycott's position was strong. With Don Wilson and Phil Sharpe increasingly unconvincing alternatives as captain and Richard Hutton's work commitments reducing his involvement – so much so that Yorkshire felt unable to name a vice-captain for 1973 – his importance to the club was arguably greater than ever. The game at home to Middlesex in August 1972, under Wilson, had been Yorkshire's only Championship win without Boycott in his first two years in charge, compared to eight defeats in 17 missed matches. Even though he only played in ten of Yorkshire's 1972 Championship games, Boycott still contributed six of their nine centuries. 'It would have been very difficult to find somebody else to take over,' Lester told me. 'Maybe that's why he kept getting reappointed.'

The 1973 campaign was Yorkshire's worst yet. They finished 14th in the Championship and became the first professional team knocked out of the Gillette Cup by a Minor Counties side, the low point of what *Wisden* called 'a disturbingly unsuccessful season'. That it was their best Sunday League finish to date – runners-up, with Boycott and John Hampshire scoring more than their 15 team-mates combined – was no consolation. Boycott made only eight Championship appearances and although his batting average of 42.25 was still Yorkshire's best it was less than half what it had been in the previous two years. The three wins they recorded in the competition all came under Phil Sharpe.

'Has Yorkshire cricket ever been so low?' asked Russell Inglis after top-scoring in Durham's five-wicket Gillette Cup win at Harrogate's St George's Road. Visiting captain Brian Lander took the only top-level five-wicket haul of his career but the historic victory was no fluke.

'They simply played better than we did: they bowled very well indeed, they batted carefully and fielded exceptionally well,' Boycott admitted. Yorkshire had been bowled out for 135. Colin Johnson made their only significant score, but hit his wickets six short of a half-century. Chris Old was out-bowled by his brother, England rugby union international Alan, who took the new ball for Durham as the professionals crawled to 18/1 in the first nine overs. That said, Chris Old and Richard Hutton were the two England cricket internationals in Yorkshire's attack, and both had four overs un-bowled as Boycott mismanaged his resources. The *Yorkshire Post*'s Terry Brindle called the defeat, 'A reminder; not a revelation.' The county had not won a game in the knockout competition since lifting the trophy four years earlier.

Other lowlights included being bowled out for 69 in May's drawn Roses match at Old Trafford, and 60 and 43 in July's innings-and-165-run defeat to Surrey at The Oval. It was Yorkshire's lowest completed total in a three-day match against another county for 108 years. Only three players reached double figures and none were specialist batsmen. Yorkshire had the Championship's joint-lowest number of batting bonus points – 28 – along with Nottinghamshire in 1973. Team-mates Nicholson, Hampshire, David Bairstow and Phil Carrick, plus the committee, all served up the dreaded vote of confidence as questions were asked of Boycott's captaincy throughout the year.

The pressure Boycott was under at county level impacted on his international career. Since having his spleen removed as an eight-year-old he had been reluctant to tour the subcontinent, and in 1972/73 he stayed at home to try and deal with his problems at Yorkshire rather than go with England to India and Pakistan. The decision would have a profound effect.

Chairman of selectors Alec Bedser later admitted had Boycott toured as Tony Lewis's vice-captain, he would probably have been made England skipper when injury forced the Welshman to retire and Ray Illingworth – who had also turned down the 1972/73 tour when complaining of tiredness – was sacked after a 2-0 home defeat to West Indies the following summer. Instead Mike Denness led England in the Caribbean despite not having been picked as a batsman for the home series and reputedly being in danger of losing the Kent captaincy. When told the news by Illingworth, Boycott had a nosebleed. Rumours would later circulate that Illingworth had favoured Denness when asked by the selectors and whether true or not, hearing such talk would have done nothing to endear Illingworth to his former – and future – Yorkshire team-mate.

Realising he would have to win Boycott over, Denness tried to get him involved by organising net practices, something he was more dedicated to than perhaps any team-mate at any stage of his career, but the opener refused, saying it was not his responsibility having not been named vice-captain. He did, however, agree to be on the selection panel for the tour. After struggling against the new ball, Boycott did not appreciate being demoted to four in the batting order to protect him from it in Bridgetown, nor did it do any good, scoring ten and 13 while the captain stepped up to do his job at the top to no great effect either.

England went into the final match of the five-match series 1-0 down with the press predicting Denness would be sacked if they lost. Restored to open, Boycott made 99 and 112 to set up a 26-run win. He told England physio Bernard Thomas at the post-match presentation, 'Bernard, that's buggered my chances of the England job,' and Denness afterwards, 'Unfortunately, that's the worst win we could have had for English cricket.' Boycott admitted in his autobiography, 'I felt sick when the significance of the situation sank in…. I had just cost myself the captaincy of England.'

A mentally fatigued Boycott would have benefited from a break but instead he and his England team-mates went straight into preparations for the new season, and his problems came with him. He briefly lost the considerable expertise of Roy Parsons as the lead fundraiser for his benefit year over 'differences of opinion', and more alarmingly his touch in the middle. He opened the season with 140 against Cambridge University, but it would take another 14 first-class innings before he next made three figures for Yorkshire. 'Sometimes he tried too hard,' comments his former team-mate for club and country, Chris Old. 'It was difficult for him to decide how he was going to play. We all go through bad patches but I think when Geoffrey had a bad spell, rather than being carefree, he would try harder and harder and get out to silly things, or get bogged down. You either lead by example or [your captaincy] makes up for what you lack in other areas, but when both don't work it's disaster.'

During this dismal run Boycott was accused of taking 'his burden of personal responsibility and [hanging] it round the neck of the Roses match at Headingley'. The *Yorkshire Post*'s Terry Brindle, normally a faithful ally and Boycott's future ghost-writer, was unimpressed with the White Rose's 114 in 54 overs having been set 244 in 74 to win by Lancashire – and particularly the captain, who at one stage crawled to 39 runs in two hours. 'A private struggle had triumphed at the expense of public entertainment,' he wrote. John Temple expressed his disappointment that Yorkshire had not taken up the challenge, arguing they were obliged to having won the toss. An appointment with a back specialist ahead of the first Test meant Boycott was absent when the game was reviewed but he made it known his senior players did not think the chase, delayed 15 minutes by rain, was a sensible one.

Caution hung heavy over Roses matches in this period. 'Both sets of supporters and the committees would be terrified if they lost so there were a lot of draws,' explains Boycott, who made 79 not out. 'Each committee used to crow over the other one because they would have drinks together and it was a big derby then. It was the supporters and the committees who were afraid of losing more than the players.' The bore draw continued a winless sequence which would extend to ten Championship games – Yorkshire's worst start since the war – before it was ended by Arthur Robinson's hat-trick and 157 not out from John Hampshire, his first century in just over a year, against Nottinghamshire at Worksop. As well as getting the side off the mark for the season, it ended a run of 43 first-class away games without a win. The sequence started under Brian Close, but Boycott had been captain for 21 of those matches.

The day after the Roses draw, Boycott made a century in either innings of the Test trial at Worcester but when he was twice out cheaply in the first Test against India a week later the *Daily Mirror* wrote, 'His once-prim, well-ordered world, is once again a shambles.' Adding to his frustration was the fact that in the second innings he had been dismissed by the innocuous left-arm medium pace of Eknath Solkar for the fourth time in three matches that summer. In all Solkar won 27 Test caps yet took just 18 wickets, and in two years at Sussex he only played first-class cricket for them once. John Woodcock of *The Times* declared, 'The best therapy would be a hundred at Lord's', but Boycott had chosen a different medicine, telling chairman of selectors Alec Bedser he was 'in no mental or emotional condition to play well for England' and making way for Lancashire's David Lloyd. It worked for him, his form picking up sufficiently to end the season fifth in the Championship averages with 1,220 runs at 58.09. In August he was named in England's winter Ashes squad. Boycott cast doubt on that in a letter to Bedser which mentioned he was considering retiring as he approached his 34th birthday. Kept at arm's length while he ummed and aahed over whether or not to tour Australia, MCC were forced to send urgent telegrams to Boycott's home demanding an answer. They had initially been under the impression it would be a 'yes', but after a two-hour meeting he opted to stay at home. Yorkshire stressed they had not been consulted.

Mounting concern over his future as Yorkshire captain was only one factor in Boycott turning down the opportunity to represent his country. His mother's rheumatoid arthritis was another and in 1977 he told the High Court, 'I was disappointed and disillusioned [to be overlooked for the England captaincy], but it was only a small element.' Australia's attack that winter was led by Dennis Lillee and Jeff Thomson, and in 1978 Tony Greig would say of Boycott, 'His ability to be where fast bowlers aren't has long been a talking point.'

The charge of ducking fast bowling is debatable. Lillee was recovering from a potential career-ending back injury, Thomson still to take a Test wicket after a solitary appearance, in 1972. Boycott never missed a Championship game against Thomson, Andy Roberts, Courtney Walsh, Mike Procter or Bob Willis unless on England duty, and his absences against Colin Croft, Joel Garner, Malcolm Marshall, Garth Le Roux, Wayne Daniel and Michael Holding – who, along with Thomson, he reckoned to be the fastest bowler he faced – came in the middle of prolonged spells of injury. Of those, Daniel was the only one he avoided more than once (playing against him six times out of nine) in county cricket. He missed Patrick Patterson in all four Championship games Yorkshire played against Lancashire in 1985 and 1986. The 1986 absences came in the middle of injuries which ruined his final season, whereas both times in 1985 he played the next game, but Patterson had not represented West Indies at that stage and it is hard to see why Boycott would fear him any more than those he did face.

The only real controversy of his county career in this respect came in August 1984 when due to face Sylvester Clarke – a West Indian clocked at over 100mph helped, some suspected, by a questionable bowling action – on a bouncy Oval pitch. Boycott walked into the dressing room after a lap of the outfield to tell captain David Bairstow he had not recovered from straining his hamstring in a benefit match two days earlier. 'The architects of the Surrey pavilion deserve to be congratulated on their sound design. The roof stayed on,' commented Bairstow, who also had fellow opener Martyn Moxon pull out with a bruised hand that morning. Boycott returned the day after that game concluded, dropped to the second team. His appearance record against 13 of county cricket's fastest bowlers between 1971 and 1986 was 46 from a possible 59 Championship games, or 78 per cent. He also toured the West Indies, home then of the quickest bowlers and therefore unsurprisingly the quickest pitches, three times – more than any Englishman at that point. The final trip saw him face Croft, Garner, Holding, Marshall and Roberts at 40, an age where he ought to have known better. As Kent's visit to Bradford Park Avenue in 1971 had highlighted, there were Yorkshire games when Boycott's absence was called into question, but rarely because of the speed of the man taking the new ball for the opposition.

Even though they told the press it was done 'for very good personal reasons', the Test and County Cricket Board did not take Boycott's decision to skip the 1974/75 Ashes too well, blocking with Yorkshire's support his request to tour South Africa with a Derrick Robbins XI in search of sun and pre-season match practice in March. In May 1975 Boycott announced he was taking an indefinite break from Test cricket. The timing was immaculate. A few hours later Denness was announced as England's captain in cricket's first World Cup. Not only was the Scotsman's appointment overshadowed, it was harder to accuse Boycott of withdrawing because of it, as Denness had by no means been certain to be chosen. 'He abstained from playing for England at a time when Lillee and Thomson were at the height of their powers, ostensibly to devote all his time to Yorkshire,' Hutton comments. 'Well, he devoted the time to himself, not to Yorkshire.'

Chris Old, who had a foot in both camps, shares Hutton's sadness. 'I thought, that's fine for Yorkshire because he's going to be available all the time,' he says. 'It would be a chance for him to get everything sorted out but I don't think we performed as well in that period.'

The *Bradford Telegraph and Argus* revealed, 'The official Yorkshire attitude to their captain's decision is that he has not acted as they would have wished and that the club policy is to bring up cricketers who want to play for their country.' By then it was clear to Boycott he faced a battle to keep the Yorkshire captaincy. Without international cricket to worry about, it could at least command his full attention.

6

The Purge

THURSDAY 12 September 1974 was a momentous day in Yorkshire sport as a charismatic, outspoken leader with the self-confidence to match his ability was sacked after consistently ruffling the feathers of his senior players without winning enough matches. As Leeds United dispensed with Brian Clough, five and a half miles north, his friend Geoffrey Boycott was fighting for his job in the face of some uncomfortable questions in Headingley's committee room.

Another difficult season had tested patience among both Boycott's Yorkshire squad and the committee members meeting to decide, among other things, who should lead it next season. Boycott was taken aback by their hostile tone as he was asked his thoughts on playing under a different captain – and specifically John Hampshire, who averaged more than 50 that summer. Don Brennan sought assurances Boycott would not revert to his cautious early-season approach the next time he was short of form and Robin Feather voiced his concern the team was suffering as a result of the captain's frequent absences. Eventually the opener was asked to leave the room while those around the table reached a decision.

It had taken the Football League champions just 44 days to decide Clough was not the man to lead them. Boycott had good cause to be thankful that cricket – even in success-hungry Yorkshire – took a far more patient approach. He was re-elected for a fifth season as captain by seven votes to six. To have any hope of justifying the lukewarm faith he would need far more support from his players than he had enjoyed so far. Fortunately for him, Don Wilson, Phil Sharpe and Richard Hutton had all left by the time the 1975 season started. As well as being Boycott's leading dressing-room critics, the trio of close friends were the best equipped to replace him as captain. Once they moved on Boycott, free from international cricket and comfortable in the company of a younger and more responsive squad, cut a more relaxed figure and Yorkshire reaped the benefits.

Wilson, a slow left-armer who relied on bowling accurately from a great height, shrugged off the disappointment of missing out on the captaincy to have an excellent 1971, claiming 60 first-class victims at 18.25, but from there his career nosedived, taking only 46 wickets in the next three years combined. Some felt he suffered without Brian Close's wily captaincy, others for the absence of Ray Illingworth's tight bowling at the opposite end, but Hutton believes the 1970/71 tour of Australia and New Zealand, where Wilson won the last of his six England caps, was his undoing. 'Don lost his action,' he explains. 'He did an awful lot of net bowling on that tour and his arm had got low. I think gradually he lost confidence. It didn't help when Boycott was at mid-off in a match against Leicestershire and took his cap off and stamped on it after Don had been hit for another four.'

Wilson's form became an embarrassment when Yorkshire reached the 1972 Benson and Hedges Cup Final. With Boycott injured, the vice-captain had not taken more than two wickets in an innings for over a month. His pre-Lord's illness offered Yorkshire a smokescreen but he would not allow them to

THE WAR OF THE WHITE ROSES

use it. In cup final week Wilson played in a Minor Counties Championship game at York's Clifton Park, taking the wickets of four frontline Cumberland batsmen in the first innings, and adding two scalps in the second as Yorkshire claimed a ten-wicket victory. Even so, the selectors decided to go with the extra seam option of Howard Cooper against Leicestershire and to avoid unnecessary awkwardness, left Wilson out of the 14-man squad, citing his flu. Wilson, though, was not playing ball. With Yorkshire paying for him and his wife Jill to travel to London, he took part in a pre-match net session and told the *Yorkshire Post*, 'There is no question of me not being fit…. I thought that I might at least have been included in the party of 14.' Wilson was brought back against Surrey and Lancashire, but when Yorkshire lost both games by an innings, he was out again.

Boycott claimed the spinner's exclusion owed more to others on the selection committee but – spurred on, his captain felt, by an ambitious wife – the 35-year-old did little to hide his resentment. It spectacularly bubbled over at Southampton's White Rose Hotel in the final week of the campaign. With Boycott and the Hampshire team in attendance, a well-oiled Wilson let forth with some home truths, and announced he was considering an offer to join Derbyshire which would kick-start an exodus. It came to nothing. Wilson did not leave, nor did any senior player, and Boycott let the incident pass.

Wilson was selected for the 1973 Championship opener at Edgbaston, with Boycott claiming he was 'under orders to bowl him'. Wilson's 14 wicketless overs cost 69 runs in the one-innings-per-side draw. 'The ball was reaching the wicketkeeper second or even third bounce; the Warwickshire batsmen plundered Wilson and then treated him with a sympathetic indifference which may have hurt him just as much,' Boycott recalled. It was the final match of the 1973 season, with Boycott absent, before Wilson appeared in Yorkshire's first team again.

Having been groomed as Brian Close's successor, it would have been perfectly understandable had Sharpe also felt a little bitter when he and Wilson were usurped by a younger man with no captaincy experience. Sharpe was one of the all-time great slip fielders and while many reckoned he owed his England caps to that alone, an average of more than 46 runs from 12 Tests suggests otherwise. The committee misgivings which cost him the Yorkshire captaincy were shared by the man chosen instead. Sharpe and Boycott were very different personalities, the former viewed as a nice, sociable person who played for enjoyment by an opening partner who tried to be tough, professional and determined to win. He proved unable to help himself, scoring only three centuries during Boycott's captaincy, two in games the skipper missed. Leading Yorkshire out at Lord's in July 1972 offered an unexpected shot at redemption and cricketing history, but with his side outplayed twice that weekend – Warwickshire thrashed them by 109 runs on the Sunday – Sharpe did not feature again in the first team that summer. From then until May 1974 the rotund batsman would only play twice in the Sunday League, his lack of mobility in the field cited as the reason.

By far the biggest personality clash in Yorkshire's dressing room, however, was between Boycott and Hutton. Sir Leonard Hutton had been Boycott's boyhood hero but he held a dislike towards the legendary batsman's son which endures to this day. Ironically, given Sir Len was England's first professional captain (a concept Yorkshire's committee took another eight years to embrace), the fact his son belonged to the 'gentleman' era rankled with Boycott. He had been made to work hard for everything and resented those, like Richard Hutton, he felt had not. Boycott failed his 11-plus before winning a place at Hemsworth Grammar School a year later. He sat his O levels, then left for a steady job at the Ministry of Pensions but gambled by giving it up in July 1963 to try and make a career in cricket. Hutton went from the prestigious Repton School to Cambridge University, then juggled cricket with an off-field career. His dressing-room nickname was 'Archie' after

Archie Andrews, the blazer-and-scarf-clad prep schoolboy ventriloquist's dummy of the 1950s. 'Sharpe was a Worksop College boy, Richard Hutton Cambridge, Don Wilson was senior to Geoffrey; I think they all had aspirations to captain Yorkshire and with the benefit of hindsight and listening to various players and what have you, there could well have been a little bit of jealousy that a kid from the sticks, a young upstart, was captain above them,' says George Hepworth, but it could just as easily be his lifelong friend Boycott speaking.

Nevertheless, Boycott recommended Hutton Jnr to England's selectors in 1971. He tells me, 'I'd always pick him in my side because he was a good slipper, a good, tall, seam-up bowler and a useful batter,' but the kind words end there. Hutton made his second XI debut in the game where Boycott scored his maiden century at that level, at Bridlington in 1961, and his views on the man two years his senior were well entrenched after a decade on the wrong end of each another's acidic tongues. 'I was appalled that Brian Close had been removed, and that Boycott had been appointed captain,' he says. 'I was very fearful of how that would play out. The next four years were really most unenjoyable compared to how the previous seven or eight had been. One or two of us did try to tackle him from time to time about his commitment to Yorkshire and the way he was running the show. I can remember being given the answer one day, "Well it's all right for you, but I've got to think about playing for England." There was no end of incidents and issues.'

Unlike Sharpe and latterly Wilson, Hutton performed well under the new captain. Despite five England appearances in 1971, he was Yorkshire's leading Championship wicket-taker and joint top of the Sunday League charts. Improbably, given everything said since, he spoke glowingly of Boycott's captaincy before his Test debut. 'There were times in the 1960s when I didn't feel I was getting the opportunity I might have liked,' he explains. 'I remember a match in which Fred [Trueman] and Illingworth had been bowling, we got stuck and I was put on. I took two wickets in fairly quick succession and was immediately taken off. Fred was put on to bowl. I was so put out I refused to take my sweater from the umpire and stood there expecting to bowl the next over, but I was just bundled out of it. One was more involved [under Boycott] because I was having to do more than previously, when I probably was making up the numbers. I always thought he relied on my bowling quite a lot.'

Junior players such as Peter Squires and Andrew Dalton were also disenchanted. Dalton, a highly-rated batsman who made three first-class centuries in 21 appearances, resigned at the end of 1972 aged 25 to concentrate on what would be a successful business career. He declined to talk further about his reasons for resignation for this book, but in an earlier interview with Leo McKinstry explained, 'I resigned from Yorkshire primarily because there was such an unpleasant atmosphere in the dressing room. In my letter of resignation I said that the relationships between the captain and the senior professionals were too poor to entice me to keep playing.'

Drawing on his experiences after professional cricket, Dalton believes the Yorkshire committee created many of its own problems by choosing Boycott for a job he was unsuited to. 'Having spent much of my working life in industry running businesses or groups of businesses and being a reasonably experienced general manager I hold a fair amount of store on the quality of judgement of management boards, and the thing that has always stood out for me with regards to this sorry chapter in Yorkshire's history was the sequence of events that led to Brian Close's sacking,' he comments. 'I just thought that the whole process was poorly handled by the committee. I'm not sure it had to get to that point. The departure of someone who had been an excellent captain who led from the front in the interests of the side was a big mistake. The committee, which was too large, then compounded matters by making a fatal error of judgement in appointing somebody who was transparently not up to the job being asked of him, lacking both leadership and man-management skills. It's not entirely fair or reasonable to blame an individual for being a poor leader if he is asked to do a job he is not suited to.'

For many in the squad, playing for Yorkshire was not just an important source of income but a lifelong ambition. Dalton and rugby union international Squires had outside interests which allowed them to view the game as just that. 'I wasn't perhaps as committed to going down one route as some might be,' explains Dalton. 'I had a degree and had spent a bit of time in business during the non-playing months, so I had other options when the playing and dressing room atmosphere became more and more unpleasant.'

Tony Nicholson and Geoff Cope were frustrated Boycott was scared to use them more – in the former's case after having a blood clot removed from his leg in 1972, the latter because Sunday League cricket might expose his action to greater scrutiny. Hutton, Wilson and Sharpe, then, were not alone in their dissatisfaction with the captain. 'Usually you'd finish, have a shower, go into the bar, meet the opposition and chat,' says Chris Old. 'Geoffrey very rarely came into the bar whereas the majority of the team would chat to people. There were sometimes little things inside the dressing room that made you feel somebody wasn't happy – not that things were necessarily said, but you could sense them.'

Despite being unofficial leader of the opposition and an obvious candidate to replace him – something he made clear could only happen if Boycott left – it was not the captain's doing that Hutton's influence diminished. His job as a chartered accountant restricted the all-rounder to six County Championship appearances in 1973, and unsurprisingly he struggled for form. He was dropped for the final match, against Kent at Bradford Park Avenue, after just 65 runs and nine wickets. 'I was torn between two stools,' he explains. 'I was under pressure from my job to pack in cricket. They wanted me to go full-time but I remember telling [England chairman of selectors] Alec Bedser I was thinking about packing it in and he said, "Don't do that, go back to Yorkshire and get it all sorted out." I suppose that inspired me to carry on. I changed my job to play full-time for Yorkshire. That was a bad move, I should have finished at the end of the 1972 season, certainly after 1973.'

By 1973, Boycott had opposition from former players as well as current ones. 'When we were playing, people like Percy Holmes, Frank Smailes, Arthur Wood, Ellis Robinson, Bill Bowes, so many of the 1930s players, used to love coming into the dressing room two or three times a season,' explains Bryan Stott, founder chairman of the Yorkshire Players' Association, which was set up in 2005 to maintain the link between generations. 'It was fabulous for us to be able to talk to them and get this continuity of the Yorkshire tradition. When Geoffrey was made captain he stopped it. That to me was the biggest mistake he ever made as far as Yorkshire cricket was concerned. He thought people were planning against him so he banned past players from going into the dressing room or sitting on the balcony.'

In October 1972 Fred Trueman wrote the *Sunday People* column Sidney Fielden later described as the start of the anti-Boycott campaign, calling the captaincy 'his only failure in a brilliant career.' It was a theme the former fast bowler often returned to, notably ten months later at a dinner to mark the end of cricket at Sheffield's Bramall Lane.

After Boycott left at 11pm, Trueman launched a furious attack on his record. At the end of the 1973 season former captain Ronnie Burnet, citing Boycott's frequent international absences, called for Hutton to be made captain. Another ex-skipper, Vic Wilson, joined the chorus at Sessay Cricket Club's annual dinner, saying, 'There is nothing the matter with the ability of the players, but it is obvious that not everything is running as smoothly as it should.' Sir Len Hutton and Herbert Sutcliffe voiced doubts, as did Don Brennan. Not that everyone jumped on the bandwagon. John Temple criticised Burnet's comments, saying he had no reservations about Boycott's captaincy, and no change had been discussed by the committee.

'I have never heard such rubbish. The atmosphere in the dressing room is magnificent, much better than in the 1960s when we were winning the Championship,' said Nicholson, one of a number of team-mates to voice support. Whether they could have done any differently in the atmosphere Hutton describes is open to question. In 1973 Hampshire claimed the whole dressing room was behind Boycott but his endorsement when buttonholed in the car park of a Hull hotel after a game against Worcestershire the following season was far from ringing, 'I supported him before, but it is up to him now.'

'There weren't many people on Geoffrey's side at that time – at least not inside the club!' commented Ted Lester, who travelled with the first team as scorer. 'One or two of the players were pro-Boycott but the majority were anti-Boycott. Maybe one or two would have been a bit better players if they had played under Geoffrey, instead of going their own way. There was rarely a match where something didn't go wrong. If I said something in Boycott's favour – even, "Well played, Geoff" – that wouldn't go well for me. At times I'd say, "Go get some runs, Geoff, get your nut down and stay in." I thought he was better staying in than being sat in the pavilion but you try telling that to the ones that didn't like him. It was very rare he got credit for scoring runs. I think he was more intent on getting runs for himself than Yorkshire but if you look at the averages, he was top every year he was captain except his last. You couldn't really expect him to carry the can all the time.

'There was never a good team spirit. Boycs wanted to go his way and other people wanted to go theirs. There was no harmony at all. They were sad days, really. He couldn't have done anything about it. The committee could have. If Brian

Sellers had taken over as team manager, things would have been different. They would have had to toe the line. Nobody toed the line. They didn't respect anybody. There was a lot of undercurrent behind the captain's back. It needed somebody like Brian Sellers who would put his foot down and say, "You'll do as I say, and if not, you're going!" A few new members of the committee would have helped, but they seemed to get the wrong ones.'

If Lester was wary of saying the wrong thing to the wrong person, young bowler Mike Bore had no such concerns. 'It was fine,' he said. 'Well, it was for me. I was brought up to just stay at the back and listen to what people say – don't cast an opinion unless it really affects you. I just took the attitude, "What can I do?" There wasn't much asking your opinion but you daren't really express it because you didn't know whose flag was flying for who. The senior players would tell you just to get on with it, keep your head down and do the best you could.'

In June 1974, with Boycott in turmoil over his international career, he again infuriated Hutton. The opener went straight from Old Trafford and what would be the final Test of part one of his international career to Bath, where Yorkshire were playing Somerset in the Championship. 'Brian Close was captain of Somerset and I think for some reason he [Boycott] was somewhat unnerved about it,' Hutton suggests. 'On the morning of the match Philip Sharpe told us Boycott wasn't going to play because he was unfit [with flu] – he didn't necessarily need to be injured to cry off. I remember the match vividly because I happened to get 100 but we lost. Philip Sharpe dropped two in two off me at first slip.'

Rather than stay with his team, Boycott spent the final day playing for local club Landsdown against Selwyn College, Cambridge, showcasing the idiosyncrasies which could so annoy his colleagues. He hogged the strike, in one early over hitting the second, third, fourth and fifth balls for four, then knocking a single off the last, and even had the ball changed.

'Not that it was out of shape, but because it was leaving bright red marks on the blade of his bat,' John Woodcock explained in *The Times*. He made 108 before retiring. The next day he scored 149 not out for Yorkshire at Sheffield. 'I found that to be quite unbelievable,' says Hutton. 'Well, no, it is believable.'

Later that month Leicestershire's Graham McKenzie broke a Boycott bone for the second time in three years. After having his finger stitched in hospital under general anaesthetic, 'He spent the rest of the match lying in the physio's room not taking any further interest in the game,' Hutton recalls. 'It was reported he complained about the noise the batters were making with their studded boots as they passed the physio's door and would they kindly tread more quietly – actually "kindly" wouldn't have entered his vocabulary. That might be apocryphal.'

Boycott was called in for what he described as 'a long and very constructive chat' with chairman John Temple and committeeman Billy Sutcliffe while Hutton, Wilson and Nicholson drew up a petition among the capped players to have him removed as captain. Sharpe refused to sign and John Hampshire headed off the rebellion by revealing he had recently spoken to Boycott, who was considering retirement. 'He was a bit like Philip, a bit of a fence-sitter,' Hutton says of Hampshire. 'Philip had a philosophical compunction about ratting on one's team-mate. I think at the time Hampshire might have been in a good position to be the replacement captain and may not have wanted to prejudice that ambition by making an issue of it. We had a number of junior players on that petition who hadn't really played more than three or four years, and it was done at a particular fixture only among those playing. We couldn't see any point in proceeding without the support of the two senior players. Whether that was right or wrong, I don't know.'

Yorkshire enjoyed a strong finish to 1974, easily beating Derbyshire away and Surrey at home. 'Judged realistically and with a view to the long term Yorkshire had a better season than for some time,' reflected the *Yorkshire Post*. Despite his poor start, Boycott was the top Englishman in the national averages, and the only Yorkshire batsman to make 1,000 first-class runs. His benefit season was also a success, raising £20,639 – nearly half as much again as the county record Nicholson set the previous year. What pleased him most, though, was seeing his dressing-room enemies depart. Wilson resigned and Sharpe was released a year early to join Derbyshire after a desperately disappointing season saw him make 1,004 fewer first-class runs than Boycott with a top score of 51. Sharpe's penultimate century for Derbyshire came against Yorkshire in 1976, before his former captain caught him off Geoff Cope for 126.

Hutton's season had been disrupted by a torn intercostal muscle which severely restricted his bowling. 'In 1974 the committee offered me terms on a match basis, which meant I wasn't going to be an automatic selection, so I decided those terms were not acceptable,' he says. 'I couldn't really envisage playing for anyone else. Warwickshire asked me if I was available, to which I said no. The thought of playing for another county after my association with Yorkshire was abhorrent.

'He [Boycott] wanted rid of us so that he could make his position even more dominant. I think he was fearful of anyone coming into the side and shooting out the lights. It would weaken his position. Basically it's a flaw in his character, among others. His insecurity could govern his approach to other people. I think he certainly saw me as a threat, even though I had no particular ambitions towards the captaincy.' Incongruously, Hutton is wearing a Middlesex fleece. His son Ben broke the family link with Yorkshire, captaining the southern county.

Boycott went into 1975 with only two of the senior players inherited in 1971, both capped on the same October 1963 day as him – Hampshire and the fading Nicholson. Hampshire saw

Nicholson as a fellow mediator, but Hutton regarded him as being in his camp. Having won the power struggle, Boycott had to prove to a divided committee they had backed the right horse.

In February 1975 he held a secret three-hour meeting with chairman Arthur Connell and president Sir Kenneth Parkinson at the offices of the *Yorkshire Post*, where the latter was chairman. Boycott complained about the public criticism he was getting from members of the committee. 'How to establish trust' was top of his agenda, 'Eliminating disloyal elements' second. He realised there was more to that than simply cutting loose Hutton, Sharpe and Wilson. In pre-season Boycott, a student of Yorkshire County Cricket Club history, quoted Lord Hawke on winning his maiden Championship as captain, '"I could have won nothing unless I had the loyal support of the team and one of the best committees it was possible to serve under." I sincerely hope to be able to say something like that in the future.' Boycott asked the committee what they wanted from him and was told to take more risks and do more to encourage his youngsters. In return he would get their backing if he faced criticism.

A new side was emerging from the wreckage of 1968–70. David Bairstow, Phil Carrick, Chris Old, Barrie Leadbeater, Tony Nicholson, Peter Squires and Richard Lumb produced career-best batting performances in 1974, Arthur Robinson doing likewise with the ball. Arnie Sidebottom, a 22-year-old Manchester United central defender, made his Yorkshire debut in 1973 but did not add to his two Championship appearances the following season. In 1975 he became a first-team regular. Bairstow, then 23, had impressed sufficiently since winning the battle with Neil Smith to replace Jimmy Binks in 1970 to be capped three years later. Slow left-armer Carrick was 22 and all-rounder Graham Stevenson 19. Sidebottom, Bairstow and Stevenson played for England in the 1980s, while Old, Bairstow and Carrick captained Yorkshire. Jim Love, who would become a mainstay of Yorkshire's batting and a one-day international, made his debut in 1975, Bill Athey and Kevin Sharp in 1976.

If Boycott got his approach right, the youngsters generally showed the necessary mental qualities too. 'My idols weren't particularly cricketers, they were probably all footballers – Sprake, Reaney, Cooper, Bremner, Charlton, Hunter, Lorimer, Clark, Jones, Giles and Gray, sub Madeley,' says Sharp, reeling off the great Leeds United team of his youth. 'These great names of Yorkshire cricket, I knew they were great names, but they weren't my idols, so I wasn't too overawed. The first time I met Norman Hunter I couldn't speak to him I was that nervous but I didn't fear Boycs. I always felt he backed me. I felt he thought I could play although there were a couple of times when I really did lack some form and confidence and that would have frustrated him.'

Boycott seemed to enjoy working with his young side – 'He'd be the top dog,' Mike Bore told me. 'When the senior players were around, he was probably the junior one, along with John Hampshire' – and in 1975 they brought the best out of him. Hampshire observed, 'He made a conscious and obvious effort to get closer to the members of the team. He let his hair grow a bit longer and took to wearing discreetly flared flannels…. He became the better half of Jekyll and Hyde.' The *Yorkshire Post* noted, 'The mean machine has shown more consideration and humanity in this season than in any since he became captain.' Wives were encouraged to attend matches, Stevenson to be the team jester.

Boycott started making an effort to appear at the team's favourite Headingley watering hole, The Original Oak, and there were reports of him enjoying a drink at Worcester and in Glasgow in May. The first was a champagne party Boycott hosted after a century against Worcestershire, completing his set against the first-class counties, although his generosity had run out by the time it came to set a declaration and the match was drawn. Boycott looks back on 1975 as his happiest year in cricket, and before April's Benson and Hedges Cup Roses match he told the press, 'For the first time in 18 months I have basically found peace and contentment in cricket. I regard my main task as that of leading Yorkshire back to cricket supremacy and the next two summers are going to be important ones. I want to concentrate on developing the future of the game in Yorkshire where I believe I am best appreciated.' The approach was never going to totally suit everyone. 'Geoffrey seemed to be leaning towards the younger players just coming into the side,' says Old. 'The older players were kind of left to go their own way. There were several of us probably in the middle!' Generally, though, results were positive.

The mood may have been lighter but that did not mean standards had been abandoned, as Sharp discovered during his first week as a professional cricketer. 'I walked into the Yorkshire dressing room on 1 April 1976 fairly relaxed and walked straight into this fella called Boycott,' he recalls. 'He asked me what my name was, then he asked me where I lived. I said, "Just up the road." He said, "How did you get here this morning?" I said on the bus. So he said, "Put your bag down in that corner, get back on that bus and put some decent clothes on." I think I was just wearing jeans and a T-shirt and that wasn't how Yorkshire cricketers dressed, not even for practice. My mother was in the kitchen when I got back and she said, "What are you doing?" I put a shirt and jacket and some trousers on and went back on the bus. I'd missed nearly all the morning practice. When I got back he looked at me, did Geoff, and said, "That's better. My name's Geoff Boycott, pleased to meet you," and he shook my hand.

'On my second day John Hampshire asked if I could catch so when I said yes he sent me over to the slip cradle. After ten minutes I'd had enough, my hands were hurting but he said, "You just stay where you are." After half an hour my hands were bruised and there was blood seeping through. He pretty much said to me if you want to be a Yorkshire cricketer, you'll have to put up with it. By the end of the week David Bairstow had me pinned up against the wall because I was being cheeky to him. That was my first week! So I kind of got the idea very quickly there were certain standards that needed to be adhered to.

'We always had to wear a shirt and tie for the first two days of a County Championship match and you would always wear a blazer for lunch – these big thick donkey jackets with either your first or second team rose on it depending if you were capped or not – even in 90-degree heat. You had to shave every morning or you were in real trouble. It's funny, on my first day as a Worcestershire coach I didn't shave and it was liberating! Even as a coach at Yorkshire I always shaved because I felt as though that's what you should do. I was kind of ingrained with these wonderful traditions and they gave you discipline.'

Playing for Nottinghamshire between 1979 and 1988 gave Bore some perspective on the Yorkshire way. 'It was more enjoyable playing at Notts,' he explained. 'Yorkshire were more strict, at Notts it was more relaxed – go out and enjoy it and if you make a mistake, don't worry. The captain Mike Smedley, a Yorkshireman, was a very quiet, unassuming chap who just left you to get on with your game, whereas Yorkshire expected things. I was a bit of a practical joker, cutting the toes out of the socks and taking shoelaces out of shoes, and there was more camaraderie at Notts, I have to say. At Yorkshire if you made a mistake you got told off but they never carried a grudge. They backed each other but if you stepped out of line the senior players told you and put you back.

'Against Lancashire at Old Trafford [in 1973] I was about to bowl to Clive Lloyd and Tony Nicholson was at mid-on. "Nick" asked if I'd bowled at this bloke before and I hadn't so he said, "Whatever you do, don't bowl at his leg stump." You never know where the first ball's going to go, you're always praying. It pitched leg stump and he hit me over the pavilion into the car park. Nick came over and said, "Don't you listen to what I have to say?" I said, "It swung," so he said, "Don't swing it!"'

The fixture compilers handed Yorkshire a tough start to 1975 so, naturally, Boycott proceeded with caution. The first five Championship matches were drawn, leaving Yorkshire unbeaten but 14th at the start of June. They were struggling in the Sunday League and had lost in the Benson and Hedges Cup quarter-finals. June, though, brought cricket's inaugural World Cup, which largely took Yorkshire's biggest handicap – overseas players – out of the equation. Old was their only representative but Gloucestershire were without Sadiq Mohammad and Zaheer Abbas, Warwickshire missing Dennis Amiss, John Jameson, Alvin Kallicharran, Rohan Kanhai and Deryck Murray. Yorkshire hammered both. In between time they played Middlesex, who had no one involved and inflicted Yorkshire's only Championship defeat of the season. A week after the final Yorkshire played a Hampshire side minus Gordon Greenidge and Andy Roberts, who had played on the winning West Indies side, and injured South African Barry Richards. Semi-finalist Old returned for Yorkshire, who won by nine wickets. On 29 July, Yorkshire went top of the Championship for the first time since 1968 after beating Surrey by 35 runs at The Oval. Not everyone was happy.

'I think it is wrong that while the rest of us do our duty and are proud to do it, whether the going is tough or not, Boycott, who made his name with England and currently tops the national averages, should be able to opt out and carry his county to the top of the table,' said John Edrich, England batsman and Surrey captain. 'If Yorkshire win the Championship this season, it will be unfair to other counties who consistently give their best men for England duty.'

Boycott scored 462 runs at an average of 115.5 in Yorkshire's three Championship matches during the World Cup, but Old was not the only player they missed on England duty in 1975. Peter Squires spent May touring Australia with the rugby union side, while John Hampshire sat out matches against Middlesex and Glamorgan having been recalled after a three-year absence for the third Ashes Test at Headingley. On the flip side, Manchester United, back in football's First Division, allowed Sidebottom to keep playing cricket at the start of 1975/76 as long as he trained with them when not playing.

After victory at The Oval, Yorkshire had six games remaining, the chasing pack seven or eight. 'There have been years of famine since they last won the title and although it's a little early yet to start feasting it does look as if the lean times are over,' David Warner wrote in the *Bradford Telegraph and Argus*. Injuries, though, were starting to take effect. A fortnight earlier Yorkshire had played Lancashire in a Sunday League game at Headingley with only two capped players, Hampshire and Bairstow. Boycott lost patience with his batsmen in mid-season, saying, 'Unfortunately Barrie Leadbeater has not been doing well and younger batsmen like Peter Squires, Andrew Townsley and Alan Hampshire have not been making the most of their opportunities.' Yorkshire put up a good fight, winning ten Championship matches in 1975, but Ray Illingworth's Leicestershire came out on top in six of their last eight to take the trophy for the first time.

Yorkshire finished eight points behind in second, points they might well have taken had the third day at Glamorgan not been rained off, but every side has a hard-luck tale or two about the weather at the end of an English season. 'The big problem was the Roses match a couple of weeks before on such a flat pitch at Headingley,' argues Boycott, looking back 40 years on. Only 17 wickets fell in the three-day draw, with Boycott, Frank Hayes and Clive Lloyd making centuries. Finishing second – three years ahead of schedule according to Boycott, who had targeted fifth – earned Yorkshire £2,000 in prize money pushing profits close to £10,000, and membership went above

12,000 for the first time. Not since 1946 had they gone through a Championship season with only one defeat.

Boycott averaged 72.73 in the Championship and 60.54 in the Sunday League, where he fell 23 short of Barry Richards's all-time record for runs in a season, and Yorkshire finished joint fifth. John Hampshire and Richard Lumb also passed 1,000 Championship runs, the latter involved in six century partnerships with Boycott, and spinners Geoff Cope and Phil Carrick took 65 and 73 wickets respectively.

'I do not want to see it happen, but if Yorkshire were to recruit one top overseas batsman they would probably be an outstanding side,' commented Illingworth. Tony Nicholson's retirement – he made himself available for limited-overs cricket, but the offer was never taken up – added to the squad's youthful feel. Yorkshire's annual report proudly declared, 'To be runners-up after four years in the lower half of the Championship table is an achievement in itself. The contribution made to the achievement by the young members of the side leads to the hope that this is the beginning of a genuine revival.' After the tight squeak of 12 months earlier, Boycott was unanimously re-elected captain for 1976. His inquisitors of the previous year, Don Brennan and Robin Feather, did not attend the meeting.

Five years into Boycott's captaincy, a platform had at last been laid, yet it would be more than a quarter of a century until Yorkshire finished as high in the Championship again.

7

Turning Point

YORKSHIRE County Cricket Club can be reticent when it comes to handing out praise, with an uncanny knack of shooting itself in the foot when things are going well. Both characteristics were evident at the end of the 1975 campaign as with success finally back in sight, they quickly lapsed into their old ways. Perversely, Geoffrey Boycott's personal glory on returning to the international arena not only further handicapped them but also reinforced his position as captain.

Yorkshire finished 1975 with a 59-run win over Essex at Acklam Park. At the end of the match the travelling supporters wanted their young team to come out and take a bow, but they declined. 'We had a wonderful match, I scored 92, but we came second [in the County Championship],' Boycott explains, his attitude not softened by hindsight. His refusal to get carried away went beyond trivialities like laps of honour. Boycott advised the committee against adding to its pool of capped players, now down to himself, David Bairstow, Geoff Cope, John Hampshire, Barrie Leadbeater, Richard Lumb and Chris Old.

With only a few exceptions, those given the honour of wearing the full 11-rose petal as opposed to the rosebud of a colt, can pride themselves in knowing it was hard-earned. Brian Close is not the only player to have appeared for England before being capped by Yorkshire. In 1975 there were calls for Arthur Robinson and Phil Carrick to be added to the elite group. 'Yorkshire caps are awarded for persistently high levels of performance over a period of time, not on the strength of one encouraging season,' cautioned Boycott. 'The ones who have done well should be told so and rewarded financially but I do not think a cap must follow automatically.'

Yorkshire's committee followed the hard taskmaster's advice, and Boycott negotiated pay rises for Cope, Leadbeater, Robinson, Mike Bore and Howard Cooper. The snub was tough on Carrick, the county's leading wicket-taker in the 1975 Championship. It was no flash in the pan. The season had been his sixth as a first-teamer, accumulating over 1,000 first-class runs and 170 wickets. With the exception of 1971, when his solitary appearance produced economical bowling but no wickets (or runs), his left-arm spin had claimed more victims each year than the last, and in 1975 his batting broke the 500-run barrier for the first time. In August he produced career-best figures with bat (87) and ball (8-72) against Derbyshire at Scarborough.

Boycott's attitude seemed like just another example of him failing to appreciate the need to encourage his Yorkshire players, particularly the younger ones. Although the decision on caps ultimately lay with the committee, the blame was put at his door. 'I played on the staff for 11 years and I never got offered a cap,' pointed out Bore, who did not feature in 1975 as Yorkshire tried to convert him from a seamer to a Derek Underwood-style medium-pace left-arm spinner. 'Boycott's the captain, he makes the recommendations, so you begin to realise where you fit.'

Carrick's mistreatment was tacitly acknowledged the following year when, after taking fewer wickets at a higher average, he belatedly got his dues.

'Carrick did have a disappointing season this year but we have taken a broad view of his playing career with Yorkshire,' explained cricket chairman John Temple. Even then the committee did not handle it well, delaying a decision until the player was in Port Elizabeth for the winter. Robinson also got his cap by following Fred Trueman and Ray Illingworth's example and threatening to leave.

Injuries were the biggest barrier to continued Yorkshire progress in 1976. Tony Nicholson's retirement put extra responsibility on to Old, their only current England international, and his body was not up to it. Injuries were a constant frustration throughout his career, and still are. As the third Test between England and India petered out into a draw at Headingley in 1979, Graham Gooch entertained spectators with his repertoire of bowling impressions. He kept his cap on for his Boycott, then did John Price, Bob Willis and Jeff Thomson before finishing with Old, who was missing through injury. Gooch ran in and pulled up with a mock thigh strain. 'The Yorkshire crowd were not slow to see the joke,' the *Bradford Telegraph and Argus* noted.

Old went on ten England tours yet the only one he completed was Australia in 1976/77. It was not much of an achievement – it consisted of a solitary warm-up game and a one-off Test. When I visit his house in Cornwall, he is signed off work at Sainsbury's after a knee operation and struggling with his shoulder, regular problem areas during a career which saw him win 46 Test and 32 one-day international caps, be the only Englishman to play in both Centenary Tests, play a vital supporting role in the 'Botham's Ashes' Test of 1981, captain his county, score nearly 8,000 first-class runs, take over 1,000 wickets and still give the impression he could have achieved more. 'I think [Boycott] believes I should have been better than I was,' he reflects. 'In hindsight I agree but you can't turn the clock back. I've had a serious problem with my knee since the early 1970s, which I've managed to keep going with. Possibly there were times when I could have been fitter. There were times when we had days off and I'd go home and totally relax when perhaps I should have put a bit more training in to keep things ticking over, but you do need to recharge the batteries. I should have worked harder on my batting too. I got into a rut of doing what I wanted to.'

Despite, that, he believes he was given leeway by his demanding captain. 'I always feel he had respect for me, especially in those three years he wasn't playing Test cricket,' he says. 'I was the only one so I think he respected me for what I was doing. After a Test match it can be very difficult the next day to get up and play but he knew I'd give it everything I'd got, even if sometimes it just wasn't there.'

Old had surgery on both knees in 1970 and 1971 but when it was decided in August 1976 to go back in to remove loose bone, there was a serious risk. 'I might still have been in a wheelchair,' he told *Wisden* in 1979, when he was named one of the book's players of the season. Old had been struggling with the problem since facing Surrey on the opening weekend of the season and made just six Championship and two Test appearances. Arnie Sidebottom played three times in the Championship after dislocating his right elbow playing for his new football club, Huddersfield Town. The most damaging absence of all, however, was the captain's.

In May against Essex Boycott suffered the indignity of two single-figure dismissals in a Championship game for the first time since the 1973 Roses match at Sheffield, but that apart he made a good start to the campaign and was in a real purple patch when taking on Lancashire once more in a Sunday League match at Old Trafford. Having filled his boots against Cambridge University earlier in the week, Boycott had taken his tally to 266 runs without being dismissed when Ossett-born Barry Wood struck him on the right hand. He batted on for seven overs before admitting defeat. His broken finger was due to keep him out for three weeks, but when he suffered a disc problem in his back playing football in the park, that extended to two months or 18 games, nine in the Championship.

Hampshire took over the captaincy and had the good grace not to break his own finger until Boycott returned, although he did damage his tendons in a Sunday League game against Kent in June, handing over to Cope rather than senior professional Leadbeater, who days earlier had taken 208 minutes to score what would be his only Yorkshire century.

A good performance as stand-in by Hampshire would have given ammunition to those committeemen who in the autumn of 1974 had toyed with handing him the captaincy full-time. The bad one that followed added to their frustration with Boycott. Two wins, two defeats and five draws was Hampshire's Championship record, but in May he presided over another limited-overs humiliation. Yorkshire's place in the Benson and Hedges Cup quarter-finals was all but guaranteed if they beat the Combined Universities in their final Group D match at Barnsley's Shaw Lane. The Oxbridge students had performed respectably in their debut season in the competition, winning two matches in 1975, but this was their last chance to take a point from the 1976 edition.

Boycott's injury had seen Bill Athey make his debut three days earlier and although he put on 53 for the first wicket with Leadbeater against the students, the runs came slowly. Sent in at three to up the scoring rate, Old made a duck, and when Hampshire was run out for nought, Yorkshire were 67/4. They totalled 185/7 in 55 overs. The students included Yorkshire second-team wicketkeeper Stephen Coverdale, who was studying at Cambridge, future England players Peter Roebuck, Vic Marks and Chris Tavare, and top-scorer Gajan Pathmanathan, who had made seven appearances for Sri Lanka in all formats. Pathmanathan took advantage when, in the words of Terry Brindle, the hosts 'bowled too badly for any words the *Yorkshire Post* would accept'.

Old conceded 36 runs in his opening four overs and admitted, 'I was dreadful, absolutely dreadful.' Brindle wrote that Yorkshire 'were beaten with embarrassing ease'. Second in the Championship, Yorkshire finished the season eighth as Hampshire and Boycott detected the team spirit which had been such an important factor in 1975 draining away. 'Without my runs and my captaincy the team really struggled,' Boycott reflects. 'It was a big factor. Once we weren't winning and I wasn't playing, all the shenanigans started up again. It was only silenced in 1975 because we were winning and I was scoring runs. It was only quiet when we were doing well. The Combined Universities game was a big disappointment but it wasn't the beginning or end of anything. The committee thought we should always be champions and the best team but other teams had overseas players and we just couldn't match that.'

Boycott was frustrated. He had been told to keep his distance from the team when injured and was not allowed a say in selection, presumably so the committee could gauge how Hampshire would fare if given the captaincy full-time. He claimed Cope, Cooper, Robinson, Carrick and Lumb approached him during his lay-off with complaints about Hampshire being too weak tactically and too tough when it came to dishing out criticism, although if Bore had a problem then, he did not by the time he spoke to me. 'John was all right, quite capable,' he says. 'He was hard, from South Yorkshire. Him and Jimmy Binks were good mates and two mentors when I first went into the set-up. He was quite popular in the dressing room. It's all to do with trying to maintain standards.'

There was just as much exasperation with Boycott's body, and in late June John Temple was forced to deny a newspaper story that Yorkshire were considering sacking him as captain. Instead the tensions came out in other ways. In July, Mel Ryan, a Yorkshire seamer in the 1950s and 1960s and Huddersfield's general committee representative since 1974, turned on

Temple, criticising the relationship between the cricket committee he was a member of and its stand-in captain. Ryan called for Temple to be replaced by someone with first-class playing experience (Temple's career had not gone beyond captaining York in the Yorkshire League), and threatened to resign and go public with his concerns. He remained an occasionally exasperated member of the cricket committee for two more years.

If the team struggled in 1976, many individuals were starting to show real potential. Athey, the son of the Acklam Park groundsman and a talented enough footballer to have been offered terms by Middlesbrough as a 16-year-old, made an important 70 not out in his third Championship appearance, a win over Kent, and followed it two matches later with an unbeaten 131 against Sussex. He was 18 years and nine months old. Some saw him as Boycott's long-term successor, others compared his strokeplay to Sir Len Hutton, the only player to have scored a Yorkshire hundred at a younger age. Graham Stevenson smashed four half-centuries and took 23 wickets in the Championship as well as recording his first five-wicket haul in one-day cricket, Bairstow and Jim Love scored maiden first-class hundreds in August, and 17-year-old Kevin Sharp made his debut in the final match. Boycott tipped all six as future England internationals in his 1980 book *Opening Up*. He was right about all but Carrick and Sharp, although whether any achieved their potential is debatable.

'One or two people I do know always felt he made life difficult for them,' Old says when I ask about Boycott's attitude towards his youngsters. 'Others it seemed no matter how they performed they were the ones.'

Bore, by contrast, believed 'he was fairly even'. Those Boycott took a shine too got his help off the field as well as on it. 'I had a very good relationship with Geoff,' Sharp reflects. 'When I got married to my first wife I lived in Wakefield not far from Geoff. I'd had five or six winters abroad but I stayed at home after that and he helped organise me some coaching in Wakefield and over Hemsworth way where he came from with some of the local lads and parents he knew, so he was good to me in that respect. I even bought a bed off him when I got married! I suppose most people had kind of a love or hate relationship with him. Half the team probably thought quite a bit about him and the other half didn't. He was very forthright, as he still is.'

Caps and contracts were the battlegrounds for Boycott's latest round of end-of-season struggles with the committee. In contrast to his attitude 12 months earlier, the captain wanted Arthur Robinson, Howard Cooper and Carrick capped on the field against Northamptonshire to reward their loyalty and lift spirits at the club. Yorkshire morale would need raising further that week, as even Carrick's 7-137 could not prevent a 198-run defeat. Rather than reward Robinson and Cooper, selection committee members Billy Sutcliffe, Don Brennan and John Temple wanted to sack them, along with Steve Oldham, Peter Squires and Colin Johnson. Perhaps their hearts were in the right place, trying to make space for the youngsters by clearing out the uncapped players who threatened to block their path, but their captain certainly did not see it that way, later calling it 'wholesale slaughter'.

Ryan and Doug Padgett supported Boycott's capping recommendations, so with the vote deadlocked the matter was referred to the wider cricket committee, which met in October, by which time the captain was in Australia. Geoff Dennis seconded Ryan's proposal to cap Robinson. Treasurer Michael Crawford suggested Robinson and Carrick – voted the club's most promising player by supporters – and carried the day 8-4. The only player to leave was Squires, although a decision on whether to offer Cooper, Yorkshire's other out-of-contract player, a new deal was delayed while he sought specialist help over his back problems. While far from spectacular, Squires's 1976 season had been the best of his five with Yorkshire in both

Championship and limited-overs terms, but at 25 it was felt he was not fulfilling his potential.

In May 1976, England selectors Ken Barrington and Sir Len Hutton travelled to Hove, where Yorkshire were playing a Sussex side led by national captain Tony Greig, to find out if Boycott was interested in returning to Test cricket. He says he discussed it with his Yorkshire players and they wanted him to themselves, so Greig was left to try to make the West Indies 'grovel' without him. Greig upped the ante, offering Boycott the vice-captaincy for the winter tour of India, Sri Lanka and Australia only for Boycott's injuries to put the issue on hold. Selector Charlie Elliott asked again at the end of the season, but Boycott was reluctant to put his name forward when he had doubts about whether he would be selected and besides, Elliott acknowledged the spin-dominated subcontinent might not be the best place for someone with an unwanted reputation for dodging fast bowling to return. In one respect, the situation was unchanged from 1974: England were still being led by someone Boycott regarded as an inferior captain who was not even English, as Greig's thick South African accent made clear. In 1977, however, the cricketing landscape changed dramatically.

Kerry Packer, owner of Australia's Channel Nine television station, was under pressure to produce more local content and saw exclusive live sport as the answer. He offered A\$2.5m to secure the television rights for Test cricket in his country between 1976 and 1981, yet the Australian Cricket Board opted to stay loyal to the government-funded Australian Broadcasting Commission for A\$210,000 over three years. Next he tried to buy the rights for the 1977 Ashes in England, but the Australian authorities recommended their Test and County Cricket Board counterparts take ABC's offer which, again, was far smaller. Packer responded in just about the most radical way possible – by trying to set up his own version of Test cricket. It was a very real threat to the sport's world order, fiercely resisted not only by Lord's but supporters across England. Leading English players Dennis Amiss, Alan Knott, John Snow and Derek Underwood were among the first to agree to join what the media and authorities disparagingly referred to as Packer's 'circus'. After an initial approach in March 1977, so did Boycott.

The appeal was obvious. Boycott was earning between £3,000 and £4,000 a year with Yorkshire, and returning to the England fold would bring in an extra £400 per Test. Packer was offering £25,000 a year. As soon as the enormity of what he had shaken hands on became clear to the Yorkshireman, he backed away. When Packer went to the High Court in September and October to stop the International Cricket Council banning his World Series Cricket players from the Test arena, Boycott recalled this conversation with the television mogul, '"Does that mean I can't play for Yorkshire?" He said, "That's right." I said, "Hang on a minute, under no circumstances. I can't sign the contract in its present form."' Boycott told the court he would happily have signed up for one series that would prolong his international exile – he had, anyway, agreed to be in Australia in 1977/78 for another winter with club side Waverley after averaging 165 for them in first-grade cricket in 1976/77 – but nothing which threatened his involvement with Yorkshire.

Dennis Lillee was suspicious, claiming the real reason Boycott turned Packer down was that he wanted to captain the Rest of the World team – or if not him, his future sparring partner Ray Illingworth – while Greig claimed when the news of WSC broke Boycott begged for a chance to reconsider. Tellingly, that story was not repeated under oath in the High Court. As the first high-profile player to shun Packer publicly, Boycott, so often to be found sitting on the other side of the fence and never on it, became an unlikely Establishment hero. His standing was confirmed when he and Illingworth, who was not offered a Packer deal, were the only current English cricketers called at the High Court by the defence, who had hoped to put Sir Don Bradman in the witness box until his wife fell ill.

If Boycott was the most high-profile English good guy, there was no question who the baddie was. Greig's role as Packer's chief recruiting officer cost him the England captaincy and left a tantalising void for a player already thinking about returning to the international scene. Boycott had outlined 'the next two summers' as crucial to Yorkshire when he spoke about his self-imposed exile at Old Trafford in April 1975, and had given them his full commitment. Now England needed their ninth-highest run-scorer and chairman of selectors Alec Bedser stressed if Boycott made himself available again, his past would not be held against him. The question was to what extent he would try to exploit his strong bargaining position.

In May 1977 Terry Brindle suggested there were only three credible replacements for the sacked Greig among the ranks of county captains – Boycott, Hampshire's Richard Gilliat and Middlesex's Mike Brearley. Gilliat had a modest first-class record but good off-field credentials – an Oxford University graduate who later taught at Charterhouse. Brearley was also a clever man – the Cambridge graduate juggled his early career with lecturing philosophy at Newcastle University – and had been given the winter vice-captaincy Boycott turned down despite only two Test caps. The wicketkeeper-turned-opener was still to make a Test century (he never would) and had scored only 340 runs in his first eight matches.

England faced a choice between proven captains with dubious playing credentials and a world-class cricketer whose captaincy skills were open to question. Some even doubted Boycott's runs could still be relied upon at the highest level. Three years was a long time to have been out of Test cricket and even with so many high-quality overseas players, the county game was no substitute. As far back as 1975 *Wisden* editor Norman Preston questioned 'whether he will ever be a force again in Test cricket'. Then there were the diplomatic questions, always important at Lord's: should Boycott be allowed to waltz back in as captain without first serving time in the ranks? Should he ever be allowed to captain the country he turned his back on? 'If England want Boycott back with the proviso that he can never be their captain, I doubt he will go,' commented Brindle in the 17 May edition of the *Yorkshire Post*.

On 11 June Boycott informed Bedser he was available but the following morning he was not named in the squad for the first Ashes Test at Lord's. Captain Brearley would open with Dennis Amiss, the Packer rebel. Both the *Yorkshire Post* and *Bradford Telegraph and Argus* took it as a sign that, three years after his last Test appearance, Boycott's international career was finally over. England were simply playing hard to get, not wanting to be seen to drop everything the minute he fluttered his eyelashes, particularly as he was yet to score a century that season. Amiss made nought and four in the rain-affected draw but the selectors reasoned it would be unfair to drop the Warwickshire opener on the strength of one game, so their only change for Old Trafford was to bring spinner Geoff Miller in for batsman Graham Barlow. Boycott put his extra time with Yorkshire to good use. The *Harrogate Herald* described his first century of the summer, 139 not out against Somerset, as 'another masterclass in batsmanship'.

A fortnight later Yorkshire faced Australia – minus the rested Jeff Thomson and Lennie Pascoe (Lillee missed the tour through injury) – at Scarborough with Boycott knowing he needed a good performance to make his case to England. He was lbw to Max Walker second ball as the hosts were bowled out for 75, but redeemed himself in the second innings. 'It was my second game,' Kevin Sharp recalls. 'He knocked one into cover when he was on 98 and I sent him back quite loudly. There would have been a run-out and it might have been him because of the angle of the ball. The crowd were enjoying it.' Boycott survived to make 103 not out, though some criticised him for being more focused on trying to prove a point to the selectors than pushing for victory. Two days later he made 117 at Lord's against Middlesex – 'probably the most colourless century of his career' according to David Warner in the *Telegraph and Argus*. A match-winning 154 against Nottinghamshire made it three in a week.

On 29 July 1977, the day Brian Close announced his retirement from county cricket, an in-form Boycott returned to Trent Bridge with England. He had played his first Test there against Australia in 1964 and 1,143 days and 31 matches after his previous appearance, this was effectively a second debut. England were 52/2 when Boycott stroked the ball down the pitch and set off for a single that was never there. Crowd favourite Derek Randall, batting on his home ground, was hopelessly run out. Boycott put his head in his hands as Randall trudged off. Greig and Miller had been and gone by the time Thomson found the edge of Boycott's bat and Ryan McCosker dropped what umpire Dickie Bird called 'a simple catch at first slip' with the opener 20 not out. He went on to score 107, then 80 not out in the second innings, standing at the non-striker's end as Randall hit the winning runs. Boycott had spent all five days on the field.

The century was the 98th of his first-class career. His 99th duly followed in his next innings, for Yorkshire at Edgbaston. 'A myopic man threading a needle could not have applied himself more diligently', Brindle wrote. Boycott did not bat in the second innings, promoting Chris Old up the order to take advantage of feeble bowling from an 'attack' more intent on improving its over-rate than taking wickets. He smashed 107 from 73 balls, the second 50 coming in nine minutes and featuring five sixes. At 37 minutes in all, it was two short of being the fastest hundred in first-class history. Once it was over Old opened the bowling with Boycott, each taking a wicket.

By not batting in the second innings of the draw, Boycott had set up the possibility of making his 100th first-class hundred against Australia at Headingley. 'I hadn't really thought about it at the time although I knew I'd got my 99th hundred, I wasn't stupid!' he says. 'There was no time [left in the game], really, and no chance of a result, so I sent Leadbeater and Lumb in to have a knock but Warwickshire were just treating it like a benefit match. Their over-rate for the season was down so they had people on the boundary throwing it back and they even bowled John Whitehouse and Alvin Kallicharan – they couldn't bowl for toffee! – just to get the rate up. That wasn't Chris Old's fault, and he just took advantage, but it was just farcical bowling. I only thought about the 100th hundred when I rang Rachel [Swinglehurst, now his wife] that night. She said, "You've done it now." I asked what she meant and she told me they were all over the radio saying I was on for my 100th hundred at Headingley. I said, "Oh no, I don't need that!" I'd had enough pressure on me in the previous Test, that was bad enough.' To ensure he did not get carried away with himself at Edgbaston, Old, Arthur Robinson, David Bairstow and Graham Stevenson had thoughtfully thrown him, clothed, into a bath of ice cubes.

Of the 17 batsmen who had reached the landmark worldwide, none had done so in a Test match, let alone in front of their home crowd. In 1951 Boycott's hero Len Hutton had to settle for 98 not out from 142/1 against South Africa when his winning shot bounced in front of the cover boundary. Even then, it would have been achieved on the wrong side of the Pennines, at Old Trafford. 'Boycott's mission is doomed to failure, if only because its success would be too fantastic,' Brindle claimed. Not for him.

He was 34 not out when the *Scarborough Evening News* went to press on 11 August declaring, 'Everything was pointing towards Boycott's 100th hundred on his home ground.' As his future Yorkshire team-mate Ashley Metcalfe put it, whenever Boycott was at the crease 'you knew full well if he got over the first half-hour he would bat all day' and most spectators had seen enough of him to understand that too. They 'seemed to regard the achievement of this landmark as inevitable' according to *Wisden*.

A drinks break was taken with Boycott 94 not out and at 5.50pm, after five hours and 20 minutes at the crease, the oldest man on either side drove Australia captain Greg Chappell through the on-side for the boundary that took him to exactly 100. 'A scoreboard showing 101 or 102 would have spoiled the symmetry of it all,' wrote Warner, summing up the perfection of the moment. It took five minutes to clear the field of celebrating fans and a loudspeaker announcement by Joe Lister to retrieve Boycott's cap.

Some 260 miles away at Hove, Yorkshire's Championship match against Sussex was held up by applause. Boycott returned the next day, when the gates had to be shut at 10.45am with 150 people already inside with nowhere to sit, and completed his highest Ashes score, 191.

If it was the apex of Boycott's career, it was the turning point of another disappointing Yorkshire season. As in 1976, they lost their way without their captain. Unbeaten in their opening 14 first-class games (they won six), Yorkshire were fifth in the Championship when Boycott made his Test comeback, but had already topped it four times. They lost five of their next six matches. On the day before the Trent Bridge Test, Middlesex's Wayne Daniel went on a rampage at Sheffield. Hampshire, Lumb and Sidebottom were forced to retire hurt after being struck by the West Indies fast bowler. The following day Jim Love could not field after jarring his hand facing Daniel, and Bairstow was unable to keep wicket after lunch having been struck on the thigh by him. Howard Cooper, Colin Johnson, Steve Oldham, Leadbeater and Old all appeared as substitute fielders. Old was only at Abbeydale Park for treatment on his injured shoulder, yet spent more than four hours fielding.

Yorkshire only used nine batsmen in the second innings, Bairstow opening so Lumb could come in at five, as Middlesex won by 157 runs. Both captains reported the pitch's uneven bounce but in that respect at least, Yorkshire avoided punishment. X-rays showed Sidebottom had fractured his left forearm, Hampshire had a severely bruised elbow, and Lumb a damaged left thumb. All three missed the next game, against Hampshire at Headingley, the first of three as stand-in captain for Geoff Cope. While Boycott was making history at Headingley, Yorkshire were losing by an innings in Sussex, immediately followed by a two-day defeat at Worcester.

Although Boycott was England's leading run-scorer of a series which pushed his Test average above 50 for the first time, his 100th hundred was his last of 1977. It took until Yorkshire's final match of the year for Hampshire to reach three figures. Without that, Boycott would have made more Championship centuries than the whole of his squad combined that summer, despite missing seven games. Mindful of jeopardising his 1979 benefit year and with the hostility towards World Series Cricket now obvious, Old also turned down Packer in August, so when the High Court ruled the rebels could not be banned from the county (or international) circuit, it was a blow to Yorkshire, who would have been unscathed.

Boycott's team-mates noticed a difference as soon as he returned to international cricket. 'He went back into making sure his performance was the key,' says Old. 'It was back to how it was before,' Mike Bore concurred. 'He was that sort of person, very selfish but he wouldn't be where he is otherwise.'

Two days after making himself available for England again, that aspect of Boycott's personality was back in the spotlight. Yorkshire lost by six wickets at Kent, where, in the words of John Callaghan, '[Derek] Underwood swept through the second innings, like a forest fire on an accommodating track' to take 7-43. Boycott scored 61 of Yorkshire's 127 but did so by dodging the chief threat, rather than protecting lesser batsmen. He faced just 20 of Underwood's 60 final-day deliveries.

For Bore, number 11 at Folkestone, it was nothing new. 'In 1973 we put on 108 for the last wicket, against Notts at Bradford,' he recalled. '[Garfield] Sobers was playing for Notts. Guess who had to face Sobers? I played and missed for a good 40 minutes and finished up two not out overnight. Geoffrey batted through and played really well. The next morning I was getting a few runs [37 not out]. He clipped one off his leg and ran but I saw who the fielder was, so I said straight away, "No, no, no, come in." He got run out. There's not many people have run him out but I've done it twice!' For the next four years Boycott's presence among the Yorkshire youngsters he had inspired over the last couple of seasons was fleeting.

As far as the English cricketing public were concerned, their returning hero was untouchable. In January 1978 Boycott's dream of captaining his country became a reality. He had been named vice-captain for his first sub-continental tour and when Brearley broke his arm in Lahore, Boycott led England in one Test against Pakistan, and three more in New Zealand. Despite Yorkshire finishing 12th in the Championship, there had been no end-of-season arguments over sackings before he set off. All 18 contracted players were awarded new deals, and Sharp received his first. Even so, there would be battles ahead.

8

Back to Fire the Bullets

DON BRENNAN saw Geoffrey Boycott's return to international cricket as an opportunity to once and for all end his tenure as Yorkshire captain. Waiting until he was at the peak of his popularity before trying to bring down a man who had survived seven years of often bitter internal opposition was doomed to failure, yet October 1977 marked the beginning of the end for Boycott as skipper. Little did he know it, but he was in the final 12 months of his captaincy, his status as the undisputed heavyweight of Yorkshire cricket about to end.

Brennan was elected one of Bradford's representatives to the Yorkshire committee in 1971 with a strong playing pedigree. Unusually tall for a wicketkeeper, he played for the Army in Egypt during World War Two and in 1947 joined Yorkshire as an amateur, making 167 County Championship appearances and captaining eight times in his final three seasons. In 1953 he retired, aged 33, to concentrate on the family textile business. Like Jimmy Binks, Brennan's batting stopped him winning more Test caps, averaging just over 11 in the Championship, but his glove-work was good enough for him to be picked ahead of Godfrey Evans for the final two Tests of the 1951 home series against South Africa. That winter he made his only first-class half-century, on the first leg of England's tour of India, Pakistan and Ceylon. Brennan also served on the board of rugby league club Bradford Northern, and in 1973/74 he was chosen to replace Brian Sellers on Yorkshire's selection committee. Ever since Boycott had been 'unanimously' chosen as captain in November 1970, elements on the Yorkshire committee had been eager to remove him.

Robin Feather, another Bradfordian who had been his second-team captain in 1962 and 1964, and Billy Sutcliffe, son of the legendary Herbert, who both served on the cricket committee throughout his captaincy, were constant critics but in Boycott's eyes, 'Brennan was the worst one of all.' He claimed, 'I walked into selection meetings knowing that Brennan would give me a rough ride just for the hell of it.' Boycott was kept well informed of what his committee opponents were up to thanks to Terry Brindle, who succeeded Jim Kilburn as the *Yorkshire Post*'s cricket correspondent in the mid-1970s. 'They didn't realise, but Terry Brindle used to drink in the same pub as them [the Half Moon in Collingham] and he'd tell me what they were up to,' he says.

Once the now-traditional end-of-season meeting for players to air their grievances to the hierarchy – this time orchestrated by Boycott – was out of the way, Brennan made his move. On 30 September in a BBC Radio Leeds interview he called for Geoff Cope to take over as Yorkshire's captain. 'It was very disappointing to finish 12th in the County Championship this year and we were diabolical in the one-day competitions,' he said. 'We must try to find out in the winter where we have gone wrong and then try to do something about it…

'We want young players to have a father figure to bring them on and lead them as a team. Next year Boycott is likely to be playing Test cricket and we will lose him as a captain during the Tests. Someone has to get a grip of the team and mould it into an efficient side. There has to be someone there encouraging them all the time and if the captain is absent for 50 per cent of the season then it isn't a very good system.'

Proposing Cope did not show a lot of faith in vice-captain John Hampshire, or the spinner's ability to win a regular England spot having been selected for that winter's Ashes. Cope had filled in as captain for three matches in 1977, all comprehensively lost, but Brennan saw in him the unselfish qualities he felt were lacking in Boycott. 'If people who say things in private are prepared to stand up and be counted in public, I know I will get a lot of support,' he commented, pledging to stand down from the cricket committee if not. As it turned out, Cope missed even more Yorkshire cricket than Boycott in 1978 after he was banned for the final eight Championship games when footage from The Oval revealed what the Test and County Cricket Board called 'substantial straightening of the arm at the elbow immediately prior to delivery'. It was a year before he was allowed to play first-team cricket again.

Arthur Connell, widely regarded as a moderating influence, called Brennan's comments 'deplorable and badly timed', though he admitted he was not alone on the Yorkshire committee – which had made great play of supporting Boycott's return to the Test fold – in being 'nervous' about regularly losing the captain to England again. Different circumstances perhaps, but it did not unduly trouble Sussex or joint champions Middlesex, who finished above Yorkshire despite Tony Greig and Mike Brearley's international commitments.

At a Variety Club dinner in honour of his former Barnsley team-mate's 100th first-class hundred, Michael Parkinson came to Boycott's defence. 'I have no doubt that if it came to the crunch of whether Geoff Boycott should be sacked or the committee jump over a cliff they would be advised to book a bus to Scarborough,' he said. With Huddersfield-born former Prime Minister Harold Wilson another paying tribute at the dinner, Boycott was not short of friends in high places. Mel

Ryan came at the debate from a different angle, threatening to resign from the cricket committee, 'Unless there is a dramatic change in the way things are run,' adding, 'We don't maintain a close enough contact with the players on a day-to-day basis.' As in 1976, Ryan did not follow through on his threat.

Not only was Brennan forced to resign from the cricket committee, he inadvertently brought about the formation of a protest movement which for years would have a big influence in steering Yorkshire in the directions Boycott wanted, widening divisions as it did so. The Action Group put together in response to Brian Close's sacking had been disbanded in 1975, bequeathing £400 to the club, but anger at Brennan's comments inspired its successor.

Huddersfield's Grade II-listed George Hotel is best known as the place where Yorkshire and Lancashire rugby union clubs met in 1895 to create rugby league, but in October 1977 it hosted another group of malcontents, this time Yorkshire cricket fans. Even before his 100th hundred, Boycott had attracted a loyal following. In an era when the county's cricket team did little worth bragging about, his consistently prolific performances were a source of Yorkshire pride. Largely unaware of the politics being played out off the field, and in many cases not interested anyway, his supporters judged him by what he did on it. Being seen to be at odds with the 'gin-and-tonic brigade' who ran English cricket – be it a Test and County Cricket Board often viewed as out of touch, the national selectors, or the Yorkshire committee who sacked Brian Close and allowed Ray Illingworth to leave – was hardly likely to damage his standing with the rank-and-file.

'Boycott was almost a caricature, extreme in what he represented,' explained barrister Matthew Caswell, who acted for the batsman and the Reform Group. 'Everyone saw in Geoffrey Boycott what they wanted to see. He was the son of a miner, he came from the mining community, his mother did too, and yet he was very much right- wing and an Establishment figure. As soon as he had any money it was Woolley [the village he moved to], and not Fitzwilliam [where he was born].'

On 9 October the first meeting of the Reform Group, attended by ten people, decided to petition against Brennan's comments. 'We are unanimously upset by the action of Mr Brennan, in whom we have no confidence as a member of the committee,' said John Featherstone, the local government official from Leeds who, along with Manchester accountant Peter Briggs, played a leading role in the early days. So did Tony Vann, to the surprise of Julian Vallance. 'He played cricket with people like Sutcliffe when he was qualifying for the MCC,' he says. 'The Boycott predicament had existed for years and in that group he was always being criticised and Vann never said a word to the contrary. He was obviously keeping his powder dry.'

The Reform Group's petition for a special general meeting and a vote of no confidence in Brennan got 828 signatures. They were wasting their time. 'When John Featherstone and Peter Briggs went to Leeds to present the petition, Joe Lister [Yorkshire's secretary] came out and said, "No use hanging about, Geoffrey's been reappointed,"' recalls George Hepworth, another early member of the group. The Yorkshire committee had met in secret seven days earlier, when Brennan resigned and the cricket committee he left behind unanimously voted Boycott in as captain for 1978. It had been so secret even Boycott did not yet know. The battle the Reformers had been set up to fight was won before they had started it, but in keeping quiet the committee allowed an organisation which would cause them considerable grief in the coming years to take hold as a powerful vehicle for airing grievances against them.

The Reform Group opened a bank account, engaged solicitors, and learnt lessons from their predecessors. 'An Action Group was formed initially by Stuart Anderson and Dr

John Turner, people like this,' explains Hepworth. 'I think that was the nucleus of people joining together to form a Reform Group. They kept that in mind. Stuart was chief of police in South Yorkshire and he came to a meeting. He told us in no way must you shout, dress smartly, treat everyone with dignity and respect, and listen to them. We had terrific guys on board like Bob Slicer and Reg Kirk, very good people and articulate speakers, along with Sidney Fielden. They did quite a good job.'

Just because the committee had not dared remove Boycott – 'The members would have torn us to pieces,' John Temple is supposed to have said – did not mean they were blind to Yorkshire's problems. On 10 November 1977 they announced a dramatic solution: Ray Illingworth as team manager. Although the idea of a Yorkshire manager had been mooted in the press before, the announcement caught the media by surprise. Throughout his negotiations with chairman Connell, treasurer Michael Crawford and finance committee member Norman Shuttleworth, Illingworth insisted as few people as possible know about them, inevitably upsetting those kept in the dark – not least his employers, Leicestershire. Yorkshire's committee was so outraged only president Sir Kenneth Parkinson's intervention stopped Connell losing his job. They were asked to approve the principle of a team manager – something they had been discussing for three or four years – at another secret meeting, on 31 October. Ten days later the news was out in the open, although Illingworth would not start until 1 April 1979 once his Leicestershire contract expired. Still there was secrecy. When asked how long Illingworth had signed up for, cricket committee chairman Temple would only tell the press conference it was 'longer than a year'. It was three.

'Raymond was such a super tactician – he got better when he went to Leicester – and we felt it needed a strong hand to pull them together,' explains Bryan Stott, a Yorkshire team-mate for 12 seasons. 'Raymond, with the clout he had, you listened.' Since leaving his home county in 1968, Illingworth had captained Leicestershire to a County Championship, a Sunday League title and two Benson and Hedges Cups, and England to an Ashes series win in Australia. News of his return was therefore well received. 'I thought at the time it was just what we needed,' says Chris Old, one of the few remaining members of Yorkshire's squad to have played alongside Illingworth. 'The first year and a half I thought it was a good thing. It was only as I got deeper involved in it that my opinions changed.' The county proudly talked about having the 'two best brains in the game', but therein lay the problem.

Boycott and Illingworth were stubborn Yorkshiremen with egos to match their immense cricketing knowledge. The question for some was whether they could work together, but many wondered if they were ever meant to. 'I felt that was the way that they were going to get rid of Geoffrey,' Old admits. 'I think deep down they hoped he would move of his own volition, rather than having to push him.' Ted Lester agreed – 'I'm certain they brought him back to get rid of Boycs' – and soon so did Illingworth. 'I was starting to develop a nagging feeling that the committee were bringing me in so that I could, among other things, do what they did not have the guts to do – that is to fire the bullets at Boycott,' he reflected.

Vallance, who was not on the committee when Illingworth's appointment was announced but was by the time it came into force, does not believe that was the motivation. 'I think we knew when Illy came back that Boycott wouldn't like it,' he concedes. 'It was a bit like bringing Brian Clough to Leeds United, it was fairly obvious Billy Bremner wasn't going to like it. I think he was appointed as a superior tactician able when he judged it necessary to over-rule Boycott's influence on the team, to mould the team. Illy was recruited to have a serious influence on the way our cricket was played, and on who played it. He was a hands-on cricket manager. He had a great say in who played and how the game was played, and he was brought in to do that. That was bound to rub Boycott up the wrong way in some respects.

'Illy had a few run-ins with Boycott when they were with England and we would have known about that. So when Illy was appointed we would have known it wouldn't be entirely to Boycott's delight. But I don't think we did it to get rid of Boycott. No. If Illy had wanted to get rid of him, he would have got rid of him quicker. It was to provide new leadership for the cricket. We had a lot of time for Illy – [Fred] Trueman did, Ronnie [Burnet] did. He was very, very highly rated. Whether he was as highly rated by the members I don't know, because they were in love with Boycott, there was no question about that.'

The role of team manager, separate from Doug Padgett's ongoing job as coach, was rare in county cricket – Colin Page had the title at Kent, while Tony Brown was Glamorgan's 'secretary-manager' – and many were highly suspicious of whether and how it could work. Boycott and Illingworth were therefore keen to sort out the division of responsibilities as soon as possible, rather than wait until 1979. The captain even suggested cricket committee member Norman Yardley – a former England and Yorkshire captain with a reputation as a soft touch – take on the role in 1978 as a dry run, but his idea never got off the ground.

Boycott had promoted the concept of a Yorkshire team manager as soon as he was made captain, but his thinking was for Lester to free him up to take control of the cricket; a heavyweight like Illingworth had not been employed at considerable expense (one unnamed team-mate claimed Yorkshire offered 'half as much again as Raymond expected') simply to organise hotels and speak to the press. Boycott's primary concern was who would have the final say on team selection. Connell had already been quoted in the *Yorkshire Post* as saying it would be Illingworth, who claimed it was written into his contract he would have the ultimate responsibility for choosing even the junior teams, but Temple claimed the last word lay with Boycott.

At a meeting in the players' dining room at Headingley on 13 November between Illingworth, Boycott, Parkinson, Crawford, Yardley and Temple, Illingworth said he would pick a squad for the captain to choose a team from, adding if he disagreed too often with his choices, he could always hand him a group of players that effectively made the decisions for him. It was clear, having enjoyed so much limited-overs success at Grace Road, that Illingworth wanted complete control of that aspect of Yorkshire's cricket, which he planned to target as the best way to end their trophy drought. Under Boycott the county won just two Gillette Cup ties against first-class opposition and although runners-up to Leicestershire in the 1972 Benson and Hedges Cup, they did not get out of their group in four of the next six seasons. Unsurprisingly given who was driving it, Leicestershire's one-day success had been built around spinners, who often played bit-part roles or none at all in the sides Boycott picked in the shorter formats.

Boycott does not think Illingworth was suited to his new job. 'As a captain, you will not find me saying anything but excellent things about Raymond,' he tells me. 'But you could see from when he became manager of England [from 1994–96], he couldn't cut it. His forte was being on the field and making decisions, but when someone else was out there having to make the decisions, he wasn't so good.' The relationship between Illingworth the manager and his Yorkshire captains would always be problematic until he cut out the middle man and took on the role himself in 1982.

'Illingworth never, ever, even when he was manager of England, wanted to be anything other than the leading voice,' points out Geoff Cook, who captained Northamptonshire in two Lord's finals and later won the four-day and 50-over competitions as Durham's coach. 'It was very much in evidence then that he wanted the big say in what was going on. It's always been my belief that the captain has to run the show. I think the game generally is coming round to the idea that the captain is the most important person. If you're going in with a group of people who you don't feel are really the right people to make your decision-making as sharp as it could be, you've got a problem. If you have people you don't really fancy it becomes a bit of a compromise. You have to use them to an extent, but you're not really behind them. That's always been one of the dangers of a coach–manager relationship.'

Illingworth's appointment was clearly going to clip Boycott's wings, and England's vice-captain was acutely aware of it. Given the contrasting fortunes of both as skippers in the 1970s, he did not have much of a case to argue against it, however, as Illingworth bluntly pointed out. 'He asked me how I would have felt if such an appointment had been made "over my head" at Leicestershire,' Illingworth recalled. '"Geoff," I said, "considering that for the past six or seven seasons Leicestershire have been one of the most successful sides in the country, there was no question of such a situation arising. Now if I had been captain for eight seasons during which the county had won nothing and only rarely looked to be in a position to win anything, I would not have been surprised at all in a new appointment. Why should you be?"'

The idea of the two working together in this way was not new. As far back as July 1973 the *Sunday Mirror*'s Ted Dexter had suggested Illingworth as England manager and Boycott as captain. Illingworth wanted Boycott as his vice-captain for the Ashes tour of 1970/71 but without consulting him the selectors opted instead for Colin Cowdrey. The subsequent years as international team-mates and county rivals had inevitably produced a few flashpoints between two strong-minded Yorkshiremen but Illingworth told the media he had no worries about the partnership, and was expecting a good working relationship. 'Rarely since Chamberlain's "Peace in Our Time" broadcast has a public utterance been more horribly demeaned by events,' reflected Leo McKinstry.

The way the club was run would have to alter with Illingworth's arrival, and the Reform Group wanted to have their say. Like the Action Group, the Reformers may have come into being because of the perceived mistreatment of a high-profile player but, as their name suggested, they were interested in more deep-rooted changes. In late January 1978 they proposed a select committee of no more than ten (half of them Reformers) be set up to discuss the constitution, rules and management of the club. Yorkshire dismissed the idea, arguing it was contrary to that constitution. Once Illingworth started picking the team there would be no need for a selection committee, and the cricket committee went with it. In its place was a management committee for Illingworth to report to on a monthly basis, made up of the various sub-committee chairmen, club officials and six elected representatives of the overarching general committee. In trying to streamline the decision-making process, Yorkshire had come up with yet another unwieldy body, too big for the liking of Illingworth, who was always keen to take on as much responsibility as possible in return for the power that came with it.

At the club's annual general meeting, in March 1978, Parkinson expressed his view that the club was 'on the verge of another golden era of Yorkshire cricket' but warned, 'We have the players in strength and depth, but we don't have a "team"… we shall not win competitions until we have committee, staff, members, public and players pulling together at the same time and in the same direction for the same purpose.' The Reform Group were an obvious threat to that happy state of affairs, but so too was the manager-in-waiting. Yorkshire had brought back an individual whose bloody-mindedness was, after all, the reason he left in the first place and put him into a system where he was expected to compromise with the captain. It was never likely to work if that person was equally obstinate, and Boycott undoubtedly was.

First, though, there was Illingworth's interminable notice period to get through. Changes were made to try and inspire an improvement in performances before he arrived. Win bonuses were increased for 1978 and National Breakdown – whose managing director Bob Slicer was a leading member of the Reform Group – gave £25 to Yorkshire's man of the match in each Championship game which would go straight into the player's pocket, rather than the team pool. There was a £200 bonus for the player who won most awards during the season and £100 for the best fielder.

Illingworth signed off at Grace Road with a disappointing summer for him and his team. He took fewer first-class wickets than in any English season since 1954, and his run tally was his poorest since 1952, when he only played six matches. As a result, the captain was dropped for three Championship games. In June, days after his 46th birthday, Illingworth was criticised for an over-generous declaration when Leicestershire set his future employers 271 to win in 115 minutes plus 20 overs. A 189-run opening partnership between Richard Lumb and Bill Athey laid the platform for Yorkshire's four-wicket win. By the time Illingworth finally started work back at his home county after more than a decade away, Boycott had been removed as captain, all the time he had spent in meetings haggling over who would do what largely wasted.

Hot on the heels of Don Brennan's failed coup attempt, Illingworth's appointment amounted to a declaration of war on Boycott by his own committee and in the Reform Group he had a volunteer army to fight it on his behalf. Boycott may have lost some important early battles, but it was Illingworth who would most live to rue the day he agreed to return to Yorkshire.

9

An Alternative
Emerges… Slowly

ONLY Lord Hawke and Brian Sellers had served longer
as Yorkshire's captain but with an average County
Championship finish of tenth and no limited-overs
silverware to soften the blow, it was not results which had kept
Geoff Boycott in the job into an eighth season. More often
than not when the committee sat down each October to select
a skipper for the following year, alternatives were thin on the
ground.

Dwindling form meant Don Wilson and Phil Sharpe could
not be relied upon as first-team regulars after 1971, while
Richard Hutton became a part-time player in 1973. Chris
Old was England's vice-captain in the first two Tests of the
1977 season but his fitness and international commitments
restricted him to 23 Championship appearances from a
possible 64 between 1976 and 1978. Geoff Cope's availability
was constantly in doubt because of the seemingly unrelenting
scrutiny his bowling action was under from the authorities.
By definition they went into games without their best player,
but none of the captains who deputised for Boycott between

1971 and 1977 particularly impressed, contributing seven of Yorkshire's 37 Championship wins. In 1978 the county at last found another player guaranteed a place in the side capable of leading them to victories. Half a year after apparently wanting to sack him as vice-captain, the committee leapt on John Hampshire's emergence as a credible candidate, and gave him the top job instead of Boycott.

Boycott and Hampshire had long been rivals – it was just the latter never realised. Born four months and 11 miles apart, the pair from the pit villages had known each other since the age of 13. They came through the ranks together and were awarded first-team caps on the same day. When batsman Alan Hampshire played alongside his brother at Worcestershire in the Sunday League on 8 June 1975 he did not bat or bowl, and rarely touched the ball in the field, yet still made history. Seamer John Hampshire Snr made just three appearances and was never capped, but is the only man to play for Yorkshire's first team and have two sons do likewise. His eldest started as a leg-spinner then developed into a second XI opener, but had settled into a new role at number four when a first-team vacancy opened up at the top of the order, so Brian Close instead asked a reticent Boycott to step up from the middle order. The positions the pair established themselves in were good fits for both – the cautious Boycott was better suited to opening, the powerful batsman from Thurnscoe ideal for coming in later, except on Sundays when the pair regularly faced the new ball together in 40-over cricket.

Unbeknown to Hampshire, the shy, insecure youngster from Fitzwilliam regarded him as a serious threat to his hopes of a career in the sport. Hampshire's talent was more obvious as a teenager and he was the first invited to Yorkshire nets, and to make his debut for the second and first teams. When he took 7-52 against Glamorgan with his leg spin in 1963 (a bowling performance he never bettered in first-class cricket),

Boycott is said to have remarked, 'What do I do now, learn to bowl slow left-arm?'

Hampshire was Boycott's room-mate on England's 1970/71 Ashes tour and even cut his hair before he returned home as Yorkshire's new captain. Both had been cruelly treated by the national selectors, in Hampshire's case given just one more game after a century on his England debut at Lord's in 1969, a unique achievement at Headquarters until Andrew Strauss matched it in 2004. Eight caps was no reflection on Hampshire's talent, but Boycott's greater concentration and consistency allowed him to make far more out of arguably less.

As bickering became a regular feature of Yorkshire's dressing room in the early 1970s Hampshire tried to act as the mediator, often speaking to Boycott about the squad's concerns. 'In many ways John Hampshire was the real Yorkshireman through and through,' argues former Northamptonshire opener Geoff Cook. 'He had a passion to play for Yorkshire purely for the cricket and he wanted the youngsters to go on without any of the obvious ego of the others. He played the good guy in many respects.' It was one of the ironies of the War of the White Roses that it was the peacemaker who brought about Boycott's downfall with an incredible act of defiance – and weeks later was rewarded with the captaincy.

The roots of Boycott's demise came when he injured his back bowling in Yorkshire's Benson and Hedges Cup defeat to Nottinghamshire on 20 May 1978, then badly bruised his thumb fielding in a one-day international against Pakistan four days later. An 'arthritic condition' set in. Hampshire led the team to four wins and two draws in seven Championship matches, plus three victories from four Sunday League games. The Championship successes included wins over the old enemy, Lancashire, and a Leicestershire side led by Yorkshire's manager-in-waiting Ray Illingworth.

It was quite a turnaround for Hampshire, whose captaincy both during Boycott's long absence in 1976 and his return to international cricket in 1977 had been unimpressive, and his relationships with the selection committee and some players poor. So unhappy were the committee that in April 1978 they had wanted to remove Hampshire as vice-captain, only for Boycott to successfully argue for him to be kept on. Not only did results justify that, Hampshire was also in fantastic form with the bat. As stand-in captain he made half-centuries against Derbyshire, Lancashire and Middlesex, and hundreds against Nottinghamshire and Northamptonshire (followed up with 76 in the second innings). It would be Hampshire's most productive season, making a total of three Championship centuries and nine 50s, as well as three half-centuries and a top score of 114 in the Sunday League, where Boycott never went beyond 40. His form and the pace of his scoring were such a concern that in July David Warner dared ask, 'Should Boycott drop out of John Player League games?'

By then, Yorkshire's frustration with their captain was building. He had turned down a two-year contract in the winter, asking for a 12-month arrangement instead and, as was usually the case when he was injured, his employers were in the dark about when he might return. They were seemingly resigned to waiting for the nod, rather than being seen to put any pressure on a player no more willing to rush his comebacks than his batting. When Boycott asked to play for the second XI against Nottinghamshire in a three-day game at Scarborough, secretary Joe Lister made no attempt to hide his irritation. He told the *Daily Mail,* 'We know no more than that. He telephoned this morning to say he now felt ready to play in the second team. As far as his long-term future is concerned, the average member knows probably as much as the committee.'

Rumours Boycott and Illingworth could swap counties in 1979 (there was also speculation about Somerset interest now Brian Close had retired) gained sufficient ground for Leicestershire to issue a statement confirming they had not made an approach, and for Boycott to write to *The Times* –

with Yorkshire's blessing. 'As my future appears to be a source of permanent speculation by members of the press, I would like to place formally on record that it is my intention to play first-class cricket for Yorkshire and England just as long as I am able to maintain a proper standard of professional ability,' he confirmed. It was not just the rumour-mongers stirring the pot, however.

Deliberately or otherwise, Illingworth opened a damaging rift between Yorkshire's two senior players. He and Hampshire had remained close friends since their time as club-mates. Hampshire was a regular visitor at the Spanish holiday home owned by Illingworth, captain for five of his eight Test caps. Although he had only played once for his country since the last of those, at The Oval in 1972, in the summer of 1978 Illingworth began promoting the idea Hampshire should captain England, and according to Boycott encouraged journalists to do likewise.

Boycott was still injured when Yorkshire travelled to Grace Road in June, and the friends met for dinner during the Championship game. There Illingworth mentioned Boycott had previously told him he did not trust Hampshire. 'I went straight up the wall,' the latter wrote. 'At the first opportunity I sought out Boycott and gave him a chance to put his side of the story. When he didn't give me a satisfactory answer I was livid… I told him exactly what I thought of him and reported the matter to the chairman.' An equally angry Boycott claimed not to remember the remark – though he did not deny making it. Yorkshire demanded an explanation from Illingworth, and when Boycott and Hampshire were summoned to the *Yorkshire Post* offices to hear it, they were told the comment had come during a meal at his house three or four years earlier. On top of his game and with the incoming manager's support, Hampshire now had the motivation to bring about something he had spent much of the last eight years trying to prevent – the removal of Boycott as captain.

On 15 July 1978 Yorkshire, eight games unbeaten in the Championship, travelled to Northamptonshire's Wantage Road. They had come straight from The Oval where Boycott, fresh from 127 for the second XI at Scarborough, featured in a five-wicket win wrapped up at 6.08pm the previous day, thanks in no small part to 48 and 39 from Hampshire. The first Test against New Zealand was 12 days away and having not played in the three-match series against Pakistan because of his injury, the *Scarborough Evening News* noted Boycott was 'anxious to establish his Test place again'. The result was, he admitted, 'pretty grim stuff'. Geoff Cook won the toss and his Northamptonshire side made 280/7 in the 100 overs permitted. Left to face the final hour and hampered, he claimed, by his injured thumb, Boycott's response was to score 17, and when play resumed after Sunday's rest day he extended it to 113 in 90 of the 100 overs. His first 50 did not include a boundary.

Fortunately Bill Athey was in fluent form, making 114, so when Boycott was out, bringing Colin Johnson to the crease, only 33 was needed from ten overs for a fourth batting point. 'I had not gone in with any idea in my mind other than playing the way I had always done,' Hampshire later explained. 'But when Boycott finally went for 113 in getting on for five hours I suddenly thought, "What the hell's it all about? We've watched slow batting for so long. Now I'm going to see what it's like."'

Between them, he and Johnson scored just 11 runs. The in-form Hampshire played four scoring shots in 59 deliveries, while his junior partner contributed six singles from 26, and had a number of others turned down. The *Yorkshire Post* called it 'an inexplicable anti-climax to Yorkshire's innings', although that did not stop bemused spectators approaching the press box in search of an answer. The *Scarborough Evening News*'s suggestion it could have been a ploy to force an early Northamptonshire declaration was generous at best.

'It was incredible,' Cook recalls. 'Like in 1971, we didn't really twig what was going on at first. The innings Boycott had played didn't seem any slower than we'd seen him play before [as a percentage of runs scored, it was his second slowest for Yorkshire]. He was the big prize and we thought we were doing okay to control him, it was quite an efficient performance. It only really came to light when John Hampshire batted with Colin Johnson. Hampshire was giving Johnson strict instructions to play as few shots as possible. It was pretty obvious after a while. I'm not quite a contemporary of John Hampshire's but we'd spent a lot of time together and I was saying, "What's going on here?" He said, "That **** cannot get away with this. It's a protest block." We were getting through with damage limitation. Our bowlers were queuing up to bowl a few maidens! At times it was amusing. People were wondering what was going on. They had set a launching pad for a huge total, then brought the game back to us. The game was a draw from a position where they were going to dominate.'

With only ten minutes between innings, Hampshire claimed nothing was said to him in the dressing room. It surprised and angered him. 'Boycott didn't say anything to me, man to man, but left it to the committee,' he wrote. With no hint of what was to come during their eight overs together Boycott claimed to be oblivious, having changed in a back room with no view of the cricket, until a furious David Bairstow burst in. 'The mood in the dressing room was murderous and I knew it would be impossible for Hampshire and myself to discuss it in front of the team without creating a mighty row, so I bit my tongue,' was his explanation. According to him, the confrontation came instead with Bairstow in the shower, '"It was a bloody disgrace what you did," said Bairstow,' Boycott recalled. '"I just couldn't score," answered Hampshire. "Come off it, in the nick you are of course you could," said Bairstow.'

If Hampshire was taken aback by the lack of reaction on the Monday, the rest of the week made up for it. Extra reporters were despatched to Wantage Road as once more rowing Yorkshire cricketers became the media's focus. With

Boycott not batting having been hit on the wrist shortly before Northamptonshire's declaration, the White Rose never got close to their victory target of 290 in 160 minutes, shaking hands on a draw at 5.30pm on 108/2. Nevertheless, the *Yorkshire Post* noted Hampshire had batted aggressively for his 38 not out.

'The final day became a real political hot potato,' Cook comments. 'The media were coming in, as were the administrators from Headingley. Boycott never changed his rather distant attitude. He'd got a hundred and he was happy with that. He'd laid the foundations for a big score. I think he said at the time it was no worse an innings than others he'd played. The cricket became a side issue. That was symptomatic of the whole era, it was like a party political show. Every game we turned up it seemed something was going to happen.' Yorkshire, third in the Championship at the start of the game, had thrown away 13 points by not passing 300 then forcing victory.

In the 1970s it was relatively rare for Yorkshire committee members to attend away games, but the match coincided with a United Newspapers board meeting, giving a horrified Sir Kenneth Parkinson the opportunity to watch Hampshire's first innings. Committee member Billy Sutcliffe was also there. Parkinson was staying at the Saxon Hotel, as was John Callaghan, cricket correspondent for the *Yorkshire Evening Post*, part of the United group. The next morning the president invited Callaghan to breakfast where he is said to have told him, 'I truly think it one of the worst days of my life. Things cannot be allowed to continue in this way.' Parkinson had always been pro-Boycott, and felt the opener's scoring rate was questionable, but Hampshire's behaviour blatant and indefensible. As the president's was an honorary role, his powers to do anything about it were limited.

The cricket committee waited for the players to return home and held an investigation at the end of the following day's play at Bradford Park Avenue. The selection committee of Sutcliffe, John Temple and Ronnie Burnet called witnesses and carried out an investigation which lasted more than four hours, then reported back to the cricket committee, who in turn updated the general committee. Dragged into Thursday by rain, the Gillette Cup tie against Nottinghamshire produced a thrilling finish and a rare win in the competition – by one wicket with three balls to spare – but for neither the first nor the last time at a Yorkshire game, the cricket was a side issue.

Sutcliffe, Temple and Burnet sided with a contrite Hampshire. They told him he should have gone for the bonus point and voiced his concerns off the field, but sympathised with his frustration at Boycott's slow scoring – not just in Northampton, but generally. Johnson told the selectors he intended to go for the point, but when his vice-captain told him he did not, thought he should follow his lead.

Boycott in turn complained he 'felt uncomfortable as though I was in the dock'. As Julian Vallance explains, the selectors were in tune with wider feelings on the general committee, who unanimously approved their action. 'It didn't really cause a big stir in the main committee, it just fuelled the anti-Boycott feeling among those who were already anti-Boycott,' he says.

The minutes of the hearing acknowledged Boycott scored too slowly, but when reference was apparently made to his 'selfish batting' in a press statement, Parkinson intervened to have it removed. Instead, the brief missive gave the *Yorkshire Post* the impression, 'The committee seemed anxious to sweep the whole affair under the brown and gold carpet of the players' room.' One reporter asked Temple what Parkinson's opinion of the go-slow had been, but the cricket chairman claimed his president had not voiced one in their ten-minute telephone conversation earlier that day. Given that Parkinson had been at Wantage Road and Temple (and Burnet) had not, it seemed highly implausible. Hampshire left the ground clutching his whites, cleaned and pressed for the next day's play, without comment.

David Warner wrote an angry comment piece in the *Bradford Telegraph and Argus*. 'The John Hampshire "go-slow" controversy was discussed for four hours by the Yorkshire selection committee at Bradford yesterday afternoon, and then dismissed in a bald three-line statement,' he began. 'The selectors have absolutely no intention at present of letting the public know why the incident occurred or what steps have been taken... The selectors may consider it closed but thousands of Yorkshire members may consider it otherwise. They may consider they have a right to know what caused Hampshire to bat 18 overs for seven runs and add 11 in the last ten overs with Colin Johnson.' Warner urged members who felt the same to lobby their committee representatives to have the information released.

Yorkshire's coyness left an information vacuum the captain seemed only too happy to fill. 'Boycott hung around at the back of the room and invited – or so I thought – questions,' an anonymous northern journalist was quoted as saying in Hampshire's book *Family Argument*. 'It turned into a muttered press conference between the captain and those members of the press he thought he could trust. Nothing was quotable but I came away with the impression that the committee had backed him and bollocked Jake [Hampshire]. As I recall, other papers shared that view. Subsequently events suggested that we all grabbed the wrong end of the stick which was proffered to us. I'm not sure who should take the blame, but Yorkshire must share it for refusing to confirm or deny the only source of information open to us.' Boycott was livid to be portrayed as the bad guy when he felt Hampshire ought to have been suspended and stripped of the vice-captaincy, Hampshire equally furious when the front page of Thursday's *Yorkshire Post* – and other pages in other newspapers – reported he had been censured.

The uncapped Johnson, who made nought the day after the enquiry, only played Championship cricket once more for Yorkshire, after Boycott was sacked as captain. He was dropped but Hampshire played against Glamorgan, where the suspended Geoff Cope was not missed thanks to 4-11 in 17 balls from debutant spinner Peter Whiteley. Johnson's only other appearance of 1978 was a Sunday League match at Old Trafford on 27 August, where he made two.

Almost a year later he made the next and last of his 86 Championship appearances, and on being released at the end of the season became second XI captain. His second-team form had done nothing to suggest he had been unfairly treated. 'Colin and I used to travel together all the time, we were good mates,' revealed Mike Bore, who was also released in 1978. 'We both got asked what we wanted to do and I said when I finished I wanted to coach so I thought I'd got the edge on Colin as second team captain but it wasn't to be.' Johnson was replaced, without explanation, by Steve Oldham in 1985. Runners-up the previous year, Yorkshire had won the 1984 Second XI Championship.

The Saturday after the go-slow it was business as usual as Boycott and Hampshire batted together against New Zealand. A fluent Hampshire contributed 90 to their 131-run partnership, while his captain was criticised for labouring more than four and a half hours over 103 not out. 'Boycott's ultra-careful approach certainly guards against batting collapses, but is it good for team morale and is it always necessary with so many talented batsmen often waiting to get to the wicket?' asked Warner. Yorkshire had a first-innings lead but although they opened with Jim Love and David Bairstow there was not time to win. Boycott made 48 from 52 overs in the next match, against Somerset at Taunton in the Championship. It was also a draw, Yorkshire only having time to take eight second-innings wickets.

The go-slow could hardly be said to have derailed Yorkshire's season – they suffered only one further

Championship defeat, to Middlesex in a rain-affected one-innings game at Lord's – but the selection committee's response mortally damaged Boycott's captaincy. A private poll of capped players by Cope – which, contrary to popular belief, Illingworth denied knowing anything about until afterwards – showed only five per cent support for the captain. Boycott, unhappy Cope had been selective in whose opinion he canvassed, conducted his own poll but instead of asking did they want him as captain, the question was would they play under him. As Illingworth pointed out, 'There is one heck of a difference – and the players answered that as members of the Yorkshire County Cricket Club team they would play under whoever was elected captain.'

Hampshire further strengthened his case by completing the Championship double over Lancashire, although the win really belonged to Chris Old. He took over the Yorkshire captaincy for the first time when Hampshire was injured and made 100 not out from number nine, including a 105-run ninth-wicket partnership with Howard Cooper. He also took match figures of 9-85 in a ten-wicket win. Phil Carrick had scored his maiden first-class century in the Headingley game, won by an innings and 32 runs with a day to spare, but Hampshire's 54 was Yorkshire's next highest on a pitch reported for inconsistent bounce.

On 8 September Boycott's run of 15 consecutive seasons at the top of Yorkshire's averages came to an end. The unique achievement was halted at Scarborough where, according to the *Yorkshire Post*, Boycott made 'the longest and unloveliest 23 of his chequered career' with 'the selective and wholly engrossed pastime of a man eating a pomegranate with a pin' in victory over Gloucestershire. He finished sixth in the national standings, Hampshire – the first England-born player to 1,000 first-class runs in 1978 – fifth. Boycott did not make the top three in the county's player of the year award, which was Hampshire, David Bairstow and Kevin Sharp, in that order.

As captains there was little to choose between the pair. Hampshire contributed as many wins (five) from ten Championship games as Boycott did from 12 to Yorkshire's fourth-place finish, and both had 50/50 Sunday League records so must share more or less equal blame for *Wisden*'s criticism that 'most of their defeats in this field reflected a lack of tactics rather than technique'. Still, seventh was Yorkshire's highest finish in the competition for five years. Both men's captaincy had come in for criticism at times, Hampshire frowned upon after settling for an early-season draw against Middlesex at Bradford. John Callaghan accused a 'trance-like' Boycott of being too focused on personal batting practise and not enough on securing a morale-boosting win for his hitherto winless team at Oxford University in May. It did not work; he made nought and three in the draw. His gamble of bowling wicketkeeper Bairstow in May's Benson and Hedges Cup tie at Nottinghamshire backfired too as his three wicketless overs cost 17 runs. Yorkshire lost by 19.

Boycott was reported to the committee for his angry reaction to, of all things, an opener scoring too slowly in the Gillette Cup. The weather made a mess of the 1978 season and hurt Yorkshire in the quarter-finals, where they hosted Sussex at Headingley. Hampshire's 90-run partnership with Sharp had put them in a good position when rain washed out the rest of the day with the score 174/8 off 52 overs. When it continued for the next two reserve days and into a third, the game was rescheduled as a ten-overs-a-side affair but a back injury meant Hampshire was unable to play.

The captain recognised he was not suited to such a short format, and dropped himself to nine in the order, with Sharp opening. Unfortunately neither was Richard Lumb, who felt the sharp end of his captain's tongue after making ten from 23 balls as Yorkshire were denied a home semi-final against Lancashire. The next day, against Hampshire in Southampton, another incident brought Lumb and Boycott into conflict.

After Barrie Leadbeater made 61 and Lumb nought, Boycott told the former he was technically the better player. It was, he said, an attempt to motivate a bit-part player, but the conversation got back to Lumb and when he returned from Test duty Boycott was asked to explain it to the committee. The case against him was mounting.

Boycott's record as leader was such that all his committee critics really needed was some reassurance that the side was no longer dependent on his captaincy, but Hampshire provided a bit more. Derbyshire were linked with him throughout 1978. With Eddie Barlow out of contract at the end of the season, they would be looking for a new captain, and Chesterfield's was the closest first-class ground to Hampshire's Todwick home. 'Naturally we would be interested in a player of Hampshire's calibre if he were available, but he isn't,' Derbyshire secretary David Harrison was quoted as saying five days after the go-slow enquiry. 'If he were released by Yorkshire that would be a different matter.'

Suddenly Hampshire, whose contract was due to expire at the end of the 1979 season, held all the cards. After seven winters where sacking the captain meant risking losing their best batsman, this time not sacking the captain would all but guarantee it. Hampshire was up front with Harrison, telling him he would take Yorkshire's captaincy if offered it, if not he would join Derbyshire.

10

The Cruellest
of Sackings

IN LESS than a week, Geoffrey Boycott lost the two things he cared most about in the world. On 15 September he headed to Bermuda on holiday knowing that, as so often, his re-election as Yorkshire captain would be anything but a formality. Twelve days later he was informed by telegram that his mother, Jane, had died of cancer. Before the week was out he had been sacked as Yorkshire captain. 'A lot of people decided that the timing was deliberate, but not even a Yorkshire committee could think up something as evil as that,' wrote David Bairstow.

September started badly and got much worse for Boycott. He had ignored a bad back to captain England to a 132-run win over Pakistan in May's first one-day international, but when the Ashes squad was announced in September Bob Willis, a 29-year-old with 41 caps to Boycott's 74, was vice-captain. Willis had been Boycott's understudy in New Zealand, where the Yorkshireman made unwanted history as the first England skipper to lose there. 'I was unable to find any aspect of his captaincy which was significantly better than Brearley's, whose more gentle and relaxed leadership brings out the best in his side,' commented Henry Blofeld.

The journalist was especially critical of the pace of Boycott's batting, which was such an issue in the second Test in Christchurch that Willis promoted Ian Botham up the order with express instructions to run out his captain. That the all-rounder so eagerly accomplished his mission speaks volumes for the respect – or lack of it – for Boycott in his own dressing room. On the morning the 1978/79 Ashes squad was announced, the *Yorkshire Post* predicted England would do without a vice-captain. 'He is such a key batsman that the committee feel he should concentrate 100 per cent on that,' was chairman of selectors Alec Bedser's diplomatic explanation for the snub, which prompted the resignation of his colleague John Murray.

Next came Scarborough, and the end of Boycott's 15-year domination of the Yorkshire averages. With John Hampshire missing, a second-innings century against Gloucestershire, or even an unbeaten 44, would have preserved it but there was no chance thanks to the rain which washed out day one and much of day two.

All of that, though, paled into insignificance alongside the loss of his beloved mother. Tom Boycott had died in 1967, four years too early to achieve his ambition of seeing his son captain Yorkshire, and Boycott lived with his mother until her death. She had always been there for him with words of support throughout his troubles with club and country, so her death was inevitably going to hit the 37-year-old hard. Her cancer had been diagnosed as terminal 13 months earlier, but Boycott had no idea when he left to recharge his batteries ahead of the winter's battles that he would never see her again. He had feared the end might come when he was due to be in Australia, either delaying his departure or causing him to fly back.

Yorkshire president Sir Kenneth Parkinson promised the *Yorkshire Evening Post*'s John Callaghan he would go in to bat for Boycott when the time came to choose a captain for 1979, saying, 'I want him and Raymond to have every chance.' Boycott felt let down over the 'go-slow', believing a fear of losing his job as president had stopped Parkinson standing up to the committee, though it is hard to see what he could do once they reached a decision. The selection committee had been due to discuss the captaincy on 22 September. A letter was sent to Boycott's house to that effect but as soon as it was realised he was in Bermuda, they sent another pushing the date back by six days, the day he returned to discover the cricket committee would make their recommendation at Headingley the next day. Rather than taking matters out of his hands on hearing of Mrs Boycott's death, Yorkshire asked their grieving captain if he would be there. He said he would. 'Despite the mounting evidence against it, I still clung to the belief that I would retain the captaincy,' he commented.

By now Boycott was familiar with the protocol. He would leave the room while the cricket committee decided their recommendation to the general committee. This time, though, Boycott noticed a difference beyond Ray Illingworth's presence. Illingworth was still seven months away from starting his new job but the decision would have a big bearing on him, and he had therefore been at the previous day's meeting too. The cricket committee headed for lunch as soon as their meeting concluded.

'[Chairman John] Temple told me their decision would have to go before the general committee that afternoon for ratification; he didn't tell me what the decision was but I knew something was wrong, if only because in previous years he had often given me a hint that the cricket committee's recommendation was for my re-appointment,' Boycott recalled. Ronnie Burnet, who succeeded Mel Ryan on the cricket committee in April having rejoined the general committee for a second spell, told the Nidderdale Cricket League's annual dinner their vote had been 10-0 in favour of a new captain, with one abstention.

Temple offered to telephone Boycott with the final decision, but he preferred to wait for it. Once told, he asked to meet the committee to discuss it, but with the rest of the agenda to get through first, he had to wait again before finally speaking to Temple, Parkinson and Arthur Connell. 'The Yorkshire County Cricket Club, after long and careful consideration, have decided that the interests of the club would be best served by offering the captaincy to J.H. Hampshire,' read the club's statement. 'The committee very much hope that Boycott will continue to extend his invaluable services as a player and have offered him a two-year contract to continue as such.'

'In many ways I think he was better off,' Ted Lester told me, but the sacking caused outrage among the members. 'I thought it was an injustice to Geoffrey at the time but when you're not inside anything you only get to see one side,' Reform Group member Russell Devy told me before his death. 'All we wanted was for him to be reinstated as captain. We thought he was just getting a team together, a young team, and that they hadn't given him the chance. Geoffrey brought some young players through and he had one of the best fast bowlers in the country in Graham Stevenson. He was a bloody good cricketer. And Kevin Sharp was a belter.' Time had mellowed Devy – 36 years earlier he wrote to the *Yorkshire Post*, 'If Geoffrey Boycott were to play under John Hampshire, I shall have lost complete faith in the human race.'

On the day Boycott was sacked, the popular Pope John Paul I died after 33 days in the Vatican, the 20th century's shortest papacy. Naturally, the *Yorkshire Post*'s front page led with the news from Headingley – His Holiness lying in state was the main picture. Although one of eight committee representatives to vote against the decision (Parkinson, Eric Baines, David Drabble, Jack Sokell, Dr John Turner, David

Welch and Ron Yeomans were the others), Tony Woodhouse was bemused by the furore. 'For months the local newspapers were full of the Boycott sacking,' he wrote. 'Looking back it all seemed so silly and irrelevant. It cannot happen anywhere else in England. In London it would not have merited a mention. In Manchester, the Lancashire member would have read it once, turned it over in his mind and forgotten it on the morrow. In Yorkshire it went on and on...'

Hampshire was due to leave for a winter playing for Tasmania the next day. When Temple rang at about 4pm to offer the captaincy, he accepted. The following day his father told the *Scarborough Evening News*, 'The decision to sack Boycott is going to cause a lot of arguing but I don't care. Last night was one of the best Friday nights I've ever had.' By the time the paper hit the newsstands, the arguing John Hampshire Snr forecast was well under way. It was hardly the most outlandish of predictions.

Reform Group chairman Peter Briggs told that morning's *Yorkshire Post*, 'The decision to appoint Hampshire as captain is ludicrous. Hampshire let himself, and the entire club, down when he batted slowly at Northampton last season... It makes you wonder if someone didn't put Hampshire up to it in the first place.' Beyond Hampshire and Boycott, though, Yorkshire had few options. Geoff Cope was again suspended over his action and while Bill Athey and Kevin Sharp – who made 260 not out at Worcester in August as England Under-19 captain in the interestingly-sponsored Agatha Christie series – were seen as future skippers, both were uncapped and far too inexperienced for such a political situation.

Hampshire was only Public Enemy number two in the Reformers' eyes once it became known Illingworth had written to the committee asking them to sort out the issue of the captaincy 'once and for all', and citing Cope's players' poll as evidence the dressing room favoured change. The last eight years had demonstrated the only way to draw a line under the matter was by terminating Boycott's captaincy, and it was clear that was what Illingworth wanted to give himself the best chance of succeeding.

Boycott took the news badly. John Callaghan said the deposed captain 'was in the depths of despair' when he contacted him. 'What's often overlooked with Boycott is that when he recalled Yorkshire cricket is his life he's telling the truth', David Bairstow wrote, recalling their phonecall. 'After a while he broke off the conversation. He was so choked up I thought he might have been crying.'

Mike Bore also got a call. 'I was sacked the same day,' he told me. 'Joe Lister, who was secretary, sent me a letter to say my contract was now up and I was no longer needed. I said, "Hang on a minute Joe, in April you asked me to sign a two-year contract." He said, "I did not," but I had a copy and I said I'd show him it so he checked in the office and rang me back that night most apologetic to say I was right. But he said, "They want rid of you. Would you accept a payment?" They offered to cover my contract and told me there was a county after me. Boycs rang me trying to get a bit of support and I said, "I'm sorry Geoffrey, after the way you've treated me over the years I won't support you. Let's keep it at that." Since then I've met him a number of times and he's always come over, shook hands and asked how the family was. There is a good side to him.' Boycott said little in public until an explosive television appearance.

BBC1's 7 October schedule was packed with the usual staples – *Multi-Coloured Swap Shop, Grandstand, Doctor Who, Larry Grayson's Generation Game, All Creatures Great and Small, Little and Large* and *Match of the Day*. After the football, at 11.15pm, came another – *Parkinson*. Appearing alongside actor Kenneth More and singer Barry Manilow, Michael Parkinson's final guest, in his Yorkshire County Cricket Club blazer and tie, was Boycott. He had appeared just over a year previously, days after the conclusion of his triumphant comeback Test series, but the consensus was that this time he came across badly.

There was certainly no holding back when Boycott spoke about the committee. 'They're small-minded people – people who think they're always right,' he said. 'The whole thing was a set-up. They knew they were going to sack me, but at least they could have postponed the meeting. They could have allowed my mother to be buried in peace, but they could not wait.' Boycott predicted that over the next five or six years the likes of Athey, Bairstow, Sharp, Phil Carrick and Richard Lumb could all be sacked, and revealed his defence of Hampshire as vice-captain in April. Despite that, he was determined to stay. 'I cannot think of playing for any other county, I cannot even contemplate it,' he insisted. 'My loyalty to Yorkshire is not in question, it is the committee's loyalty that is in question.' There was also a rallying cry, 'If they [Yorkshire's members] want me to return as captain they must do something about it. They have got to get together, get off their bottoms and do what they have to do.' Boycott had not given up on the captaincy, and Britain's most famous chat show host warned, 'The Yorkshire committee have picked on the wrong man this time.'

Parkinson and the *Yorkshire Post* were the only media Boycott spoke to. Paid £100 by the BBC, he turned down £10,000 from a national Sunday newspaper, saying the future of Yorkshire County Cricket Club – which he regarded as being at stake – was far more important than money. As the *Bradford Telegraph and Argus* pointed out, taking it would have risked the fate of Jonny Wardle, scratched from England's Ashes tour party and sacked by Yorkshire 20 years earlier for an unauthorised newspaper article. He spoke at Delph Working Men's Club in Huddersfield shortly after *Parkinson* but David Warner claimed when Boycott saw him and a national journalist in the audience, he toned his speech down.

The Reform Group responded to the call to arms. One feature of it and its successor organisations was the quality of legal representation they were able to call on. As well as Boycott's solicitor Duncan Mutch, the likes of Steven Frieze and Brian Walsh, the QC who defended Jon Venables in the Jamie Bulger trial, fought their corner. Walsh's junior, Matthew Caswell, had been introduced to Boycott in May. 'I was invited to some function as a guest speaker, and met Geoffrey Boycott,' he recalls from his front room, overlooking Leeds's Roundhay Park. 'Geoffrey was with the [Yorkshire] team playing cricket at Oxford and my daughter was the secretary of the union at the college. He and Duncan Mutch went along to see if I would help.

'What I didn't realise was why. Geoffrey – with all his ability, with all his eminence as a public figure – had very few friends. He's not good at making friends. When he came to me as an outsider, he was obviously thinking I would be able to help him, which I did. In a sense I was flattered that Geoffrey Boycott was coming to me for advice. He came to my house with Duncan Mutch. Geoffrey was paranoid – with some justification – that people were out to get him but even those who were not, he was always very wary of them. So he was assured by Duncan Mutch that I would be on his side.

'I helped as an adviser to begin with, thinking that would be the end of the matter but one thing led to another and I got deeper and deeper into the whole thing. I was a member of the club but really my interest after that was not cricket, not Geoffrey Boycott, it was the excitement of the movement itself.' Caswell's first impressions of the Reformers were underwhelming. 'They did not know what's what,' he tells me. 'The stupid motion they put forward was not realistic at all. It was hopeless. They wanted an order that Geoffrey Boycott be restored as captain. No court would do that. This room became more like the centre of the organisation. When Geoffrey's contract was cancelled we requisitioned a special general meeting of the club and I drafted cautiously two resolutions. One was what the court could not do but the members could.

The court cannot say you must have Geoffrey as club captain, but the members' meeting could, so there was a resolution that Geoffrey be restored as captain. The next one was a vote of no confidence in the cricket committee.'

Five days after Boycott's appeal, four hours before the next committee meeting, Sidney Fielden, John Featherstone and Peter Briggs presented a petition to the club. 'We, the undersigned, request the convening of a special general meeting of members of the Yorkshire County Cricket Club within 21 days for the purpose of discussing the decision of the club committee to appoint J.H. Hampshire as captain in place of G. Boycott and for the purpose of making recommendations to the committee,' it read. Lister picked up the phone to Featherstone to suggest a meeting that day but the Reform Group secretary insisted they communicate in writing. In the subsequent committee meeting, Yorkshire were more preoccupied with Boycott's outburst.

Temple had made his view known on the Sunday – 'It seems, from what he said, that nobody knows anything about the game but Boycott,' he commented. 'There comes a time when we must defend ourselves.' Lister wrote to the *Yorkshire Post*, 'I… hope Yorkshire members and others who saw the interview would be surprised at Geoffrey Boycott's claims that I am lacking in compassion and that I was probably acting on committee instructions. Whatever my shortcomings, I had hoped the image I have endeavoured to create is not this.' Ronnie Burnet had said before Boycott's appearance on *Parkinson* that backing down would be a victory for 'mob rule'.

Burnet was on a business course but the rest of the cricket committee – Temple, Arthur Connell, Michael Crawford, Geoff Dennis, Robin Feather, Harry McIlvenny, Frank Melling, Mel Ryan, Sir Kenneth Parkinson, Brian Sellers, Billy Sutcliffe and Norman Yardley – decided to send a letter urgently demanding Boycott come and explain his comments. It was hand-delivered the next day by Lister's assistant David

Ryder but Boycott was not at home, seemingly more concerned with finding some decent bowlers to provide pre-Ashes net practice at Johnny Lawrence's indoor school. His contract had expired – early in 1978 all capped players were sent draft contracts running until 31 March 1980, but without warning his was returned with the date amended to 20 September 1978 – and believed this left him free to say what he liked. As far as Yorkshire were concerned, if he wished to keep his TCCB registration he had to abide by their rules, which stated, 'Before making any public pronouncement a registered cricketer must obtain the prior consent of his county cricket club'.

In his letter, Lister told Boycott that rather than simply report the matter, Yorkshire would give him the chance to explain. Boycott took that as a threat and only when the secretary assured him it was not, did he accept – but with strings attached. Temple did weigh in with a threat, that Yorkshire's two-year contract offer could be torn up, but this was later dropped. The committee declined Boycott's offer to make his correspondence public but chief among its demands was that he be heard by the general committee, rather than the cricket committee. 'The bigger assembly may favour a softer approach,' the *Scarborough Evening News* speculated. He got his wish. A meeting was called for 4pm on 23 October, the day before Boycott headed to London *en route* to Australia.

Boycott's old adversaries joined the debate. A 'vindicated' Don Brennan said he would happily put himself forward to return to the cricket committee, Fred Trueman revealed Richard Hutton had been asked at the 1972 Headingley Test match if he would captain Yorkshire, and Hutton wrote a scathing critique of Boycott's captaincy. Tony Nicholson said the only surprise was it had taken the committee so long to sack him. It was, he said, 'Boycott first, Boycott second and the team third.'

Ahead of the meeting, Boycott and Trueman slugged it out in *The Times*. Boycott wrote to the newspaper about one of his hobby horses, committee disloyalty, arguing only his 100th hundred had saved him from the sack 12 months earlier. 'My team has never had a chance (and they are beginning to be a real force in county cricket) for no team can serve two masters and gain success: disruption and success are poor bedfellows', he wrote. He reiterated what he told the paper in June: he intended to play for Yorkshire and England for as long as possible.

Trueman wrote back that Boycott's letter was 'manifest rubbish' and continued, 'If, as he claims, he intends to play for Yorkshire "as long as he can maintain his ability" all he has to do is to accept the Yorkshire committee's offer of a contract and make his batting talent available to the team. One hopes he will, but fears he won't. If he doesn't perhaps he will tell us why.' He added for good measure, 'Since 1878 Yorkshire's position in the Championship table has been in double figures only eight times and five of those have been during Boycott's captaincy. My only quarrel with the Yorkshire committee is that they have put up with Boycott as captain for too long.'

Duncan Mutch, a Yorkshire member since 1962 and part of the Reform Group, called on the general committee meeting to 'change this unjust decision' in an impassioned speech lasting nearly two hours. It was accompanied by a dossier highlighting, 'The professionalism of the captain and the obvious disloyalty of his cricket chairman and committee throughout at least seven of those eight years.'

'Unsupportive' might have been a more accurate if less dramatic word than 'disloyal' to describe many of the incidents cited – the removal of the word 'enthusiastic' from the 1973 press release, Temple's criticism when Boycott refused to chase victory in the May 1974 Roses, the hostile questioning at the end-of-season committee meeting, the refusal to cap players at Scarborough in September 1976 and a ten-day delay between reappointing him captain for 1978 and informing him. Mutch concluded, 'If you do not reappoint this man to his coveted office and see that he has a completely loyal committee behind him and the freedom to act in accordance with his instinct… you will, I fear, destroy Yorkshire cricket for years ahead.' Boycott sat in the kitchens drinking tea for 85 minutes while the committee reached a decision. They refused to back down.

Planning was under way on both sides for the inevitable battle. The Reformers drafted a letter to all 13,000 Yorkshire members outlining their aims and asking for financial support. The group's income in October 1978 was £1,053.75, as opposed to expenditure of £1,392, so the decision was taken to charge subscriptions – £5 for a vice-president, £1 for full members and 50p for juniors. With a second letter planned nearer the time of the proposed special general meeting at a cost of £1,800, they hoped to negotiate a special rate with the Post Office, but were prepared to deliver them by hand if not. They were also considering laying on special coaches to get members to any SGM. Add in legal costs, and it would be an expensive fight.

Dinners were organised to raise funds, with 400 at the first in Sheffield. 'I was one of the people who arranged them,' Russell Devy told me. 'It wasn't difficult – I got too many [speakers] in fact. I got Jim Laker, Sonny Ramadhin, quite a few turned up. They only wanted a hotel and expenses. We didn't have to go around flogging tickets, people applied for them.' Over 2,000 members responded to the initial letter, 1,077 in support. Others were in favour of the cricket committee resigning, but not Boycott's reappointment. Unsurprisingly, the mood was much stronger at the meetings – a vote on who should be captain for 1979 produced a 125-5 win for Boycott over Hampshire.

Yorkshire consistently argued an SGM would cost a great deal of money (then estimated at £11,000) without achieving anything, but even before Boycott appeared in front of the general committee, they provisionally booked Leeds Town Hall for 18 November. Ken Harvey discussed the possibility of an anti-Reform group, but only as a last resort, while Rev David

Warner, the rector of Wombwell and honorary president of its Cricket Lovers' Society, optimistically called for mediation.

In a sign of battles to come, the committee disputed the Reformers had enough signatories to force an SGM because some of the 504 members were not up to date with their subscriptions, then called one themselves on 2 December. It would be fought on their terms – a vote of confidence in the general committee – rather than the Reformers'. Boycott said he would return from Australia to attend. 'I want to stay on as Yorkshire captain but whether I would stay as a player under Hampshire is another matter,' he said. 'I am not at this stage interested in playing for another county.' Not that it deterred them.

'If he was on the market I think most counties would be interested and, of course, Mr Packer,' Surrey secretary Ian Scott-Brown had said earlier in the month. 'I am confident Surrey would be one of the clubs interested.' Others speculated Boycott might retire and take up the media position which would eventually provide his second career. Under club rules all members could attend the SGM, but only those who had been so for six months were entitled to vote. Also ineligible were those who had not paid their subscription by 23 October – the date the meeting was called. 'The October deadline must have been a relief to Mr Featherstone, who would otherwise have been ineligible to vote,' Lister mischievously noted. In all, 11,262 Yorkshire members were entitled to register their opinions.

The Reformers went from demanding an SGM to trying to get it cancelled. Brian Walsh argued by calling for a vote of confidence in themselves, the general committee were ignoring 'the specific issues'. It was the cricket committee the rebels had a problem with. Lister argued the Reform Group's resolutions could not be heard on a technicality, even though Featherstone had sent an amended requisition a week later. Vice-chancellor Jim Blackett-Ord, a judge who would become increasingly familiar with Yorkshire's bickering over the next five years, awarded the Reformers costs and ruled an SGM must be called over Boycott's sacking. He urged Connell to use 'his best endeavours' to announce it by 28 November. The Reformers offered a combined meeting to discuss both sides' resolutions and the original SGM was put back seven days to allow a new agenda to be drawn up with three resolutions: a vote of confidence in the general committee, one of no confidence in the cricket committee, and a demand for Boycott's reinstatement as captain. With Leeds Town Hall undergoing 'structural alterations' by then, Harrogate's Royal Hall was its venue.

With the battleground at last defined, the propaganda war could begin in earnest. The first significant shot was fired by Richard Hutton in December's issue of *The Cricketer*. 'Neither party to the present dispute warrants sympathy although one's feelings incline towards the committee', he commented.

Hutton's article responded to the 'emotional nonsense' spouted in Boycott's defence with many of the criticisms he outlined in earlier chapters of this book – that Boycott's selfish attitude was at odds with the team ethic promoted by Brian Close, switching the focus from the collective to the individual, and his 'one-paced' batting harmed a side already handicapped by a cull of its experience and the infusion of overseas players into rival counties. He argued, 'The approach adopted by the committee played straight into Boycott's hands and by 1977 they appeared to have lost control of him.' There were statistics to back up his points, notably that between 1878 and 1970 Yorkshire had only finished outside of the County Championship's top four 15 times, but they had done so in six of Boycott's eight seasons in charge. Acknowledgement of Boycott's popularity among English cricket fans came on page 11 of the magazine, a full-page advert for a commemorative bronze of the shot which brought up his 100th hundred. Nine inches high on a green marble plinth, it and a certificate signed by Boycott and the artist were available for £165.

In November Yorkshire called a press conference to make their case, and pulled no punches. They released a statement signed by Connell and distributed to members which featured what would virtually be their motto that winter, and the crux of their argument, 'The committee's decision has nothing to do with what Geoffrey Boycott has or has not done as a cricketer, but rather with what he has not achieved as a leader.' It accused Boycott of being indecisive and 'so dedicated to the perfection and exploitation of his own batting technique that he is sometimes oblivious to the feelings and aspirations of his team-mates', making him incapable of drawing the best out of them. It noted, 'It is significant that not one present or former Yorkshire player has expressed support for the appointment of Geoffrey Boycott for next season' and drew attention to the fact he had not been chosen as England's Ashes vice-captain.

Yorkshire stressed their patience in the face of incidents largely hidden from public view of capped players complaining to the committee about Boycott's leadership and countless reprimands – over the pace of his batting, his handling of players and even for criticising their ability in front of 'outsiders'. The committee admitted, 'He has never been seen to be an ideal captain, though in the early days it was hoped he might become one.' It argued the selection committee had over-ruled Boycott once in eight years, and emphasised Hampshire was appointed not by the cricket committee the Reformers were targeting and which Ray Illingworth's appointment would anyway make more or less redundant, but the general committee which was the subject of its SGM resolution. Nevertheless, there was no questioning Boycott's playing credentials, which is why they offered him the longest contract they were permitted to. The two-year limit was self-imposed but it did not seem unreasonable to assess how Boycott would react to being back in the ranks.

The tone was not entirely negative, however, declaring, 'Yorkshire has a crop of young players at the moment whose potential is as high as any of the overseas stars who have contributed so much to the success of other counties.' In its end-of-season report the committee had also been keen to stress, 'At no time has lack of finance been an inhibiting factor in obtaining and retaining the best available Yorkshire-born players,' although the county had yet to sign any of the many talented Yorkshiremen playing for the other 16 first-class counties. Bringing Illingworth back from Leicestershire was a welcome first step towards addressing the insularity which saw a squad composed entirely of Yorkshire-born players who had never played for any other county coached only by Yorkshire-born former players who had also never experienced life elsewhere. Only when on international duty were players exposed to different ideas, and few in the late 1970s did that very often.

There was more to keeping their best players than mere finance, and Connell warned the press conference some might leave were Boycott reinstated, adding one anonymous player had told him so personally. Whether or not he was referring to him, it was clear Hampshire's Yorkshire career was at risk. The committee was keen to stress, however, this was about more than individuals. 'There is much at stake, not only the future of Yorkshire cricket, but also the future of the club as a democratic institution,' it warned. 'The committee of the club is democratically elected and must be allowed to make decisions, even unpopular ones. If the members, on largely sentimental ground, are to call such decisions in questions, other than through the regular elections of committee members, or at the annual general meeting, the club will destroy itself.'

The Reformers were not spared either. 'They are a self-appointed body,' the statement declared. 'They have no first-hand knowledge of first-class cricket nor have they any knowledge of its administration.' Connell repeated Hutton's phrase that they were 'a personality cult'. The Reformers were unhappy that copies of Trueman's letter to *The Times* and Illingworth's to the committee were included with Yorkshire's statement, but nothing putting the opposing point of view. Featherstone asked Yorkshire to redress the balance by paying for Reform Group advertisements in the local newspapers. Lister dismissed the argument, but said had the Reformers asked to include their literature in the mail-out, Yorkshire would have done so.

Featherstone also pointed out six of the ten cricket committee members had been in place at the time of the disastrous decisions to release Illingworth and sack Close, and argued Boycott deserved at least a year to see how he worked with the new manager, who they criticised for acting as a 'spokesman' for the players. 'The club must be living in a fool's paradise if they feel they can sack a man as captain and expect him to continue playing under someone else,' Featherstone said. If they were, so were Derbyshire, Kent, Lancashire, Surrey, Sussex and Warwickshire, as Bob Taylor, Asif Iqbal, David Lloyd, John Edrich, Tony Greig and David Brown had done just that in 1978.

Boycott's hand could be detected in a *Yorkshire Post* spread two days later outlining the case for him and printing his correspondence with the committee during the period Mutch spoke about. Connell told Radio Hallam the committee were distinctly unimpressed. A more direct response to what Boycott called 'the smear campaign' came from Brisbane with an eight-page statement of his own. 'The Reform Group is right in every respect,' it declared. 'Indeed I do not feel that their resolutions go far enough, for the whole leadership of the club, with certain honourable exceptions, needs to be removed.'

Boycott defended his record as captain, pointing out Illingworth and Trueman had both said it would take ten years to win another trophy after Close left, and dismissed the players' poll Illingworth cited in his letter – 'They are not free agents – they could put their jobs at risk if they admit to disagreeing with the committee.' The general committee, 'pawns of the cricket committee', was labelled disloyal (Boycott's buzzword), dishonest and undemocratic for trying to deny the Reformers an SGM to discuss their resolution, and he argued most had played cricket at no higher a level than those members whose opinions they were over-ruling. Yorkshire could have pointed out the cricket committee which advised and sat on the wider committee included four former Yorkshire captains (one of whom, Norman Yardley, had also captained England), two ex-second XI captains and a capped player in Mel Ryan, but refrained from responding.

Boycott also tried to widen the debate beyond his own future. 'All thinking members and people know that the real question is – who is responsible for the present state of Yorkshire cricket?' he stated. If allowed two more years at the helm (taking him to ten in all), he pledged to 'gladly' stand down at the end of it if he failed to bring silverware back to the county. 'I say this because of my confidence in Yorkshire cricket and in my young team,' he explained.

The deposed captain had changed his mind about attending the SGM, despite enduring his worst Test series. Hampered by a knee injury, his top score was 90 not out and in December he was reported for calling umpire Don Weser a 'fucking cheat' after Ian Botham's lbw appeal against Western Australia's Kim Hughes was turned down in a tour match. That evening the management refused his request to miss the second Test but *The Guardian* speculated he might not see the tour out. When Mike Brearley and Bob Willis missed the next warm-up game, inexperienced wicketkeeper Bob Taylor captained rather than Boycott. He made his first Test duck since 1969 in the fourth Test at the Sydney Cricket Ground in January. Boycott was not in a good place – 'These last few months have been the worst of my life,' he had written to Ted Lester from the flight to Australia.

Finally it was time for the membership to decide. Over 1,300 were at the Royal Hall, where Mutch had to step in when pro-committee speakers were booed and jeered. Jack Mewies, now on the committee's side having led the 1970/71 rebellion, was heckled when he called Boycott's captaincy record, 'The worst in the history of Yorkshire cricket.'

Author and Yorkshire member Derrick Boothroyd found the committee's confidence motion problematic. '[I] finally plumped for the committee because in this instance I supported their action,' he explained. 'But I was far from having "confidence in the committee of the club as now constituted." The wording of the resolution was tantamount to a confidence trick. If the committee had been completely honest and straightforward the resolution would have specified that one was supporting the committee in this particular issue and not in general terms. I am quite sure a great many of the members who voted for the committee's resolution did so with great reluctance.'

Whatever the thinking, Yorkshire's committee won on all three counts. Brian Walsh proposed the vote of no confidence in the cricket committee, and Sidney Fielden's speech drew a standing ovation, but even their oratory could not sway the decision. Their time would come. The committee were supported by 4,422 voters (3,952 of them by proxy), with 3,067 against (2,196 proxies). The vote of no confidence in the cricket committee was defeated 4,216 (3,820) to 3,346 (2,401), and the biggest margin was over Boycott. The attempt to reinstate him was supported by 2,602 (1,902) and opposed by 4,826 (4,279).

At last Hampshire could celebrate being Yorkshire's captain. 'I was rooming with him in Brisbane [where Tasmania were playing Queensland in Australia's Gillette Cup] when he got the phonecall from the secretary to tell him he'd got the Yorkshire captaincy,' recalls Tasmania captain Jack Simmons. 'We were just getting into bed and he said, "Let's retire to the bar." He bought a bottle of champagne. He rated getting the captaincy of Yorkshire as an even bigger honour than playing for England.' It is a great tragedy of the period that many who regarded the captaincy in such a light rued taking it. Hampshire would be no exception.

11

'Oh Christ,
They're Back!'

ASK Kevin Sharp to describe John Hampshire and one
word instantly springs to his lips, 'Tough.' That even
Hampshire was soon frightened to make a decision
and reluctant to leave his house shows the strain Yorkshire's
new captain and his family were put under by Geoffrey
Boycott's more militant supporters. Eventually the abuse
forced him to give up the captaincy, and a year later leave the
club altogether.

'I began to feel that about 98 per cent of the crowd were
against me and wanting, hoping, for me to make a mistake,'
Hampshire later confessed. 'That seems a big percentage, I
know, but that's how I felt and it got worse in the second year.
Yet I couldn't jack it in at the end of the first year after all the
strife and controversy which had surrounded my appointment.
That would have been letting down the people who had faith
in me and, I thought, plunging us into another crisis.' He took
the hostility – not necessarily from the Reform Group, but
certainly Boycott fans – so badly that by halfway through his
first season, he did not want to leave home at night. Much

Fred Trueman makes a one-handed catch to remove Doug Walters off the bowling of Richard Hutton. Yorkshire's crushing victory over Australia in 1968, which he captained, was a glorious swansong for the retiring fast bowler *(courtesy Press Association)*

Batsman Ken Taylor retired from first-class cricket in 1968, compounding the loss of Fred Trueman and Ray Illingworth. He is pictured right with future committee member Bryan Stott in April 1961 *(courtesy Mirrorpix)*

Brian Sellers, left with future Yorkshire president Norman Yardley in 1947, was the authoritarian cricket chairman responsible for the hugely damaging departures of Ray Illingworth and Brian Close *(courtesy Getty Images)*

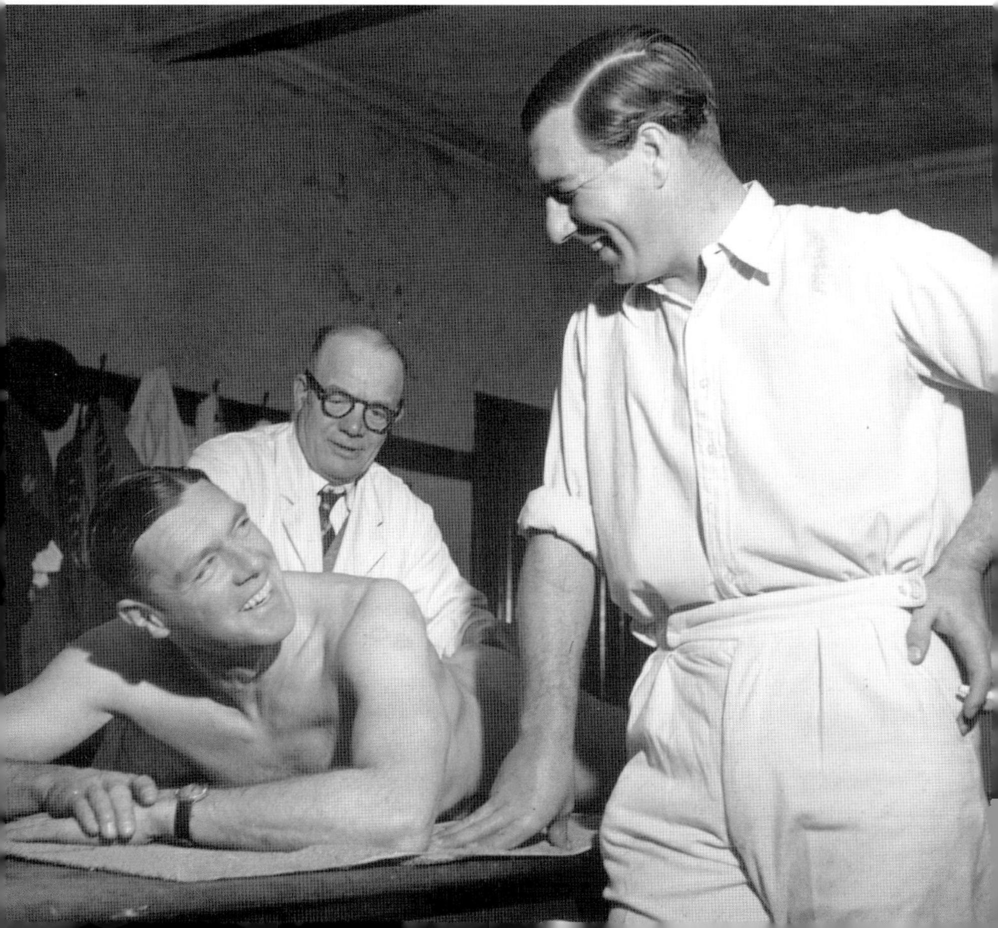

Geoff Cope was seen as Ray Illingworth's natural successor in 1968, but doubts about the legality of his bowling action stopped the spinner fulfilling his potential *(courtesy Adelphi Archive)*

Wicketkeeper Jimmy Binks was a huge loss when he became the latest Yorkshire player to retire, in 1969 *(courtesy Adelphi Archive)*

Yorkshire team-mates Illingworth (left) and Close. Some feel Close might have been able to remain as captain beyond 1970 had his trusted friend not left for Leicestershire *(courtesy Mirrorpix)*

New Yorkshire captain Geoffrey Boycott with his squad in 1971. In ability and profile, the opening batsman would overshadow his team-mates *(courtesy Getty Images)*

Boycott valued Doug Padgett as a senior professional, but he was soon taken away to work with the second team *(courtesy Adelphi Archive)*

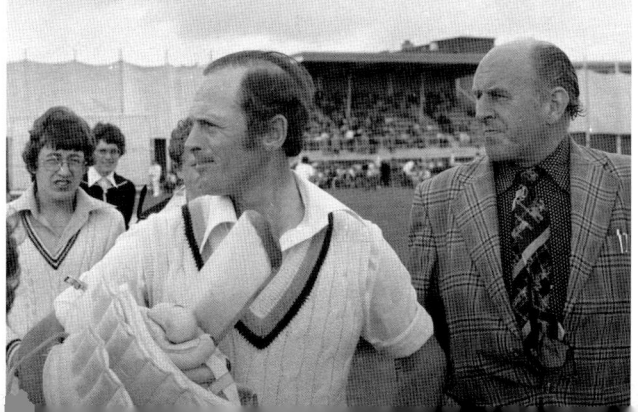

Scorer Ted Lester, pictured right with Boycott in 1978, was a trusted confidant of Yorkshire's captain, but the committee refused to make him team manager in 1971 *(courtesy Mirrorpix)*

Yorkshire captain Phil Sharpe and Leicestershire's Ray Illingworth toss up before the 1972 Benson and Hedges Final. Yorkshire, minus the injured Boycott, were soundly beaten
(courtesy Press Association)

Don Wilson missed out on the Yorkshire captaincy by one vote, and became a leading dressing-room critic of Boycott
(courtesy Adelphi Archive)

Richard Hutton, pictured right with his legendary father Sir Leonard, was seen as an alternative captain to Boycott, even after outside interests began to take priority over cricket
(courtesy Adelphi Archive)

Then-England captain Mike Denness chats with Boycott in May 1975. Boycott's contempt for the Scotsman and his shaky grip on the Yorkshire captaincy were factors in his refusal to play for England from 1974 to 1977 *(courtesy Mirrorpix)*

Despite being Brian Close's vice-captain Phil Sharpe, pictured batting against Surrey in 1971, was overlooked as his replacement *(courtesy Adelphi Archive)*

Boycott grew his hair and became more relaxed during his voluntary three-year exile from international cricket in the 1970s, and in 1975 Yorkshire felt the benefit *(courtesy Mirrorpix)*

Boycott's Yorkshire team-mates detected a more selfish attitude after he returned to Test cricket, scoring his 100th first-class hundred against Australia at Headingley in 1977 *(courtesy Adelphi Archive)*

A badly-timed attempt by former Yorkshire and England wicketkeeper Don Brennan (far right) to unseat Boycott as captain led to the formation of the Reform Group *(courtesy Adelphi Archive)*

Yorkshire secretary Joe Lister and chairman John Temple in 1978. Dealing with the pro-Boycott Reform Group took up a lot of their time *(courtesy Press Association)*

Yorkshire's committee meet at Headingley in 1978 to discuss what action to take following criticism by deposed captain Boycott in a television interview with Michael Parkinson *(courtesy Press Association)*

New Yorkshire captain John Hampshire, new manager Ray Illingworth and deposed skipper Geoffrey Boycott pose for the cameras in pre-season, 1979. Hampshire remarked it led to captions of '"All is forgiven" and that sort of rubbish.' (*courtesy Press Association*)

Boycott back in pre-season training in 1979, his first session since being sacked as captain (*courtesy Press Association*)

As his long-time opening partner, Richard Lumb had a fraught relationship with Boycott and his unwillingness to get involved in Yorkshire's politics stopped him captaining the county (*courtesy Adelphi Archive*)

Neil Hartley was seen by Ray Illingworth as a future Yorkshire captain but pushed into the job at an early age, his playing ability never justified the role and his affair with Illingworth's daughter added to the pressure (*courtesy Adelphi Archive*)

David Bairstow was hurt when Illingworth preferred the uncapped Hartley as Yorkshire's stand-in captain, prompting a very public row in a Scarborough cocktail bar, but his friendship with Boycott eventually got him the job *(courtesy Getty Images)*

In partnership with Geoff Cook, Northamptonshire's Wayne Larkins destroyed Yorkshire at Middlesbrough in 1982, bringing about the end of Chris Old's captaincy. Geoffrey Boycott, Bill Athey and David Bairstow appeal in vain for his wicket *(courtesy The Gazette)*

Ray Illingworth with the 1983 Sunday League trophy, Yorkshire's first major silverware since 1969. Later that winter he was sacked as manager *(courtesy Getty Images)*

Teessiders Bill Athey (left) and Chris Old (right) both left Yorkshire in the early 1980s – Athey disillusioned with the dressing-room politics, Old released after being sacked as captain *(courtesy Getty Images)*

Julian Vallance sat on the Dobson committee which looked into the running of the club in the winter of 1981-82. He describes himself as Yorkshire's 'chairman of public relations – failed!' during the Revolution *(courtesy Getty Images)*

Devoted Boycott fan Phyllis Culpan's
financial support for Sidney Fielden was
used against him in 1985
(courtesy George Hepworth)

Martyn Moxon, Kevin Sharp and Phil Carrick
in the slips at Middlesbrough in July 1986.
Moxon learnt from Boycott by watching,
Sharp by chauffeuring him *(courtesy Mirrorpix)*

In the 1980s Yorkshire's team contained a number
of younger players Boycott was close to. Graham
Stevenson (front left) chats to him during a 1984
Headingley photocall with Steve Oldham, Arnie
Sidebottom, Simon Dennis and Jim Love behind
(courtesy Getty Images)

Ashley Metcalfe was seen as a potential
batting successor to Boycott at
Yorkshire, but his links to Illingworth
put him in an awkward position
politically *(courtesy Getty Images)*

of it came via the letters pages of the *Yorkshire Post* and its sister paper the *Yorkshire Evening Post*, but some was far more personal. Manager Ray Illingworth suffered too, to the point where by the end of the 1979 season his wife Shirley told him, 'The day you come home and tell me you have packed it in will be the happiest day of my life.' Boycott's supporters may have lost the battle the Reform Group was created to fight, but the war was far from over. If only the team had been so hard to defeat.

The lead headline on the *Yorkshire Post*'s front page was very clear about the outcome of the 1978 special general meeting, 'Boycott's last stroke'. The introduction asserted, 'Geoff Boycott has almost certainly played his last match for Yorkshire.' Not for the last time, the obituaries on his career had been written too soon. Although county cricketers were technically allowed to wait until 31 March to decide whether they would re-sign for the following season, Yorkshire gave Boycott until New Year's Eve to agree to their two-year contract offer.

The deposed captain claimed Northamptonshire and Gloucestershire approaches, secretary Mike Vockins confirmed Worcestershire would consider one too if the contract went unsigned, and Lancashire League club Accrington ambitiously offered a way out which avoided having to play against Yorkshire. In the winter of 1981/82 a committee set up to look into all aspects of Yorkshire cricket was told Boycott approached Lancashire's Jack Bond about the possibility of wearing the Red Rose, but dismissed the story because it could not be substantiated. Boycott denies it when I put it to him, Bond tells me he has no recollection and his then-colleague Jack Simmons adds, 'It must have happened three or four times when people played well and started saying they were interested in joining Lancashire so they got a bit of an increase in salary but I knew Boycs quite well and he never mentioned that to me. I can't believe he wanted to leave.' Chairman Cedric

Rhoades told Lancashire's annual general meeting they had no interest and Nottinghamshire secretary Philip Carling claimed to be 'baffled and bewildered' by reports Boycott could play for them.

A move would have made everyone's life a lot less fractious but David Hall, until recently director of the Yorkshire County Cricket Club museum, does not think it was a realistic option. 'He was always keen to play for Yorkshire – and I think his father was very keen too,' he says. 'His commitment in the early years was intense. He never had any aspirations to play for anybody else.' Some friends recommended a clean break, but the *Yorkshire Evening Post* organised a petition for Boycott to stay, and when David Bairstow flew to Australia to join England's limited-overs squad, he did so with a message from Reformer Bob Slicer – 'Come back unconditionally.' By then Yorkshire had extended their deadline until 31 January, but they were not prepared to wait any longer. Those already in Australia were none the wiser. 'Geoffrey didn't talk to me about it at all,' his team-mate for club and country, Chris Old, tells me. 'Geoffrey made these decisions on his own.'

Hampshire insisted it was entirely up to Boycott, but his attitude had to be right if he returned. The signs from Australia had not been encouraging in that respect. Fate decreed Hampshire's Tasmania would face England in two January matches in Hobart ahead of the third one-day international. 'There was a lot of non-talking,' explains Old. 'I was quite friendly with John. When I went into the side he looked after me and throughout my career with Yorkshire he was one of the people I would tend to go out with. When we were in Tasmania it was just natural for me to socialise with him. David Bairstow was friendly with John too. If we didn't go out we were making an issue of it, whereas we just wanted to play cricket. In the early days I was more interested in what I was doing, so the politics of it just went over my head. It was only in the later years that you pick up on certain things. Being the next senior player after John suddenly I had a bit of responsibility so I was very mindful of trying to sort of keep the peace and keep talking to people so they weren't isolated.'

Keeping the peace was easier said than done with Yorkshire's former and future captains adamant it was not up to them to make the first move. Some felt Hampshire should have been at the airport to greet Boycott when England touched down but that and the 40-over match between the sides were dodged when his son Paul was hospitalised after being hit on the head by a cricket ball. He did, though, play in the three-day encounter, giving the press pack a chance to monitor how the pair interacted. 'The closest they came to each other was when Hampshire came out to bat and had to walk around Boycott, who was standing with the other fieldsmen near the wicket', said a report in the *Scarborough Evening News*. The *Yorkshire Post*'s Terry Brindle was in Hobart, and reported Hampshire 'passed within inches of Boycott when he walked out to bat but the pair did not seem to exchange any greetings'. He was soon walking back again, caught behind off Old for nought.

Day one ended with Boycott batting for two and a half hours on his way to a score of 90 while his successor fielded at slip. Again Brindle did not notice any words exchanged. The journalist tried to break the ice, asking if Hampshire was going to speak to Boycott, something Old also encouraged. 'I'm not going to go cap in hand,' was the response. His answer was a lot less polite when Old told Hampshire's wife, Judy, Boycott was prepared to meet him so long as Brindle was present, 'Bollocks!' Not unreasonably, he asked, 'Why would a personal meeting between Boycott and myself depend upon the presence of the *Yorkshire Post*'s cricket correspondent? What was Boycott trying to do?'

At 3.10am UK time on 31 January, Boycott cabled his acceptance of the two-year contract. The news was announced during lunch on day four of the fifth Ashes Test, but he had told Brindle in advance so it could make the front page of that morning's *Yorkshire Post*. 'Whatever the disappointments of the past few months there is no way I could let the true supporters of Yorkshire cricket down,' Boycott said. 'If the people who watch matches and pay at the gate to show their loyalty had said the county would be better off without me, I would have packed my bags.' The Reformers sent back a telex – 'Thanks a million.'

'I felt all along he would accept the club's offer, even though he has left it to the 11th hour,' insisted Joe Lister. The *Yorkshire Post*'s editorial 'greatly... hoped that controversy will swiftly be buried and that Headingley will cease to be a centre of intrigue and return to being an establishment which specialises in cricket.' Fat chance.

Even such a happy moment for the Reformers caused more bickering. Ray Illingworth tipped fuel on to the smouldering embers, saying he hoped Boycott's decision was not down to a lack of interest from other counties. The Reformers claimed their hero had turned down a far more lucrative offer and Slicer snapped back at the 'very snide remarks', warning, 'The cancer is still there and has to be removed.' Management committee member Ronnie Burnet continued the tit-for-tat by claiming 'the upsurge of vitriolic comments' showed nothing had changed.

Four Reformers stood in the 1979 committee elections but the anti-Boycott wing emerged strengthened. Hull's Reg Kirk was the Reform Group's only success and Slicer, who tried to portray himself as a 'mediator', was one of those defeated. 'Optimist' might have been a better word, standing four years running without success until a technicality stopped him making it five in a row in 1983. Others voted on to the committee for the first time were former vice-captain Phil Sharpe, who triumphed over Reformer Peter Mouncey and incumbent W.A. Hodgson in York, and Julian Vallance in Leeds. Fred Trueman was unopposed in Craven following the retirement of Brian Sellers's brother Godfrey. All opposed

Boycott, none more so than Trueman, on a self-avowed mission to stop him getting a new contract. The former fast bowler had been so resentful at the way Yorkshire treated him during and after his career he did not become a member until January 1976. In his autobiography published the following year he wrote of standing for the committee, 'I don't fancy spending half my life trading abuse across a polished oak table.'

Former Harrogate captain Vallance, who made his Yorkshire League debut as an 18-year-old in 1956, had always been more positive about serving. 'I'd been a Yorkshire member since I was 14, when my mother's pass ran out,' he recalls. 'I'd played a lot of cricket with the old Yorkshire players and I was happy to help where I could. I stood for election and lost in the first place to Tony Woodhouse, it was a close-run thing [losing by nine votes in March 1978]. We had a recount and it got worse, he won by a few more so I said I don't want any more recounts or it'll soon be unanimous! In 1979 I beat a chap called Cooper. I was just interested. I didn't lead the cricketing views, there was [Don] Brennan, Trueman, [Billy] Sutcliffe and all sorts of better players, proper players, and Illingworth as manager. The difficulties with Boycott were all cricket-led and in terms of cricketing expertise I was a follower. I accepted the cricketing logic and wisdoms as sound. I thought the people who were against Boycott as a player within the team were right. They all referred to selfishness and slow play and so on. That was a very divisive influence.'

Two days after Boycott agreed his new contract, Hampshire engineered a rapprochement. 'There was a little bit of frostiness around those games in Hobart but because we won the [Australian] Gillette Cup the prize was playing against England at the MCG,' then-Tasmania captain Jack Simmons explains. 'Boycott was batting in the nets and Hampshire had a ball in his hand and went into the England net. The England camp didn't know what was going on, I don't think. He just said, "Come on 'Fiery!" and bowled three or four balls to him.

That broke the ice.' Afterwards Yorkshire's new captain spoke positively to the media about his predecessor. The Reformers were delighted. Not that Boycott's miserable winter was completely over – he made one in the match, and thieves took his favourite bat from the dressing room, along with a pair of Old's pads and one of Bairstow's bats.

The media were out in force at Carnegie College of Physical Education in Leeds for the first official day of pre-season. 'We had to put up with the staged pictures of Illingworth with Boycott and myself, all with our arms around each other's shoulders and captions reading "All is forgiven" and that sort of rubbish,' Hampshire noted. David Warner of the *Bradford Telegraph and Argus* observed Boycott – who had reported back for training a week early – and Hampshire were 'soon chatting' although in the dressing room the new captain claimed Boycott would more often than not give the silent treatment not only to him but anyone he thought was on his side. 'While I did not get any help from him in the voluntary sense, if I did approach him, then more often than not he gave me the answer I wanted,' Hampshire explained. That, though, was generally the way when it came to Boycott dispensing advice. He was told that as the senior professional he would fill in when Hampshire was absent, although this did not prove to be the case.

Pre-season is a time of optimism, and chairman Arthur Connell summed up the mood when he said, 'A lot of rude things have been said by all sides over the last six months. What we need to do now is forget all that nonsense and concentrate on producing a successful cricket team... We have had our barney and now we must get together.' Hampshire took a similar line at Yorkshire's annual pre-season luncheon, where Illingworth declared the squad to be 'stronger than in any other county'.

The 1979 campaign started on 2 May with a Championship match at home to Northamptonshire at the county's most northerly outpost. Snow stopped play and Yorkshire dropped ten catches in the draw. 'We went up to Middlesbrough to see him [Boycott] and as we walked in the gate he fielded the ball at backward point,' Reformer George Hepworth recalls. 'Everyone to a man applauded and now we have it on record that one of the players said, "'Oh Christ, they're back!" It was just a spontaneous gesture to let the lad know that we were all behind him. We didn't want any trouble as such, we just wanted to see justice done.' Well-meaning or not, it did not gladden the heart of Yorkshire's manager. 'Support was welcome, sabotage we would well do without,' Illingworth commented.

John Featherstone had decided before the elections to resign as Reform Group secretary, but it was not announced until afterwards. He believed some supporters were too militant, and so it would prove. He told the *Yorkshire Post* after quitting, 'I feel it is time for all those with Yorkshire's true interests at heart to get together rather than run the risk of pulling apart with the season a matter of weeks away. It's time to stop the in-fighting and remember that the important thing is the welfare and success of the team on and off the field.' Joe Lister had been to South Yorkshire Police about the abusive correspondence he received among letters alleging pro-committee vote-rigging at the SGM. The author was anonymous but the handwriting familiar. The police informed Lister, 'The officer who interviewed the lady concerned felt that her apologies and undertakings were genuine and he was reasonably satisfied that the letters will now cease.'

Yorkshire would have liked nothing more than for Boycott to persuade his followers to quietly go away, but he had no intention of abandoning those who had fought his corner so determinedly. He missed Yorkshire's final three-day practice match against Worcestershire because of a long-standing engagement at a Reform Group dinner on the second evening. Club rules stated players could not attend such events during a match, so while the county did not tell him he could not go, it was one or the other. Chris Old had cancelled a benefit function for the same reason, but Boycott had accepted the invitation when his Yorkshire future was still in question, and Peter Briggs had made arrangements to pick him up from New Road. Hepworth says, 'As a friend, if you asked Geoffrey Boycott to do something for you in six months' time, I would put my life on the line that in six months' time he would deliver.'

Hampshire was just as strong-willed as Boycott, straining his friendship with the hands-on Illingworth. 'When I say he was tough, I mean a very independent person, quite forthright,' Kevin Sharp explains. 'He believed in his decisions. He always kept me in my place because I was always a cheeky little sod. Right up until his death [in March 2017] whenever I saw him there was a great deal of respect but almost a little bit of fear as well because it was always like that. If I was to step out of line he would nail me. There was also an element of care. I think he rated me and backed me, although he might not always tell you that! He was almost a bit of a father figure, really. Whenever I saw him I'd know where the line was drawn.'

Tough or not, the captaincy had a negative effect on Hampshire's form as well as his enjoyment of the game. He finished sixth in Yorkshire's 1979 batting averages, and went two years and 29 days without a century – a run that actually started in July of his great summer of 1978. In his first season back in the ranks he topped the county's averages again. Giving Hampshire the captaincy when he was Yorkshire's best batsman only stopped him being Yorkshire's best batsman. The White Rose's first defeat of 1979 did not come until late June at Worcester, their longest unbeaten start for 25 years, but the first seven matches of a wet summer were all drawn and they would play 11 before tasting victory. 'John Hampshire's captaincy provided a negative lead,' argued *Wisden*. It would be a common complaint.

As usual, injuries played their part. Boycott and Old were on 1979 World Cup duty when Hampshire broke a finger fielding at Cambridge University in June. Bairstow took over the captaincy but Hampshire confounded expectations by returning for the next match, at Northampton.

Others did not show the same resilience. Old wrenched a rib muscle while sneezing and was unable to bowl on the final day of the Championship game with Somerset at Harrogate, and Boycott was unable to bat in the second innings. He had strained his hamstring turning for the second run which brought up his first-innings century. After consulting with Hampshire he batted on for ten overs with Peter Whiteley as a runner, adding 30 to his score and taking his opening partnership with Richard Lumb to 288, Yorkshire's biggest since 1939. That was Monday, and on Wednesday they had a Benson and Hedges semi-final at Essex.

That morning Illingworth told Boycott he was prepared to risk him at 'three-quarter pace' but the batsman said he could not even jog around the ground, then told the media he had been left out. Hampshire put on 107 for the first wicket with the in-form Lumb, soon to be the country's first player to 1,000 first-class runs that summer, but Yorkshire collapsed to 173/9 from 55 overs. Sharp, Bill Athey and Jim Love made three between them, Bairstow had taken ten overs to score ten, and having declared himself fit the equally explosive Old came in at ten and faced just eight balls, though all they reaped was a single. Former Yorkshire wicketkeeper Neil Smith scored the winning runs as Essex triumphed by three wickets with an over to spare. Boycott watched from the television commentary box and criticised his team-mates on air. His candid views angered Illingworth and led to a ban on Yorkshire players commentating on their team.

Boycott returned to the side three days later against Derbyshire and made 167 on the opening day, the second of three consecutive centuries in another outstanding season for him. The back injury he suffered in the fourth Test against India caused him to miss Yorkshire's final match of 1979, against Essex at Scarborough, keeping his first-class average over 100 – for Yorkshire it was 116. The country's next highest was Younis Ahmed's 69.95 for Worcestershire. Boycott also made an important contribution with the ball.

The batsman had been second in England's bowling averages on the 1964/65 tour of South Africa but as Yorkshire captain he only turned his arm over in four Championship and four limited-overs games, all in his final two seasons. 'I didn't rate my bowling,' Boycott tells me. 'I used to be quite a decent fast-medium bowler as a lad but it was such a very good side I played in during the 1960s. Playing on uncovered pitches with two great bowlers in Fred Trueman and Ray Illingworth, we never needed a fill-in bowler. Nowadays, in four-day cricket on covered pitches, those sort of bowlers are ideal but Yorkshire just didn't need them then because Fred Trueman could clean up the tail-enders in no time. Ken Taylor was a good bowler and he hardly ever bowled. If we needed anybody it would be Closey because he could bowl spin or seam up. For the best part of ten years I hardly bowled. I had medium-slow in-swingers when I picked it up again for the [1979] World Cup because Mike Brearley wanted me to bowl in that. I had lost whatever [pace] I had because I hadn't used it for so long.'

In 1979 Boycott became the first player to top Yorkshire's seasonal batting and bowling averages since George Hirst in 1910. He only took nine first-class wickets but a tenth would have put him top nationally. Bowling was a real weakness of Hampshire's side. Yorkshire conceded 350 no-balls in the 1979 Championship and because ten wickets were needed to qualify, Old was their only representative in the top 50 of the national averages. Boycott took a career-best 4-14 at Headingley as Hampshire enjoyed another Roses win in August. He followed it with 94 made with a black eye after top-edging a sweep at Colin Johnson in the nets. The real hero, however, was Neil Hartley, bringing up his half-century with the winning runs in only his third first-class game as the hosts chased 104 in

13.3 overs. That, followed by victory over Essex, meant Yorkshire finished on a high, seventh in the Championship. David Warner reflected, 'Yorkshire's first season under the Hampshire–Illingworth regime has not been the success one would have hoped for, even taking the poor weather into account. On the other hand, it has hardly been worse than last season – in many ways it has been better.'

In October Boycott, who had a year left on his contract, revealed four counties wanted him to join them for 1980, but again he stayed. For all the division his mere presence was causing, his form was still making him impossible to remove, and his desire to play for Yorkshire meant he was not going to walk away. Others did. Steve Oldham rejected a new contract and joined Derbyshire, and in March's annual general meeting Illingworth faced awkward questions about why England Under-19 captain Tim Boon had been allowed to leave, along with future England international Neil Mallender. On Boon, Illingworth explained, 'I believe that Yorkshire have five or six better uncapped players at the moment and I could not see how he could make the first team for a year or two.' Unwilling to wait that long, Boon joined Leicestershire. Illingworth's teenage namesake Richard, another who would play for England, signed for Worcestershire.

Ashley Metcalfe grew up with them. 'It was always a concern and leaving was always potentially an option,' he says of the competition for places. 'I wanted to play for Yorkshire at all costs. Other opportunities weren't quite as appealing. I was still at school and potentially going to university, so my personal timescale and ambitions were slightly different. I hadn't left school at 16 with a desire to be playing first-class cricket from that age onwards, I was trying to find a balance. I thought opportunities would potentially come along and I was a great believer that if they did it was up to the individual to take them. People like Neil Mallender, Tim Boon, Richard Illingworth, Steven Rhodes, the gaps didn't quite work for them and there were changes within the club that meant those gaps were even harder to find. Sadly you can only play 11. There were lots of people knocking on the door and some weren't as patient as others.'

Illingworth worked hard to build links with the Yorkshire Cricket Association and persuaded Berger Paints to sponsor a competition to unearth future players. Those that try to defend Yorkshire's post-1968 struggles often point to the lack of available talent, but the list of 20 finalists for the 1981 competition is impressive. Among those receiving £100 equipment vouchers (more in the case of the top four) were Richard Illingworth, future Northamptonshire and Durham bowler Alan Walker, plus Metcalfe, Phil Berry and Ian Swallow, who would play for Yorkshire's first team. Andrew Arundell and Mark Brearley (who kept wicket for the USA in 1987) had already played for the second XI, Andrew Tate and John Whitehouse would go on to. Paul Jarvis and Nick Taylor won one-year contracts after emerging the victors from a two-hour final in the Headingley nets. Jarvis made nine Test appearances for England. 'Given the chance I would have offered contracts to six of them without hesitation,' the manager commented.

'I played a couple of games for Yorkshire Under-19s but I had no beef because they had so many to choose from and you make a call on someone – sometimes they kick on, sometimes they don't,' reflects Walker, from Emley, near Huddersfield. 'We used to play a horrendous fixture at Scarborough, Yorkshire against Yorkshire Exiles. We used to beat them and I used to think, "What a terrible fixture for them." The coaching network now is better so you're getting the right players through more or less, and they've got so many to choose from. Now if someone else takes one of their players who wasn't in the system and they do well it's fair enough, but they used to hate that. I got on well with Doug Padgett towards the end but he would be a classic. I've heard him say when I was playing against Yorkshire seconds, "Don't let Walker get you out!" It just reflects badly, I suppose.'

Despite the off-field distractions, Yorkshire went into the 1980 season with Illingworth declaring them '200 per cent better prepared' than in 1979. Hampshire's pre-season speech was about how the squad could no longer use inexperience as an excuse. The positivity was soon knocked out of them. Yorkshire at least managed to beat the Combined Universities, but it was the only win from their opening ten limited-overs games. They made their highest Benson and Hedges Cup score against Worcestershire in the group stages – 269, Boycott top-scoring with 142 – but lost by four wickets. They scored one less against Warwickshire and lost by one wicket with a ball to spare. With Alan Ramage unable to bat, last pair Arnie Sidebottom and Howard Cooper were at the crease when Northamptonshire beat them by two runs.

The near-misses saw Yorkshire finish lowest of the first-class sides in the five-team group. Luck was against Hampshire in the Sunday League too, losing the first six tosses and games as Yorkshire again finished one from bottom. Boycott was dropped from the 40-over team at Essex in July, viewed by some as 'the first move to get rid of him at the end of the season'.

Peter Ingham took his chance with 53 not out in Yorkshire's best opening partnership of the Sunday League season – 98, with Hampshire – and Boycott made only two more appearances in the competition that summer. After such a prolific 1979, Boycott did not hit his next Championship century until August 1980, although an unbeaten 154 in the final game nudged his average above 50 for the 11th successive season.

The Gillette Cup was more promising. Bill Athey contributed man-of-the-match scores of 115 and 93 not out to consecutive wins which took Yorkshire into the semi-final. Boycott missed collecting an OBE from the Queen to play in the seven-wicket quarter-final victory at Hampshire, although he only contributed seven runs. The semi-final against Surrey at The Oval was spread over two days and Yorkshire had the worst of the conditions. After losing the toss they were bowled out for 135 on a newly-laid pitch in poor light. Surrey's Sylvester Clarke was warned for bowling too many bouncers. Old returned magnificent figures of 12-7-11-2 and Sidebottom, capped with Athey in July, took 3-37 from ten overs but the *Telegraph and Argus* reckoned Yorkshire 'were at least one genuine fast bowler short' as they lost by four wickets.

May's Roses match saw Lancashire's first Championship win over Yorkshire in eight years and ended with Hampshire off the field nursing the broken finger which would keep him out of the next six three-day matches. A captain often criticised for negativity suffered for trying to win, setting the hosts 302 in 250 minutes. Yorkshire finished sixth, although but for the rain on their final day, when only nine overs were possible at Scarborough, they could have picked up the £1,000 cheque for finishing fourth.

Wisden's view of the season was that 'no real discipline has been imposed' and Hampshire felt the divisions opened up by the Reform Group created 'a sort of anarchy'. In July Yorkshire inadvertently added to the unrest when, in an attempt to head off rumours about the latter's future, they agreed new two-year contracts with Hampshire, Old and Boycott. The rest of the squad voiced their displeasure in a meeting with new chairman Michael Crawford at Sheffield.

Crawford was Yorkshire's second-team captain in 1951 and, jointly with Ronnie Burnet, 1952. He had experience of working with Boycott, having persuaded him to join Leeds when captain there. On the committee since 1954, he had been the unanimous choice when Arthur Connell stood down in March. He promised Yorkshire would revert to their traditional arrangement of leaving all such decisions until the end of the season. If it seemed sensible, it would come back to bite him three years later. David Welch had replaced Crawford as treasurer and Brian Sellers, approaching 73, stood down from the general committee so grounds committee chairman Frank Melling, a key figure in the ultimately unsuccessful attempt to build a new venue at Sheffield's Bawtry Road, could stay on as an elected member after serving the maximum 21 years representing Sheffield. As a vice-president, Sellers could still attend meetings until his death in February 1981.

Kevin Sharp missed the second half of the 1980 season with nervous stress and while he insists it had nothing to do with the politics, from speaking to him and others it appears its distracting effect on Illingworth exacerbated his problems. 'I made my first [Yorkshire] hundred against Middlesex at Lord's in June 1980, then it went downhill from there,' Sharp recalls. 'I went through the growing-up period. I finished up going to Australia to play [in the winter of 1981/82] and pull myself back together. I suppose people who have been so mentally strong – like Boycs, like Illy, like Close, like Trueman – didn't get the vulnerability of some people. Emotional intelligence wasn't on the agenda. Perhaps the fragility of people was seen as a weakness. I suppose it is to a degree but look at people in the modern game who have gone through some harsh times and still been successful, like Marcus Trescothick. There's a more humane feel now, there's more support – psychologists and all these people – and it's not a stigma any more to get some advice and some help.

'It was no more than growing up but there weren't really many shoulders to lean on then. It was a tough school – sink or swim. If you can't cope with it, get out of it. If you weren't in the right frame of mind to play, then come back when you are. I was left to my own devices a little bit. Illy had got a great reputation as a cricketer and as a captain but for me it was an emotional thing and Yorkshire cricket didn't do emotion. As a young guy talked about as being on the brink of the England team at 18 years old, I needed a different type of support that wasn't available. That's a tactful way of putting it, isn't it? I had a really tough couple of years and probably never quite recovered from it as a player.

'I was mentally tough up to 18 but I went off the rails for a year or two and I don't think I ever really became mentally strong as a player again. There was always a touch of fragility and things would then perhaps bother me more than they might have done as a youngster. It probably wasn't until I ended up leaving Yorkshire as a player that I started to find my feet, which was a bit sad but that's life. I'm not sure the Boycott–Illingworth–Hampshire scenarios really affected me directly but perhaps that environment affected you in other ways. I needed to communicate. I needed someone to support and help me as a kid. Doug Padgett was brilliant, a really good man, but the coach in those days went with the second team and the first team ran itself through the captain and the senior players.'

Martyn Moxon did not make his first-class debut until 1981 but looking back at the early part of his career he says, 'During Illy's time as manager a lot of his energy was taken up in the battle with Boycott. It was a huge distraction to the team. As a young player off the field you didn't really get much off Illy because he was busy battling Geoffrey, which was a shame. Just generally it was a shame at that time that all our so-called greats were kind of at loggerheads with each other – Close, Trueman, Illingworth, Boycott just didn't get on and they weren't working together for the benefit of Yorkshire cricket. It was about their characters, their egos and their individual personal battles.'

Ashley Metcalfe's first appearance was later still, in Illingworth's final season, and marrying the manager's daughter Diane in 1986 made his circumstances rather different. 'I got a huge amount of help from Raymond,' he says. 'The people I got the most help from were Raymond and Doug Padgett and I'm immensely grateful to both. They had the confidence to believe I could play and got it across in a really nice manner that kept you really level-headed. The people that disappointed me were people like Boycs that could have given me far more.'

When Hampshire was left out of Yorkshire's final Sunday League game of the 1980 season at Canterbury, some took it as a sign Illingworth had decided to dispense with his captain. The man who pushed for him to replace Mike Brearley as England skipper two years earlier would later concede that his old friend 'did not have a lot of flair as captain'. Hampshire had already resigned. The final straw came in a local supermarket, where his wife was abused by a Boycott supporter. The job he had been so honoured to take in Brisbane had become more hassle than it was worth. The more militant followers of the Reform Group had claimed a first victim. 'I had no knowledge of that at all,' Matthew Caswell says of the abuse. 'None of the people [from the Reform Group's leadership] would do that. I nor anyone else I was involved with would ever have put up with that.'

Yorkshire's July impatience had left an unhappy Hampshire with two years on his contract. After two captains in 16 seasons, the county were looking for a third in three years.

12

Caught in the Crossfire

I F THE choice of John Hampshire's successor as Yorkshire captain was relatively straightforward, deciding who should replace the replacement during Chris Old's frequent absences left a number of key players alienated and disgruntled. When Old emerged from 1980's trial runs as the new skipper it was as an England international with a dubious fitness record, so the question of who should lead the side was bound to reappear pretty quickly.

Old had started the decade with his future at Yorkshire in doubt. He opted out of the 1979/80 Ashes tour to give his creaking body a winter's rest, and had only been offered a county contract – with fitness clauses – for the following year. Old was Hampshire's unofficial vice-captain in 1979 but manager Ray Illingworth also viewed 30-year-old opener Richard Lumb as a candidate to replace his increasingly beleaguered skipper. When Hampshire missed 11 games in all competitions with a broken finger, it was an opportunity to see what the pair could do. Yorkshire handled it with their usual complete lack of sensitivity.

'There was a game towards the end of that season against Glamorgan at Swansea on the Sunday,' recalls Old, who was taking charge of his sixth consecutive match. 'I said to the lads I was travelling down early on Saturday, so if anyone wanted a lift I had room. Richard Lumb, who lived in the Doncaster area, said he'd drop his car off at John Hampshire's, just off the M1 in the Sheffield area. Ted Lester, the scorer, said he'd do that too. At the last minute Ray Illingworth asked if I could pick him up. So I drove all the way down in horrendous weather – a howling gale and torrential rain – and we went for a meal.' The next day, rain reduced Yorkshire's innings to 25 overs, Glamorgan's to 18, and the game ran into the evening before the hosts completed a six-wicket win.

'I dropped Ted and Richard off at John's at about one o'clock, then I dropped Illingworth off where he lived,' Old continues. 'Just as I got to his he said, "Oh, by the way, John's told me he doesn't want to captain next season so I've got to make a decision on who I want. On Wednesday for the game at Bradford [against Worcestershire] I'm making Richard Lumb captain instead of you," then got out of the car and left. We'd driven 250 miles and it was late at night. My mind wasn't working overtime so I said, "Okay, that's fine." At nine o'clock the next morning the phone rang and David Bairstow was absolutely fuming. I agreed to meet him at lunchtime to talk about it. David was annoyed that he was the next senior player and he hadn't been asked to do the job. I kind of calmed him down and said, "It's his [Illingworth's] decision, he's not going to change it, don't get yourself all worked up and get into bother. We've just got to go out there and play." He wanted to try somebody else – that was okay by me.'

Bairstow was 19 months younger than Lumb (and nearly three years Old's junior), but had been capped a year earlier, in 1973. Illingworth was firmly of the opinion that captaining in the County Championship was too much to ask of a wicketkeeper – he regarded it as 'untidy' – and harboured doubts about Bairstow specifically. 'An enthusiastic and loyal Tyke, but never a captain as long as he breathes' was his damning verdict of a player who would eventually lead the side for three years. With Geoff Cope released in 1980 after his bowling action was scrutinised for a fourth time, it left a straight choice between two very different personalities.

'Chris was very sociable,' Kevin Sharp says. 'He is just a nice fella who was a very, very good cricketer.' If Old was one of the boys, Lumb was not. 'Richard was difficult to get to know,' Old comments. 'I could have a drink with him but I think he was insecure at times. His wife had been brought up in South Africa and he was possibly thinking about moving out there [he did after retiring in 1984], and things outside of cricket.'

Geoff Cook, who played against both many times for Northamptonshire, says, 'Richard Lumb was a real individual. He had a few outstanding seasons because he was very single-minded and I always felt he pushed himself away from all the politics and just got on with his batting. Unfortunately he opened with Boycott on a number of occasions and suffered from it, but I'm sure he would also say he benefited by it as well. He wasn't a typical Yorkshire person like the Bairstows, the Carricks and the Stevensons, who carried a lot of the legacies of Yorkshire cricket. He seemed to stand aside from all that. Everybody else just suffered.' The biggest difference between Old and Lumb, though, was that only one of them really wanted to be Yorkshire's next captain.

A huge part of the job was man-managing Geoffrey Boycott and although Lumb's 29 century opening stands with him are second only to Percy Holmes and Herbert Sutcliffe for Yorkshire, there were plenty of flashpoints. Batting regularly with Boycott inevitably meant being run out by him. At times it could be laughed off. 'Richard Lumb and Barrie Leadbeater knew he was going to run on the fifth or sixth ball [of each over], so at times they literally went down into a sprinting pose ready to go,' chuckled Mike Bore. 'He didn't like that.'

On other occasions it was more serious, such as at Bradford Park Avenue in 1983 when Boycott ran Lumb out for two and

14. Leo McKinstry reported that Lumb yelled, 'That's 11-0 on run-outs now!' at Boycott in the dressing room afterwards. When a contrite Boycott innocently asked what he should do, Lumb replied, 'You should fuck off like you should have done ten years ago!' Lumb enjoyed his brief captaincy audition, but Boycott was on international duty for all the games he took charge of and he did not have the appetite to deal with him or the political circus surrounding him. Lumb could not hold down a Sunday League place, featuring in only six matches during Hampshire's captaincy, and when he matched Old's Championship record of won one, drawn two, the England international was the obvious choice.

Julian Vallance was one of three Leeds representatives on the committee which had to make the decision. 'I drove to the meeting which was going to appoint the captain,' he recalls. 'The cricket committee had met the night before to decide whom to recommend to the main committee. I heard on the radio news that Old had been appointed – and the committee hadn't met! Old was duly put forward!' The bowling all-rounder felt ready for the challenge. 'I knew I was probably coming to the end of my international career and I felt I had a good rapport with a lot of the youngsters who were coming through,' he says. 'I could work with the bowlers, talk with the batsmen about what the bowlers were looking at, and do something for the club. It actually gave me something more to do than just get up and play cricket. I could have an input into what was going on so I was really relishing the thought of it but it was a bit of a poisoned chalice. There were lots of things happening that were beyond my control. The important thing to me was the players seemed happy that I'd got it. That was a big boost. It helps if you've got that support.'

There was one player in particular Old knew he had to get on his side. He first played alongside Boycott in the 1967 Gillette Cup quarter-finals but although long-standing, their relationship never got above lukewarm. 'Throughout my career you couldn't say we were friends,' he explains. 'I always admired him as a player but he wasn't the player I would go out for a meal or a drink with. He did annoy me at times. In the dressing room he wanted his own little space and everyone had to do what he wanted. When you've had a bad time it's up to you to go and find your own space, not expect everybody to move out. But Yorkshire's always had different characters and they've always managed to succeed with them. He knew what it took for him to be the batsman that broke all these records. For 95, 96 per cent of the time, if Geoffrey did well, Yorkshire did well. There was the odd occasion where you felt he could have done a little more for the team, rather than himself, but overall his performance for Yorkshire was tremendous.'

The pair toured West Indies with England in 1980/81 and on their return, Old made a point of engaging his senior professional. 'I spoke to Geoffrey and said all I wanted him to do was go out and play and I would like to be able to come to him and ask for advice at times, particularly on the field when you need people you can trust,' he recalls. 'He seemed quite happy. I said the same to the other players, and not to be offended if I didn't take their advice. I felt as if it worked pretty well.'

More than one account identified 27 May 1981 at Dartford as the day their relationship broke down, but Old insists that was not the case. Boycott was in a bad mood having been told off when he and Bairstow left the ground during a heavy rain shower and were caught out by an earlier than expected resumption. When Old asked for advice on the field it was apparently met with, 'It's nothing to do with me. You get on with it, you're the captain.' He was by no means the only skipper to get that response from Boycott and while it registered with others, when I ask Old about it all I get back is a blank look. 'He just got on and played,' he insists. 'I think he went out there thinking, "I won't get involved in anything, I'll just do what I can." The games I captained, he seemed reasonably okay. There was once or twice where I got that response. I half-expected it in a way but at least he couldn't say I hadn't asked him.'

Earlier that month Derbyshire asked for Boycott to be disciplined for using a V-sign and offensive language when warming up before a Benson and Hedges Cup game at Derby. When Boycott, Illingworth and others ignored signs in the dressing room asking them not to practice on the playing area, chief executive David Harrison took to the tannoy to request they stop, adding, 'And that includes you, Mr Boycott.' Yorkshire decided not to act in light of what they saw as Harrison's provocation.

Old's relationship with Illingworth was more troublesome. The previous summer the manager had written *Yorkshire and Back*. One of the autobiography's more damning passages read, 'I did not think "Chilly" [Old's nickname] has ever been prepared in his life to grit his teeth and say, "I know I am feeling twinges but the side needs me to bowl well and quickly in this situation so I'll do it." I just wish he had more heart.' Old did not regard it as an issue. 'I've never read a cricket book,' he tells me. 'I wasn't really aware of what he'd written. People have their opinions, but what happened out on those 22 yards was what was important to me.' Illingworth was not the only one who questioned Old's personality. 'A bit like Norman Yardley, Chilly was probably a bit too nice to be captain,' Ted Lester argued. 'He kept out of the way whenever he could but it needed somebody a bit stronger. I think gradually he went the same way as the rest of them!'

Illingworth's determination to run the show was the main source of friction. 'To start with it seemed fine,' says Old, 'but I did end up speaking about it to the committee. If I went away for a Test match I walked into the dressing room for the next game and I didn't know which players were there, there was no communication. There was one Test match I came back from at ten or 11 o'clock at night and I got a phonecall from

Richard Lumb, saying, "Why am I not playing tomorrow?" I said, "Aren't you?" In the same [England] dressing room Bob Willis was captaining Warwickshire and two or three times when we were away the phone would ring and David Brown, the manager, would be speaking to him about various things. He seemed to be a lot more aware of what was going on. I would just be presented with a squad. I had the choice of the final XI, but I didn't necessarily have the 12 that I wanted. John [Hampshire] and Geoffrey just got on with it and Richard only complained the once. After that I think he possibly realised I didn't often have a say.'

Kevin Sharp believes the effect the politics had on the team can be overplayed. 'It was a bit of a sideshow,' he stresses. 'In the dressing room people got on with each other. The management had their issues and there might have been individuals at war with each other but bloody hell, we socialised well together! There was lots of respect.' Lester was quite clear, though, 'They didn't do nearly as well as they ought to have with the talent there was.'

Old's squad contained 14 players with first-class centuries, two England bowlers (himself and Graham Stevenson), and an international wicketkeeper, yet finished tenth in the Championship. Questions were inevitably asked of Old, but injuries were a major factor. Not until 22 August did Yorkshire have a full squad to choose from, and even then the captain was not at 100 per cent. Old was the only capped bowler fit for the NatWest Trophy first-round defeat at Kent and eight players fractured bones during the season. It at least created opportunities for others, Paul Jarvis following a wicket-taking Sunday League debut by becoming Yorkshire's youngest first-class debutant aged 16 years and 75 days. The fast bowler from Redcar had only made five second-team appearances.

By helping Ian Botham pull off one of the great Ashes victories at Headingley in July, Old unwittingly caused more political upheaval. Vice-captain Lumb was out with his second broken finger of the season – it was not his year, he also fractured a toe in the opening game at Oxford – so the only capped players making the Championship trip to Cardiff were Stevenson, returning from a groin injury, Bairstow, Hampshire, and Jim Love and Bill Athey, who had both been capped less than a year. Illingworth rang Hampshire before the game to say, 'I know you'll think I've gone round the back of the moon but I'm thinking of making Neil Hartley captain.' Hampshire's reply was typically blunt, 'I don't know whether you are trying to hang yourself or get yourself sacked, but you're wrong.' The uncapped 25-year-old all-rounder had come into the team for the previous match, a home win over Surrey, but it was only his second Championship appearance that season and 22nd since his debut in 1978. Illingworth, though, saw something in Hartley.

A talented all-round sportsman – he played football for Bradford City and rugby for Bingley – he was 19 when he captained Bingley to cricket's Bradford League and Priestley Cup double. He showed his big-match temperament against Lancashire at Headingley during Illingworth's first season as manager. The *Bradford Telegraph and Argus* described Hartley's maiden half-century, a match-winning 53 not out after being dropped on 24 by David Hughes, as 'one of the great knocks in Yorkshire cricket'. A fortnight earlier he had been England's 12th man against India. Hartley had only captained Yorkshire's second XI once, against Worcestershire in 1980, and had never taken charge of the first XI. Even with all their injuries, Yorkshire's team in Cardiff still contained five England internationals – Athey had made his Test debut the previous summer, Love his only one-day international appearances in June – and a former England Under-19 captain in Sharp.

Further complicating matters was Hartley's relationship with Illingworth's 20-year-old daughter, Vicky, which his wife Julie revealed to *The Sun* in September 1981. 'We had a very nice boy-girl relationship for a while, but it cooled and we separated in a friendly way,' explained Neil, who was going through a divorce having separated from Julie two years earlier. Yorkshire's manager, who unsuccessfully applied for an injunction to stop the story, claimed Neil and Vicky had not been an item for six weeks but that had not registered with the former team-mates I spoke to. When I point it out to Boycott, he replies, 'He [Illingworth] could argue he put his personal feelings to one side but the greatest writer of all, Shakespeare, wrote that Caesar's wife, "Must not just be above suspicion, she must be seen to be above suspicion." What's perceived is as important as what actually happens.' Kerry Packer used the same quote during his High Court case against the International Cricket Council in 1977.

When Illingworth refused Hampshire's suggestion that Bairstow lead the side, the former skipper offered to do it himself until Old returned. Hampshire top-scored in both innings at Glamorgan, and made 82 against Nottinghamshire, but Yorkshire lost by ten and eight wickets respectively. More worryingly, Hampshire suffered chest pains in South Wales. 'Whether it was the pressure of being back in command I don't know, but it was distinctly unpleasant,' he recalled. The only Yorkshire player to outscore his captain at Trent Bridge had been Hartley, making the first of three career centuries in the Championship.

When Lumb and Hampshire failed fitness tests before the next Championship match, against Warwickshire at Scarborough eight days later, Illingworth put Hartley in charge. The *Yorkshire Post*'s Terry Brindle called it 'the latest bizarre twist in a Yorkshire season where anything but success seems possible'. Sports editor Bill Bridge described it as 'bad politics, bad timing or both'. Hartley had little to work with. Boycott and Old were preparing for the fourth Ashes Test, seamers Arnie Sidebottom and Simon Dennis (son of local committee representative Geoff and cousin of Richard Hutton) also failed fitness tests, and Derby County Football

Club refused Illingworth's request for Alan Ramage to stay with Yorkshire for the rest of the campaign. Three years after his maiden first-class appearance, Steve Stuchbury, a left-arm seamer and computer operator at Rolls-Royce's Derby plant, made his Championship debut.

A 7,500 crowd watched the opening day. Quite apart from all the Yorkshire fans who ritually made a holiday out of their team's trips to the seaside, Wednesday was a national holiday and it was either watch the cricket or sit through Prince Charles's wedding to Lady Diana Spencer on the television. Warwickshire won the toss and Hartley's depleted attack bowled them out for 288. Sharp and Martyn Moxon saw Yorkshire to 71/0 by the close. In the *Yorkshire Post*, Peter Snape reflected, 'Hartley led the side with quiet authority, several of his tactical moves came off and he was never afraid to use his spinners,' although of course, 'The all-seeing critics on the Popular Bank noisily disputed some of his field placings.'

When he batted, the stand-in captain took 30 minutes getting off the mark but made 59, adding 116 for the fifth wicket with Bairstow. A weasel, not a black cat, ran across the field on the final morning to stop play but it brought Hartley bad luck nonetheless. Asif Din was nine not out when the umpires turned down Yorkshire's appeals for a bat-pad catch, and batted for another 40 minutes as Warwickshire fought to save the game. They were 85 runs ahead, six wickets down, with three hours remaining when Philip Oliver was dropped by the stretching right hand of Bairstow. 'It was a chance only by Bairstow's high standards,' wrote Snape. Hartley was denied victory but made a favourable impression. 'Neil has done all that could be expected of him,' Illingworth commented. 'It is not easy for a young captain to handle senior capped players. He made virtually all the bowling changes I would have made and set an excellent example in the field.' The next day Hartley was in charge again, overseeing a 167-run defeat to Somerset at Abbeydale Park before Old returned at home to Hampshire.

Athey had to take over wicketkeeping duties on day one at Scarborough because of a shoulder injury which left Bairstow needing painkillers to score his 62 runs. He had recently had a hole drilled in his right thumb to ease the pressure caused by a flake of bone. 'Bairstow's thumb will heal quickly enough; it is the threat to his heart Yorkshire should worry about,' Brindle warned. Bairstow later described choosing Hartley to lead the side at Scarborough as, 'Tantamount to Illingworth saying that he did not rate me or any other of the capped players as a possible captain of Yorkshire. And that hurt.' His anger spilled out when he confronted his manager in the cocktail bar of Scarborough's Royal Hotel, giving the holidaymakers an argument to gossip about. It was the opposite on the field. 'During the game Willie Hogg turned to Hartley and me and asked, "What's the matter with you two? Aren't you speaking?"' recalled Bairstow, who led a side including Hartley on the Sunday. 'Willie thought he was joking but he had in fact spotted the truth of the situation. Hartley felt more embarrassed than anything.' Bairstow was by no means the only disillusioned player.

Lumb returned for August's trip to Northamptonshire's Wellingborough School, yet Hartley again led the side. In pandering to Boycott, Old had alienated his deputy. 'I feel I have not been able to play a full part on the field,' Lumb told the *Yorkshire Post*. 'I don't consider myself sufficiently in the picture to lead the side at the moment. Before I was injured I fielded in the deep a lot and was not involved in decision-making.' When Old had gone off injured at Acklam Park in the previous game it was Boycott, not Hartley, who took the reins, and Yorkshire came close to winning. Now the opener was on international duty at Old Trafford. 'Provided he [Hartley] is selected in the side he will be captain when Old is away – at least until the end of the season,' Illingworth confirmed the following week. 'But that does not mean his place is certain.' Therein lay the problem as Yorkshire chopped and changed between Old, Bairstow, Hampshire, Boycott and Hartley – but not the official vice-captain.

When chosen to lead the side in August/September's Roses match, Brindle wrote, 'Hartley ought, in conscience, to be the embodiment of Close, Bradman and Sobers to deserve the honour… The fact he clearly is not – and would not claim to be – saddles him with responsibilities beyond his 25 years and arguably beyond his ability.' Hartley was the only Yorkshire player to make a half-century as they were blown away by West Indians Clive Lloyd (145) and Michael Holding (6-76) in a first innings defeat to Lancashire since 1932. Yorkshire had not lost at home to the Red Rose since 1970, and never by such a wide margin at Headingley. They had won at Wellingborough, but the other five Championship matches Hartley took charge of in 1981 were lost. When he became second XI captain in 1988, his Championship record as captain was one win from eight, plus two from five in limited-overs cricket.

'People like Kevin Sharp, Jim Love and Bill Athey were pissed off because they thought he wasn't as good a player as them and now he was guaranteed a place in the side,' Boycott argues. If it sounds like he is putting words in other people's mouths, Sharp more or less confirms it. 'My statistics in first-class cricket weren't particularly high, I have to say, but I don't think Neil's were great,' he reflects. 'He seemed to be guaranteed a place in the side for a while. He was quite a decent one-day cricketer but Championship cricket is an awful lot different. I was ready for my turn again and I saw someone playing who wasn't particularly making many runs. I thought, "I need to go, then."

'There was a point where I wanted to go to Worcestershire in 1983. I'd been capped in 1982 [on the same day as Hartley] and I was starting to find my feet after a tough couple of years. Illy was playing Neil in the first team and I was in the seconds, where I'd made a couple of hundreds [against Glamorgan and Warwickshire]. Duncan Fearnley [Worcestershire's Yorkshire-

205

born chairman] was my sponsor since I'd been 15 and I played league cricket with his brother Mike for Bingley in the Bradford League. I played a second-team game at Worcester [in late June] and Duncan asked what was going on. I said, "I can't get in the team," so he said, "Come and play here, you'll get in the team here." I said to Illy I'd like him to release me at the end of the year because I'd like to play for Worcestershire. I explained that I felt I needed to be playing first-team cricket now because I wasn't developing in the second team but he advised me to stick it out. Within a reasonable amount of time I was playing first-team cricket again. I made a century at Cheltenham, then another against Surrey at Scarborough and I was in the team for a long time after that. That was the end of Worcestershire, really.'

There does not seem to be much animosity towards Hartley. 'Neil was quite a balanced lad, he was a good cricketer,' says Sharp. 'You'd have to ask Illy what he saw in him as a captain.' Ashley Metcalfe goes further. 'He was a brilliant captain,' he tells me. 'He had a great cricketing mind and people just didn't give him a chance. In public he dealt with it really well but I'm sure internally it would have been really difficult. He was a far better player than his record showed. There were several young players who found it difficult to stand up and deliver in that side. You had to have a real mental strength to cope with it.'

For those looking for a stick to beat Illingworth with, Hartley was an easy option. 'I felt sorry for him,' says Old. 'I always thought he was a very useful cricketer but he was under so much pressure from the manager to produce the goods, and from other people probably expecting him to be better than he was. It made life very difficult for him, and then to be thrown in as a captain, having not really established himself in the team…' Martyn Moxon adds, 'Neil was one of my best mates in the dressing room but from a senior players' perspective it was a very unsettling decision and a little bit left-field. Only Illy knows the true reasons why Neil was made captain. It made it very awkward for Neil because he wasn't a regular in the three-day team.'

Old played in just three of Yorkshire's last 11 Championship matches of 1981 but kept his job. The lack of alternatives was so glaring David Warner suggested Colin Johnson, with one Championship appearance since the 1978 'go-slow', be promoted from second- to first-team captain for 1982. Illingworth decided the senior professional would deputise during Old's absences, except in the Sunday League, where it would be Hartley. When he was capped in May, the *Telegraph and Argus* noted, 'At the start of this campaign, Hartley had made 1,163 first-class runs for Yorkshire, which is probably as few as any professional player on receiving his cap.' With Old's days as captain numbered thanks in no small part to another farcical episode in Yorkshire's history, more arguments were looming.

13

Pantomime by the Seaside

THE tension simmering between Ray Illingworth and Geoffrey Boycott bubbled to the surface at the end of the 1981 season.

Scarborough's annual cricket festival ought to have seen another unfulfilling summer of Yorkshire cricket reach a gentle conclusion. Instead it provided the perfect stage for a pantomime which kicked off another winter of in-fighting. A suspension, a petition, an on-pitch protest and a secret recording made it impossible to turn a blind eye to the latest fall-out between Yorkshire's manager and senior professional, yet a winter-long inquiry managed to once more sweep the county's problems under the carpet.

Boycott featured in only eight of 22 County Championship matches in 1981 but it was his absence from the limited-overs side which aggravated him. Midway through the season, Illingworth had decided to blood youngsters in the Sunday League and although Boycott comfortably headed Yorkshire's seasonal averages (he was top in the Championship too), his slow 36 in the NatWest Trophy defeat at Canterbury showed why. With Martyn Moxon out early, Yorkshire made only six runs in as many overs, and Derek Underwood conceded just ten in his 12 overs. When Boycott and John Hampshire were left out of August's Sunday League game against Hampshire at Acklam Park, David Warner speculated in the *Bradford Telegraph and Argus,* 'It could be that their careers in 40-overs-a-side cricket are virtually over.' He was wrong about Boycott, but Hampshire never played for Yorkshire again in the format.

Boycott was also left out for the 50-over Fenner Trophy, a Scarborough Cricket Festival staple but essentially trumped-up friendlies. He asked to play in the three-day match against a Barbados XI which followed – a game which did not even have first-class status – but Illingworth said the youngsters would feature instead. 'He didn't tell the truth,' Boycott says. 'I told him I wanted to play because I always wanted to play but he said he wanted to play the youngsters. That was fine, fair enough, but then he played John Hampshire, Chris Old, Richard Lumb – everyone but me. He wasn't straight with me. I was bloody angry. I thought it was wrong when other people were playing but I wasn't.' Lumb, 31, tripled his limited-overs appearances for the season in the four-team competition, which Old's Yorkshire won thanks to 84 not out from 40-year-old Hampshire.

Communication was at the heart of everything which went wrong between Boycott and Illingworth in 1981. The former complained his manager, 'Barely spoke to me or to any Yorkshire player who he thought was a friend of mine.' He claimed he found out he was not playing against Hampshire from a local radio reporter. On the other hand, Illingworth pointed out Arnie Sidebottom was the only member of the squad – himself included – to have Boycott's telephone number, and then only briefly. If Illingworth wanted to get hold of his senior professional he had to phone a friend. Confirmation Boycott was not part of Yorkshire's Fenner Trophy plans was relayed via team-mate Mike Gatting while the pair were in the nets preparing for the sixth Ashes Test at The Oval, even though Yorkshire were staying at the same hotel as they were playing Middlesex at Lord's. Illingworth regarded it as Boycott's responsibility to get in touch with him about the Barbados game, and told the *Yorkshire Post* by the time that happened, 'I had already picked a team.' Boycott played instead for Castleford, making 30 in a draw.

He is unrepentant when I ask if he should have made it easier for Illingworth to contact him. 'He had me seven days a week at the cricket and he could have said anything to me because he was my boss,' he replies. 'We'd [often] play two Championship matches and a Sunday League game in a week so I saw him every day for eight hours minimum, probably nine, six days a week, and Sunday for another seven hours. If he needed to say anything to me he could do it then. The real reason why my supporters and friends didn't want me to get involved with Raymond at night was there was no trust after all that had gone on. I and my supporters believed he was fairly instrumental in getting me sacked in 1978, so you don't want to get involved in conversations on the phone when there's no one there to back up what was said.'

When it came to voicing his concerns to others, Boycott managed just fine. The day before Yorkshire's match against Northamptonshire, he was at WH Smith in York for a book-signing arranged two weeks earlier. 'I feel I am not getting a fair deal from the team manager and I am determined to have a showdown with him soon,' he said in a television interview. 'I prefer to leave this until after our last two Championship matches against Northamptonshire and Sussex so as to avoid anything that may affect our chances of winning points in those games. But there has to be some straight talking because I am tired of having my livelihood undermined.' That evening Illingworth played in a 30-over floodlight charity match at Scarborough's Seamer Road football ground, so the matter was dealt with at the breakfast table the next morning.

'I felt strongly about it,' Old says. 'I found it very strange. He'd spoken earlier in the year that he'd quite understand if he wasn't going to be selected for the Fenner Trophy because some of the youngsters should be given the opportunity. We thought it was an opportunity to bring them in. I asked the manager to have breakfast early on the morning of the match and I asked did he have permission to do the interview? He said, "No." I said, "If Graham Stevenson wrote that article, what would your decision be?" He said, "Oh, he wouldn't play for the rest of the season." I said, "That's fine, we should treat Geoffrey exactly the same." We were in a no-win situation. But I did say to him that as manager it was his job to tell Geoffrey he wasn't playing.' Illingworth told the press later that morning, 'If Geoff had been a footballer I could have slapped him on the transfer list.'

The decision left Yorkshire a batsman short. 'I'd played in the festival games but wasn't due to play in the Championship game,' Martyn Moxon recalls. 'I was staying with Simon Dennis at his house. About nine o'clock on the morning of the game I got a phonecall from Ray Illingworth basically saying, "Get to the ground, you're playing," so it was a bit of a "blummin' heck, what's happened?" I got to the ground and there was an eerie sort of atmosphere. I went into the dressing room and said, "What's happened?" and they were all very sheepish. They said, "Illy's dropped Boycs." I thought, "Oh shit!"'

Moxon made two first-team appearances in the 1980 Sunday League without batting or bowling, and only batted three times in seven matches the following year, but in June he had scored 116 against Essex at Headingley on his Championship debut. 'It was beyond my wildest dreams,' he admits. 'I got five in the first innings but to then get a hundred in my second, it just helps you settle in and relax into that environment. Once you've got a few runs behind you it gives you a lot of confidence that you can perform at that level.'

Moxon was only the second player to make 100 for Yorkshire on his maiden Championship appearance. He had just turned 21 whereas 60 years earlier Cec Tyson was 32 and a leading Yorkshire League batsman who worked as coach/groundsman with Whitwood Colliery. Tyson made a first-innings duck against Lancashire the following week and, unable to agree terms with Yorkshire, returned to his day job and club cricket with Castleford. It would be five years before he (briefly) played first-class cricket again, for Glamorgan. Moxon's reward for his match-saving display was to lose his place once Boycott returned from England duty, but during the third Test his 111 against Nottinghamshire made him the first Yorkshire player to score centuries in each of his first two Championship home matches. Only then was he awarded his second team cap.

'I was usually one of the first to get to the ground and when I got there I looked up and you could see the Scarborough office,' Old says. 'Geoffrey was in there on the phone in his whites. At nine o'clock in the morning before an 11 o'clock start, that was relatively unheard of. Yes, he'd get there early but not that early. It was a very difficult morning.' Hampshire arrived at his usual spot next to Boycott's in the home changing room, having been tipped off as to what would happen. 'We'd had "atmospheres" in the dressing room in the past but nothing like this one,' he commented.

As soon as word got out that Boycott had been dropped, there was uproar inside the ground. 'When he [Illingworth] asked me to leave I took my gear outside,' he explains. 'I think [Sidney] Fielden advised me to go and leave it to him. I didn't know what to do. I'd come to play cricket.' In the lead-up to the game the Reformers – rebranded the Yorkshire Cricket Supporters' Association – had threatened to call a special general meeting to push for a vote of no confidence in Illingworth. 'If the committee are not prepared to act then the members must,' said Peter Briggs, who stood down as chairman when the movement became a supporters' club.

'I am always prepared to listen to any constructive suggestion from the Reform Group, but I will not be browbeaten,' was chairman Michael Crawford's response. 'We cannot have two organisations running this club.' Fielden produced a petition calling for Illingworth's sacking which soon gathered more than 400 signatures – 'I reckon we could get 1,000 if we had to,' he said – and television crews arrived from Leeds with suspicious speed. Angry Boycott supporters took to the pitch.

'I remember walking [Northamptonshire captain] Geoff Cook out to the middle and he said, "What's going on?"' recalls Old. 'I said, "I'll tell you when we get to the middle," because the square was roped off and we could talk in private. I apologised for what was going to happen, but there was going to be a lot of anti-feeling. He said, "Why?" so I showed him my team. He said, "Ah… yes." When the coin came down heads and he shouted tails I said, "I'm very sorry Geoffrey, but you're going to have to field. I'm only going to allow two of my players on the field at any one time!" I felt sorry for the openers. John Hampshire was sat in the dressing room shaking. He said, "Do you realise what you've done?" I said, "Yes, but there were good reasons."'

The start of the game was held up for five minutes. 'People started sitting on the field, saying we're not allowing this game to start if Boycott's not playing,' says Kevin Sharp. Eventually Yorkshire's openers were allowed to bat. 'As I was walking out with Richard Lumb I'll never forget a guy came up to us and said, "We haven't come to watch you, we've come to watch Geoffrey," so they weren't very happy,' says Moxon, dryly. There was a suggestion some might demand their money back.

The start of the game was not the end of the pantomime. Boycott hung around for another 70 minutes, signing bats for David Bairstow's benefit fund and copies of his latest book while he held court. 'Boycott was soon swamped by sympathisers, many of them women,' the *Telegraph and Argus* noted. Cook did his best to ignore it. 'I would say the vast majority of the Yorkshire fans were Boycott followers, they idolised him,' he comments. 'It was doubly difficult for myself after the euphoria of having been picked the previous day for my first England tour. My enjoyment and pride was quickly brought back to earth by this ongoing drama – it was farce.'

The North Marine Road pavilion is tucked away in the north-east corner of the characterful ground. To the right of the away dressing room is a set of turnstiles allowing a quick and discreet getaway on to Woodall Avenue, between some of the many guesthouses circling the ground. Rising to the left of the home dressing room is the Popular Bank – a mass of wooden benches which, as the name suggests, holds the majority of spectators. At its apex stand the main gates, opening on to the road which gives the ground its name. No professional cricketer, let alone England's most famous, could make that walk during a county game without being noticed. At 12.10pm, in full view of players and spectators, Boycott chose that route to make his grand exit.

'I remember the crowd going absolutely berserk,' says Cook. 'They were his disciples and he absolutely milked it. It was like leaving home so all the family could see. It was at moments like that you realised what a king of Yorkshire cricket he was. We'd seen two or three times before the selfishness of the whole thing so that act in itself didn't surprise us. By that time we were all laughing at his selfishness but in terms of it being a County Championship match of some import, it was all rather sad.' *The Times* reported, 'Most of the 5,000 spectators rose to their feet and applauded him as he passed out of the gates'. The *Daily Telegraph* commented, 'Even if someone had taken all ten wickets, made a hundred before lunch or scored 300 in the day, it would probably have been overshadowed by events off the field.' That Bairstow became only the second Yorkshire wicketkeeper to score 1,000 first-class runs in a season was little more than a footnote.

Generally, the more experienced the player, the more it affected them. 'It was a really odd atmosphere,' Moxon admits. 'It didn't overly bother me but it was a weird situation. Being a young player, you were just playing. Fortunately. But I think as a senior player it must have been really distracting. In hindsight it was a farce.'

Some quite enjoyed it. Kevin Sharp and Bill Athey were given the job of smuggling Illingworth's wife Shirley and daughter Vicky out the back well before the close of play so they could slip away unnoticed to the hotel in nearby Kirkbymoorside Old organised through his friends the owners. 'Me and Bill Athey found it more amusing than anything else,' Sharp admits. 'It was an end-of-season game and I was getting ready to play. The team had been announced and we knew Boycs wasn't in the team. I can't say we were really affected by it. We were young lads in our early 20s so why would you get your knickers in a twist about it?' Hampshire did. 'I was so tense and nervous when my turn came to bat,' he wrote. 'It was appalling.'

The veteran rose above it, making the game's only century as the hosts won by 156 runs, but it would be his final innings for Yorkshire in Yorkshire. The incident convinced him to leave. He made 53 against Sussex in the season's final match then, midway through a two-year contract, the county's tenth-highest run-scorer and their batsman of the year finally joined Derbyshire. 'Sadly, my lasting memory will be of the greatest of all counties reduced to a squabbling rabble; of squalid, petty arguments; of supporters, once the most loyal and sane of all memberships, torn apart by a cult which regarded one man as greater than the club and even the game itself; and of a committee which made a terrible mistake and didn't try to put things right until it was too late,' he commented.

Illingworth bore the brunt of the Reformers' ire. Bob Slicer claimed double standards as Bairstow had not been suspended for his cocktail bar outburst during Yorkshire's previous visit to the town. 'I was very disappointed with quite a lot of the members' reactions,' admits Old. 'I was lucky that they didn't really take it out on me, it was more on the manager. I always tried to be open with them about what was happening, explaining there were good reasons. I always felt it was important that as a player you speak to the members and as a captain that you were available most of the time to not necessarily explain things but give them an idea of what the thoughts were.'

Illingworth and Old both believe the incident was an ambush by the Reformers. 'Oh yeah, he [Boycott] saw it coming,' the captain tells me. 'If we'd allowed him to play he'd done the interview and we'd not done anything about it. If we did something about it, it's a story anyway. But I didn't envisage the amount of feeling among the membership. It was quite hostile.' Illingworth later claimed Boycott had spoken to Brian Close at the Oval Test the previous week to ask if he would be interested in managing Yorkshire were the job to become vacant. 'Not true,' Boycott insists.

He had been suspended until the end of the season for breaching a contract clause which did not exist. When Illingworth handed the players their contracts in pre-season, they were supposed to sign and return them to him. Boycott read his, crossed out the standard TCCB clause that players must have permission from their counties before giving interviews, and returned it to Joe Lister. Only Lister, Boycott, his solicitor Duncan Mutch and chairman Michael Crawford knew. With Crawford uncontactable in Scotland on a golfing holiday, Illingworth spoke to Fred Trueman and Don Brennan before suspending Boycott but not Lister, who had been told in advance about the WH Smith interview.

It begs the question if Boycott was suspended for something he was not guilty of, why did he not tell Illingworth or Old? 'I left it to my solicitor Duncan Mutch and when they came to read my contract they were amazed it [the clause] wasn't there,' he replies. 'Having sent me home they couldn't take that back but it didn't go any further, shall we say. It soon became clear that they didn't have a leg to stand on. It being the end of the season they quietly forgot about it.' Boycott had some sharp legal minds in his camp and Yorkshire's solicitor, John Bosomworth, told Illingworth if he disciplined the batsman in future it should be in writing, and minuted by the club.

With Boycott out of the picture – he spent day two of the game at the Wakefield Districts stand at the CBI's Enterprise Zones Exhibition in London – Lady Luck rubbed salt into Yorkshire's wounds. Moxon was fielding at silly point when a George Sharp shot hit him in the nose. He did not open in the second innings yet added 92 with Hampshire for the seventh wicket despite needing a runner after tea because he was having so much difficulty breathing. He went in first at Sussex but was finally sent to hospital after making one, and did not reappear once a double fracture was diagnosed. Moxon's opening partner, Richard Lumb, did not bat in the second innings either after breaking a knuckle on his left hand, so Peter Ingham and Phil Carrick were sent out instead. Athey did not feature in the final two games after needing stitches in his right thumb having broken into his parents' house when locked out. The final game of the season was a nonsense anyway, Yorkshire losing by eight wickets as Carrick and part-timer Jim Love bowled 20 overs to improve their seasonal over rate. They had been fined £1,000 for dropping below 19 per hour in the first half of the campaign, but got the second punishment down from £800 to £600.

It was off the field where the real contests were taking place. The players joined the debate after John Callaghan suggested they preferred Boycott to the under-pressure Old as captain. 'The time has come to sort it out decisively and the only answer is in player power, however unpleasant that expression may sound in the corridors of administrative power,' Callaghan wrote in the *Yorkshire Evening Post*. 'From my own observations, Boycott is re-established as the team favourite, but the way to prove or disprove that theory is via the "ballot box".'

'I was asked at Scarborough [the week before Boycott's suspension] to take a poll by Doug Padgett, who was coach and a very close friend of Raymond's,' Old reveals. 'It didn't sit easily with me. I talked to one or two of the lads and they seemed quite happy with it. I was also under the impression that it wasn't going into the public domain. It was kind of intimated that it wasn't, it was for committee use.' After the Fenner Trophy Final, 18 players were asked if they wanted Boycott as captain. Fifteen said no, three abstained. The three contracted players not asked were first-year professionals. Although injured, Old travelled to Hove for the final game of the season where two further questions were posed. Two capped players not at the game could not be contacted. Asked if Boycott should be in the team next season the result was 10-2 against, with four abstentions, while 13 wanted Illingworth as manager, with three keeping their counsel. On 23 September the results were made public, Crawford arguing, 'Certain sections of the media already knew about the findings and we did not want things to leak out haphazardly.'

By then the management committee had discussed the Scarborough pantomime. They were presented with a 37-point dossier outlining why the Reformers thought Illingworth should be sacked, and a manager's report which stressed, 'We have a weed in the ground which must be removed to let the roses bloom.' A ten-hour meeting at Headingley could not even come up with a statement. Illingworth, Boycott and his legal team raised objections to the one drawn up by the committee, so in yet another communications triumph for Yorkshire, a statement explaining why there was no statement was issued. Crawford did, however, reveal, 'We have pulled back from the brink of sacking someone.'

It was agreed by all parties there would be no further comment, so when the players' poll was made public, Mutch cried foul. 'I just do not understand how a player, who has shown such unparalleled loyalty and dignity, and who is still one of the best opening batsmen in the world and Yorkshire's best professional cricketer, can be treated in such a disgraceful way,' he complained. Eric Baines resigned as Doncaster's committee representative, 'Very upset about it all,' according to his wife. Sidney Fielden rang his friend Jonny Wardle and urged him to stand as Baines's successor. The legendary former spinner thought about it for three days, decided against, and persuaded Fielden to instead. He won a three-way contest with Mike Bell and Harry Riley, taking 359 of 498 votes.

The management also set up a committee of inquiry into 'all aspects of Yorkshire cricket'. It ran all winter and achieved very little. Peter Dobson, a 64-year-old Leeds magistrate and retired accountant from Wetherby, was chosen to head it. 'No doubt the fact I have chaired a lot of meetings and I am clearly impartial was important,' he said. 'I want our investigations to go far deeper than just the way in which the team has been playing.' Dobson had an interest in cricket but no direct links since he stopped playing recreationally. He was picked as an independent voice, but Boycott disputes that. 'There was nothing about that committee that was true!' he insists. 'It was set up to get me. Peter Dobson was a close friend of and lived near Michael Crawford. There was no independence. There were people on the committee who didn't like me. This was the committee looking into the committee.'

Julian Vallance takes the point but thinks the Dobson committee he sat on was well chosen. Reformer Reg Kirk, Sheffield solicitor Tim Reed, vice-president John Temple, treasurer David Welch and former players Phil Sharpe and Billy Sutcliffe were his colleagues. Sutcliffe had replaced Don Brennan when business commitments made him unavailable. 'I don't know where you'd draw the other voices from,' says

Vallance. 'I suppose one can see Boycott's point of view but you had an independent chairman, the [general committee] chairman wasn't on it, and it did contain a number of what I'd call independent voices. We could have had more strident people either way. It wasn't as unbiased as it might have been but the majority of the committee, from which the Dobson committee was drawn, were not in the Boycott camp. They were *bona fide* appointments, it wasn't malicious or a deliberate attempt to produce an unbalanced committee.

'Brennan, Sutcliffe, Vallance, Sharpe were anti-Boycott – not anti-Boycott, but you know what I mean. Kirk's the other way. David Welch was not hopelessly anti-Boycott – I don't think he was hopelessly for him either. Tim Reed will have been brought on as an intelligent man, he was not a crony of the anti-Boycott brigade. Dobson had no bias – he was quite a strong man, a good, independent man. So you've got four anti-Boycott, one pro and three plus the chairman quite neutral. The pro-Boycotts didn't have a majority, but it wasn't a bad group and we didn't have the noisiest ones – Trueman, [Tony] Vann, Fielden and [Capt Desmond] Bailey. It wasn't a bad effort, unless you go outside the committee. I don't know how carefully that was considered, if at all.' It did not wash with the Reformers, who declared from the off the committee was weighted against them, and they would not support its findings.

The main question for Dobson appeared to be who should be sacked – Boycott or Illingworth. It was far from straightforward. It was widely believed the manager's contract expired at the end of the season but he had signed a one-year extension which would cost £20,000 to pay off. Berger Paints director John Sutton hinted strongly the new three-year £300,000 sponsorship deal they had offered would be removed if the manager was. In April they pulled out regardless but Home Charm Paints took over. On the other hand, one committeeman estimated the total cost of removing Boycott as being 'at least £150,000'. With his rank-and-file popularity underlined by local media opinion polls – 91.3 per cent responding to a *Yorkshire Evening Post* telephone vote said Boycott should not be sacked and 92.6 per cent felt Illingworth should – Bob Slicer offered £1,000 towards the cost of a referendum on the batsman's future. By leaving, Hampshire had made it harder to get rid of Boycott. The top two in Yorkshire's averages had made centuries in four of their five Championship wins that season (neither played in Northamptonshire), so being without either was discomforting. Old was thinking the unthinkable, however.

'The night before I flew out to South Africa coaching for the winter I spent four hours with this committee going through how I saw Yorkshire cricket and the best way forward,' Old recalls. 'I hoped it would actually help to sort out the problems. There were too many big characters fighting one another. It was an opportunity for the committee to say, "Right, let's sort this out once and for all and start afresh." My final thing to them was that their best way forward was to get rid of both Geoffrey and Raymond. Yes, we were going to struggle for a while but I felt we had on the committee people who'd played at the highest level who could help the captain out, make the selections with the captain and the coach, and run it from there. Martyn Moxon was coming through, Bill Athey was, and there were hopefully some quite useful youngsters kicking around that could possibly be given an opportunity. You're only going to learn how good they are by them playing – not just the odd game but a run of games.' I asked Moxon what he thinks of Old's drastic solution. 'They were big characters weren't they?' he says. 'They needed either to get rid of them, or to make them work together. That's the sad thing for me – that they didn't.'

The inquiry was given a moment of Watergate-esque drama when it was presented with a talk Illingworth gave to the Saddleworth Cricket League's annual dinner in November, secretly taped by the Reformers and also revealed

221

to the *Telegraph and Argus*. It was an attempt to discredit the manager, but added to the misgivings Vallance and others had about Boycott. 'Illingworth said he didn't think any county in the Championship would want Boycott,' Vallance recalls. 'There was a lot of talk about Boycott having approached other counties, which he always fiercely denied. The in-depth enquiry saw a letter from Alec Leggat, Lancashire's treasurer, confirming that he [Boycott] approached Jackie Bond about playing for them, but that couldn't be used because that was hearsay. Don Brennan had that letter. Where he got it from or to whom it was addressed – maybe Don – I don't know.

'The word among my group was that Boycott applied to every county but the only sources I heard quoted were Jim Laker, whom we all knew and would confide in people like Illy and Stotty [Bryan Stott], and Alec Leggat. Where they got the thought that he approached widely I don't know, but it annoyed them because he was always very strong in saying he never wanted to play for anyone but Yorkshire. That's what kept the Reform Group onside, they loved that. I was satisfied at the time that he had expressed interest in playing elsewhere. That's not to say he was necessarily going to do it, it could have just been a negotiating position, but it resonated, that's the point.' When I ask Bond about this alleged approach, which Boycott denies, the former Lancashire captain replies, 'It's not something I can remember but players like that are always in great demand because there's not many about.'

There were lighter moments too, Vallance recalls. 'I remember Vic Wilson's testimony, a written letter, in which Vic said something very good about Boycott's playing,' he laughs. 'Reg Kirk said, "There you are, that's Vic Wilson in favour." I said, "Well turn it over, Reg, because if you look at the rest it said 'obviously he must never play for Yorkshire again'!"'

In 15 meetings the Dobson committee interviewed 32 people and took written submissions from 32 more, as well as six leagues and three cricket associations but one man proved frustratingly elusive. Dobson wrote to Boycott in October, shortly before he left for Hong Kong on a business trip *en route* to joining England in India. While on tour a questionnaire was sent to Duncan Mutch, but Boycott followed the TCCB's advice to concentrate on the job in hand. Unlike the cricket, the tour was eventful for Boycott, even before it started. The Indian government thought it 'unacceptable' he and Geoff Cook were picked because of their links with South Africa, and only when both spoke out about apartheid was it allowed to go ahead. Nevertheless, *Wisden* reported Boycott being spoken to by tour manager Subba Row over 'a tactless comment to an Indian journalist about South Africa'. During the third Test in Delhi, the opener surpassed Sir Garfield Sobers as Test cricket's highest run-scorer, equalling Walter Hammond and Colin Cowdrey's 22 centuries as he did so. He then fell ill – a consequence, Fielden claimed, of his problems with Yorkshire – and was accused of losing all interest in the tour.

'He got sent home for playing golf when he said he couldn't play [on the final day of the fourth Test]. He asked me to play,' says Cook, although Boycott insisted he only walked the Tollygunge course for the fresh air his doctor told him to get. 'It was awkward for me but hopefully you can see what is right and wrong. I think they [England] were looking for an excuse to ease him out, so when they found out he'd snuck off and played golf they had one. His first target for that tour was to break the world record. He did that and I remember him saying, "That's what I've come for." He had no desire to be part of the touring party. He would rarely contribute to any team talks. Individuals' opinions were always sought and I know [England captain Keith] Fletcher found it very difficult to bring him on board on a regular basis. There were one or two instances where Boycott's cricketing intelligence really came to the fore but they were far too few and far between.'

As Boycott flew home, leaving back-up opener Cook to win his first Test caps, Row told the media, 'To some extent the effect of two weeks of physical health problems has affected his perspective and his mental approach.' Row claimed several doctors pronounced Boycott physically fit and blood and other tests had come back negative but the mystery illness kept him away from Dobson. Much to the inquiry's frustration, Boycott followed Dr Mohammed Zaman's advice not to venture beyond his garden.

In late January 1982 a 22-page interim report was produced without him. More streamlined management – something Crawford supported – was recommended, with a ten-strong committee (plus the treasurer) and no elected members, a powerful chief executive/secretary and a commercial instead of a team manager. Yorkshire had decided against such an appointment in June, despite calls for it at their annual general meeting, and while Illingworth had been successful at attracting sponsorship, concentrating on that was neither something he wanted to do nor the best use of his expertise. Dobson also called for the Yorkshire Cricket Supporters' Association to be disbanded, arguing it had 'done untold harm'. He recommended the club invoke rule 36, which allowed them to expel members for misconduct. With Dobson pushing Yorkshire to withhold his contract until he appeared, Boycott finally showed on 4 February, the last of the four dates offered, and complained later about the 'superficiality of the questions'. The final report was sent to all committee members a week ahead of the meeting to discuss it, and quickly leaked to Radio Leeds. Arthur Connell was 'appalled'. 'All committees leak,' shrugs Vallance.

'It is indisputable that all is not well in the dressing room,' the report concluded, and the blame was spread. The club's entire leadership was criticised, with the committee accused of not doing enough to resolve the problems that occurred during Boycott's time. Dobson recommended he be sacked 'as soon as economically acceptable'. If that was not immediately there would be more trouble, and possibly departures. Two-thirds of those who spoke to Dobson were said to favour dismissing Boycott. 'If that in-depth enquiry had said Boycott should be kept on as a player for the foreseeable future, I think that would have been very powerful,' comments Vallance. 'There were some relatively independent people of credibility, like Welch and Reed, and if they had said, "He's been a good player and you can't get rid of him," that would have counted for a lot. But they didn't.'

In the absence of a 'first-class captain' – Dobson did not think it was his place to look further afield for one – he concluded Illingworth had to be kept on for at least another year while the club was restructured, but should be told to address his failings. He was criticised for his handling of Boycott, a lack of player discipline and for having too many favourites. Even his dress was condemned. 'I felt Raymond had his favourites, but you could probably say that throughout,' Old reflects. 'There were some very good players that didn't seem to be given the opportunities others were. When they were, they were expected to score hundreds or take five wickets straight away and if they didn't they were back out again. Some who you felt were okay seemed to be given a longer run than some who perhaps had slightly more ability.' A referendum on ending the Yorkshire-born players policy, something the Dobson committee supported, was suggested. The club eagerly took up the smokescreen.

Three days after the report was leaked, and without having told Yorkshire, Boycott departed on a rebel tour of South Africa, something sports teams were not supposed to do until the country dropped its apartheid policy. Old and Arnie Sidebottom, who were there already, were also in the unofficial England squad. His last-minute decision suggested Boycott – already blacklisted by the United Nations for playing in South Africa – felt he had nothing to lose, either with Yorkshire or England, and although there was nothing in the county's rules against it, it was further ammunition for those who wanted rid of him. 'I think you'd have been daft not to realise the consequences,' says Cook, who initially agreed to tour before changing his mind.

Cook's Northamptonshire led calls for the rebels to be sacked by their counties but Boycott insists he was not worried. 'If we had all stuck together as the original idea had been they would have had to ban the whole England team,' he reasons. 'We weren't concerned about getting banned because BA were still flying out to South Africa and Barclays were doing business there. We thought it would be unfair to single us out.' Instead the punishment was a three-year suspension from Test cricket, which Yorkshire supported.

After March's six-hour meeting, the general committee rejected Dobson's report and decided to honour Illingworth and Boycott's contracts. 'It is about time they buried the hatchet — and not in each other's backs,' said Crawford. Some felt the leaks had saved Boycott. Police were called to the annual general meeting in Sheffield but it was something of nothing, Peter Briggs attempting to get it cancelled when he and committee member Tony Cawdry were among 100 members locked out of the 522-capacity hall. Another expensive special general meeting and a referendum on Boycott had been averted, although with his and Illingworth's contracts in their final 12 months, the issues had been put on ice rather than resolved. *The Sun* surveyed the other counties and claimed only Glamorgan were interested in signing Boycott, although four did not comment.

The Yorkshiremen returned from a lucrative but unsuccessful tour personally and for their rebel team and Dobson's report never saw the light of day. 'When they got it written up as an attempt to vilify me and sack me I think they got a letter from my barrister and they didn't dare print it because it would have cost them a lot of money,' Boycott explains. He had survived but his captain was a lame duck.

14

Player-Manager

FROM the moment he became Yorkshire's first manager, Raymond Illingworth gave the impression he was desperate to play cricket again. His eagerness to once more pull on his whites cost Chris Old the captaincy. Old survived a fractious end to the 1981 season but the navel-gazing which followed left him in desperate need of a good start to 1982. That he did not get it allowed Illingworth the total control he craved.

On returning to Yorkshire, Illingworth told the *Bradford Telegraph and Argus*, 'I did not come here with the intention of being a player but if the occasion demands it I might well turn out.' With Geoff Cope banned again, Peter Whiteley was Yorkshire's only recognised off-spinner and they were considering registering Illingworth. When John Hampshire broke his finger in June with Old and Geoffrey Boycott at the World Cup, it looked like the former England captain could lead the side against Northamptonshire. In the end Hampshire played, but Sidney Fielden wrote to Arthur Connell expressing concern that the idea had even been floated, as it would have cost 24-year-old Whiteley his place.

At the start of Illingworth's fourth season back he had still not made his second Yorkshire debut, but the side was looking increasingly in need of on-field leadership. Even before the Dobson committee could, Old cast doubt over his captaincy. Much to the Reform Group's anger, he said from Transvaal, 'I admit I would find it difficult to have Geoff in the dressing room after the players have said they are against him.' Crucially, however, he added, 'That does not automatically mean I would resign.' It made for an awkward winter.

'I got a long letter in South Africa to say the only thing that hadn't been decided was if Geoffrey was going to stay,' Old tells me. 'What made it slightly worse was that winter was the first England rebel tour. I'd been asked months before to be part of it. I said yes and I hadn't heard anything so I completely thought it had gone. All of a sudden I got told to report to Jo'burg straight away – they'd all arrived. I'd always wanted to go out to South Africa to play and when I hadn't made the England team, I thought, "Well that's it, my England career is now finished." I thought it wouldn't make any difference. It was quite enjoyable, very interesting.'

Once he was confirmed as Yorkshire captain for 1982, Old knew he had to build bridges in case Boycott was not sacked. 'I don't think Geoffrey was resigned to it,' says Old. 'I think at that time he held me responsible, especially with the players' poll, and thought I was very anti-him. I'd walk into a room and if Geoffrey was in there, he'd walk out or make sure he was in the farthest corner. I'd try to say hello and he'd not hear me. Some of the England lads we'd known for years found it amusing. I'd seen him behave like that before. I just thought, "Well you carry on Geoffrey, do what you want."

'Things changed when we got on board a plane from Durban to Cape Town. We were sat next to one another! His lady friend Ann [Wyatt] was with us, the three of us in a row. It was a little bit frosty, as you can imagine. She turned around and said, "Look you two, why don't you talk to one another and get things sorted out?" I think we talked all the way through the flight. We kind of agreed to disagree on certain things and I said to him if he wanted to come back and play for Yorkshire, I had no problems with it. All I would ask was that he gave me 100 per cent effort and did the best for Yorkshire so we could pull together to get Yorkshire to the top again. For the rest of the tour we went back to how we had been – we'd talk, we'd have a drink.' Old publicly admitted the players' poll had been a mistake, which went down badly with Illingworth.

Old limped into the new season a damaged man, a back injury at times limiting him to his Sunday League run-up. He also returned to contact lenses after eyesight trouble in South Africa. His body was in better shape than his captaincy. Dobson had been scathing about the lack of a 'strong captain' at Yorkshire. 'I didn't know that until later on,' Old reveals. 'It wasn't long after I got home that I found out what was really happening.' One of the few concrete developments from the winter was the creation of a sub-committee, dubbed the "Peacekeepers", to quickly and effectively step in when the next battle inevitably broke out. At least one of Fred Trueman, Billy Sutcliffe and Ronnie Burnet would be at every away game.

'When they announced this three-man committee that was going to be a link between the manager, the players, the committee and the captain I thought that was possibly a very good thing,' Old reflects. 'It was three people who had played at the highest level. If I wanted to talk to them I could, or they could talk to me. But the only times I saw them was when the manager was there, and I was being hauled over the coals. Raymond had played with all three and was very friendly with them.' The Peacekeepers shared a low opinion of Old. 'People like Fred, Billy and maybe others who were proper cricketers were probably quite old-fashioned in believing you want a good captain because they'd played with Closey and Illy,' Dobson committee member Julian Vallance explains. 'They were of the view that Closey didn't need a manager, and Illy didn't need a manager and if we had a strong captain we wouldn't need a manager because cricket is the one game where the captain really does influence what goes on on the field.'

Trueman the Peacekeeper was a classic poacher-turned-gamekeeper. His lack of diplomacy was key to the fast bowler's popularity in Yorkshire during and after his playing career. Boycott had been an admirer from the day in 1952 he watched Trueman's England debut at Headingley, but his hero used his weekly *Sunday People* column to become Boycott's most high-profile critic. After Boycott's sacking as captain, the column was headlined, 'In the name of God (and Yorkshire) go!' His attitude towards his former team-mate was simple, 'As a batsman, yes; as a man, no' and he joined the committee in 1979 with the express mission to get rid of Boycott as quickly as possible. Former Yorkshire captain Sutcliffe had also played with him, though not in county cricket. The Leeds skipper who persuaded Boycott to become an opener had been on the cricket committee throughout his captaincy and was equally unsympathetic.

Burnet had first-hand experience of dealing with brilliant but outspoken South Yorkshiremen. In 1958, as a 39-year-old chemical engineer who had never played first-class cricket, he stepped up from title-winning second XI captain to first-team skipper. Johnny Wardle, a slow left-armer from Barnsley, was bitter at being overlooked simply because he was not an amateur, describing Burnet as 'a quite hopeless old man'. Billy Sutcliffe had captained for the previous two seasons in preference to Wardle, who was the choice of players such as Brian Close and Bob Appleyard. The popular view, as with Illingworth 20 years later, was Burnet had been brought in to weed out a problem player but Vallance tells me, 'I knew Ronnie Burnet very well. He told me that he learned of Wardle being sacked when he was in his car. He was very disappointed.'

Former team-mate Bryan Stott says, 'Johnny disagreed entirely that Ronnie Burnet should be made captain and made it public in the winter so he was on the wrong foot straight away. Ronnie pulled a muscle badly in his calf early on in 1958 and was not able to play for seven games so Johnny skippered the side and did it very well because he knew his job. When they went out to toss up Ronnie kept on going out with them. It came to a head at Leeds [against Lancashire] when Johnny told him to go back.'

Having been asked by the committee to guide him, Wardle grew increasingly frustrated that a fit-again Burnet was ignoring his advice and the captain accused him of not trying against Somerset at Sheffield in August. 'We came in at the end of a session and a call came through would Johnny go and see Mr Nash [Yorkshire's secretary] in the committee room,' explains Stott. 'Johnny popped his blazer on. He came back and his face was ashen white. He had a letter in his hand. He threw it on to the table and someone asked, "What's wrong, John?" He said, "I've been sacked." This letter was two sentences to tell him his services would not be required for the following season and thank you for what you've done. It was incredible – bang, just like that.

'The following day John said the *Daily Mail* and the *Express* had been on for his story. We then went to Old Trafford for the next game. Ronnie comes into the dressing room and pins up the team-sheet. Johnny looks at it and says, "Sorry skipper, I'm not playing." He said these articles are coming out on Monday and I don't want to be in the dressing room. Ronnie goes out, Herbert Sutcliffe comes in and calls Johnny into the next room. Next thing Johnny puts his head around the door and says, "Cheerio lads, I'll be seeing you," and that was it. The articles weren't unduly a problem, there wasn't much there, but the county sacked him straight away and we lost Johnny, probably one of the best professionals we'd ever had – difficult to handle but I could name you one or two who caused a lot more trouble pre-Ronnie Burnet.'

Wardle's sacking, which ended his first-class and Test careers in one fell swoop, worked. Yorkshire won the County

Championship in 1959, their first in 13 seasons (the same barren spell they were in at the end of 1981), and for six of the next nine summers. The moral was that sometimes even the best player could be sacrificed to strengthen the team. Ex-England internationals Appleyard, Willie Watson and Frank Lowson had also been let go in the previous 12 months.

If it all seemed a threat to Boycott he was quite satisfied with the new system and settled straight back into post-Dobson life with 138 in a draw at Northamptonshire. It was Old who felt targeted. 'David Bairstow had a golf day up at Catterick,' he recalls. 'While we were there Howard Booth from the *Daily Mirror* rang and asked me what was happening. I said I'd sat down with Geoffrey, we'd agreed to disagree on everything else, but we were going to do our best to get Yorkshire back to the top. I didn't think too much of it.

'At half past eight the next morning I got a phonecall from the Yorkshire secretary to say there was a meeting I was expected at in half an hour with the three-man committee. The manager was there. The first thing he said was, "What do you think you're saying?" I said it was important the members knew Geoffrey and I had talked, we'd got over our differences, agreed to disagree and we just wanted everybody to realise we'd started with a clean slate to try and win things for Yorkshire cricket. I was told if I was going to speak to the public I'd got to do it with the manager there. I said, "Fine." I thought they were going to look foolish when people rang me to ask about so-and-so. They obviously hadn't thought about it. From that moment I thought, "I've got to be careful."'

Old was feeling increasingly marginalised. 'At the start of that season they were presenting caps and Neil Hartley was given one,' he recalls. 'I'd been told there was no need for me to go to this meeting because there was nothing important to discuss. If the discussion about caps isn't an important decision… We started well in the Championship but we couldn't win a one-day game. We managed to beat the Minor

Counties [at Bradford Park Avenue in May] and we had a major bust-up [about bowling changes] in the dressing room, the manager and I. It's the first time I've seen Geoffrey run out of the dressing room because nobody had ever seen me lose my temper. That's when I realised the manager wanted to captain the side, manage the side, and do everything. I went to a committee meeting and had to defend myself against this situation in Bradford and one or two others. I wasn't getting any support from the manager – in fact, all the things being queried were things the manager and I disagreed on, so it was obvious he was feeding them the information.'

Yorkshire finished bottom of Benson and Hedges Cup Group A, level on points with the Minor Counties but having taken their wickets at a slower rate. Ever-present Old had the poorest strike rate of all the Yorkshire bowlers to take a wicket. Man of the match John Hampshire had clinched Derbyshire's victory at Chesterfield with a six off Steve Stuchbury and the *Yorkshire Post* was critical of muddled thinking in a six-wicket defeat at Leicestershire. '[Richard] Lumb, whose ability against the new ball is his asset in one-day cricket, came in at an insulting number nine that made a nonsense of his selection in the first place with a specialist bowler Carrick as 12th man,' it noted. '[Jim] Love… was frustratingly held back to number six.'

Old later claimed captaining Yorkshire caused him to drink heavily, arguing, 'It was the only way I could sleep.' It would have problems beyond his own performances. 'Graham Stevenson was a talented cricketer, a bit of a loose cannon, liked his drink too much, but skilful,' points out his future Northamptonshire team-mate Alan Walker. 'He could hit a ball miles, Stevo, win you a game with the bat or the ball. Did he do it enough? Was he handled well enough? If your captain likes a pint he can't say, "You don't have a pint."'

In June Yorkshire played what ought to have been a nondescript 60-overs-a-side friendly against Zimbabwe at Abbeydale Park. With Old, Stevenson, Stuchbury, Peter Ingham, Martyn Moxon and Alan Ramage injured, Ashley Metcalfe made his debut. Two days after his 50th birthday, Illingworth also played – as captain. It was, he told the *Yorkshire Post*, a 'one-off', but the old magic was still there. Jack Heron swept his first ball and top-edged to Kevin Sharp at long-leg to give Illingworth his 1,429th Yorkshire wicket, 14 years after the 1,428th, and the hosts claimed a rare win. Two days later Old was back in charge for Middlesex's Championship visit to Sheffield. 'It was rained off with a very good chance of beating them,' he recalls. 'I stayed behind and sat talking to Mike Brearley about what sort of a job he felt I was doing. He was very aware I wasn't very happy. A few weeks earlier I'd spoken to a member of the committee I was very friendly with and said I was seriously considering resigning because I wasn't getting any support. I was due to meet some people that evening and I was an hour and a half late because as I came past the dressing room Geoffrey called me in to ask what that was all about. He talked me out of resigning!' On the rest day Yorkshire played a reduced-overs Sunday League game against Nottinghamshire. In his report, the *Yorkshire Post*'s Bill Bridge referred to 'Boycott directing everyone but himself, Old retaining that vestige of captaincy'.

The following week Old was back in his home town of Middlesbrough for Championship and Sunday League games against Northamptonshire. After a rain-delayed start, he won the toss in the three-day game. It was one of the last things to go right for him all weekend. Northamptonshire put on 278 from 61 overs for the first wicket, and were 302/1 at the close. Wayne Larkins made 186 while another man from Middlesbrough, Geoff Cook, finished 112 not out.

'That was an amazing weekend,' Cook tells me. 'You could tell there was an over-current, never mind an under-current going on. Poor old Chris had a bad start to the season with all the politics and unfortunately he won the toss on both occasions and put us in to bat – whether it was on the advice of Illingworth I never knew. We hardly lost a wicket all weekend.' Illingworth reflected, 'It wasn't the size of the stand that angered me – it was the way the runs came… I felt thoroughly ashamed.'

Cook and Larkins put on what Terry Brindle called 'a contemptuously dismissive stand of 128' for Sunday's first wicket. 'When we started the last over I walked past David Bairstow,' Old recalls. 'They were on 251 and he said, "I think we've got away with that. I thought they were going to get 270-odd." Lamby [Allan Lamb] then took 31 off Graham Stevenson's over [helped by four wides] and they finished up with 282/4. I'd been on the boundary at the opposite end to David and as we crossed I just turned to him and said, "Don't you ever open your mouth again!" We both burst out laughing. Of course that's what the manager saw.' Northamptonshire's combined weekend score was 584/5 in 106 overs, Old's overall figures 1-101.

'By the end of the Sunday game the stick the Yorkshire team were getting made me thankful that I wasn't in that environment,' Cook admits. 'Even though I was a Yorkshireman and had played a little bit of representative stuff I was so happy to be out of that. I felt really sorry for Chris. They were incensed by the perceived inadequacies of Yorkshire.' The rain which washed out the final day of the Championship game spared Yorkshire defeat, but two wins from 16 matches that season ensured Old's fate had already been sealed.

'I was called over by Illingworth,' he says. 'We went out to the groundsman's room and he said the committee had decided he was going to come back and captain the side. I said I thought he'd better tell the players but he didn't want to. I said if there was going to be an article in the papers that night, it was important the players were aware of what was going to happen and they could plan if they wanted to say anything, so he reluctantly agreed. I got all the players in the dressing room. Geoffrey was sat in his car doing his post. I knocked on his window and said, "Meeting in ten minutes." He said he had all that to do so I said, "Ten minutes, it's very important," and walked away.

'It was a square dressing room. I was sat behind the door and everyone else was on two sides, with windows on another. I just said, "Thanks everybody for dropping everything, the manager's got something to tell you," and laid on the bench. The four people opposite me were Boycott, Bairstow, Graham Stevenson and Arnie Sidebottom. David's face when Illingworth told them he was going to be captain for the rest of the season… I just had to put my fingers to my lips. Geoffrey said, "I'm sorry, I should have let you resign." If I'd have resigned I could have given my statement as to why, instead of which there was a prepared statement which, to be quite honest, I didn't really read, I just signed it. Part of it was that they thanked me for a job that I wasn't really capable of. That really hurt. In a way I should have walked away and said, "Just leave me on my own," but I played the next day and the press were around. It was very difficult. I was in and out of the side from then on, even though he [Illingworth] kept telling me I was an important part of the team. From that moment on I certainly started to talk with a county about moving on.'

Cook is full of sympathy. 'We were both from Middlesbrough and I played a little bit of cricket against him there,' he tells me. 'But I mainly knew him through playing first-class cricket against him for ten years. With somebody as powerful as Illingworth coming in it was never going to be easy to contend with that ego. Chris was the type of guy who thought, "I'll take on this challenge because I think I can get us back on track." I think everybody who sets out on that sort of challenge has similar feelings. It's a crusade and if they do the right things with the right people it will be easier but it just doesn't happen. One or two didn't have that misguided impression. Neil Hartley would always say, "I'm going to be dependent on one or two people," but others would say, "I'm going to come out of this the champion."

'Chris was a sensitive guy getting to the end of his tether. That reflected in the scoreboard and probably how he bowled. It was an absolutely impossible task for him, especially with Illingworth sitting on the touchline. He was always a big articulator about the game to anyone who would listen but also very open in his criticism. To have him watching your every move, analysing every decision – I'm sure Illingworth was very supportive but the potential was there for that destructive, deflating environment.'

With Boycott and Richard Lumb unwilling to take the captaincy and too much hostility towards his preferred option, Neil Hartley, Illingworth did the job himself. As Ronnie Burnet, chairman of the resurrected cricket committee, put it, 'Desperate measures need desperate remedies.' Yorkshire's statement described it as 'a temporary measure', hopefully until the end of the season. Terry Brindle called it 'an admission of defeat', adding, 'It is also an admission – though they will deny it to the last drop of the team's blood – that the decision to appoint a team manager was a serious misjudgement.' It was, as David Warner outlined in the *Telegraph and Argus*, a gamble. 'So far, Illingworth has not succeeded as team manager alone,' he wrote. 'If he now fails as captain, he cannot expect to remain with the club for much longer than this season.' As Cook says, 'It was a terrible indictment of Yorkshire cricket that he was playing at 50 but a terrific compliment to him that he still performed well.'

Illingworth's first game as Yorkshire's full-time captain, against Essex at Ilford, was a non-event. Four hours and five minutes was lost to rain on day one and only seven balls bowled on day two. Illingworth did not bat, bowl or even take a catch. He soon made a good impression, though, and after six weeks which had seen Yorkshire qualify for the NatWest Trophy semi-finals, Burnet was already talking about the arrangement being extended into 1983. It was a sign of progress that when he missed the Championship match against Gloucestershire at Bradford Park Avenue with a pulled left thigh muscle, Boycott could captain a side containing Hartley, Bairstow, Old and Lumb, albeit a batting collapse condemned Yorkshire to defeat. As in 1981, they finished tenth in the Championship.

Despite everything, Old was second in Yorkshire's bowling averages and their second-highest wicket-taker (behind Sidebottom on both), but when he missed the season's final games – both at Surrey – with sciatica, having only felt fit enough for the Sunday League encounter, a distinguished Yorkshire career was limping to a sad conclusion. Boycott, the top Englishman in that summer's first-class averages after scoring 1,913 runs, was unanimously awarded a new contract.

Peter Whiteley's was 'amicably' cut a year short and Peter Ingham and Steve Coverdale were released, but Old was the only senior player shown the door. 'So all the problems of that season were mine!' jokes Old, who was in South Africa when he found out. Burnet called him a 'victim of circumstance', explaining, 'The committee feel that he has lost a yard of pace. Although he might still do a reasonable job in the one-day competitions it is impossible to find the money in the present income climate to justify keeping him on that basis.'

Old had his say in May's three-part interview with *The Sun*. The then-Warwickshire player spoke of 'a private battle between Boycott, the obsessive chaser of records, and Illingworth, the captain-manager, which has nothing to do with putting Yorkshire cricket back on top again'. He was scathing about the politics, writing, 'Behind the scenes at the most famous cricket club in the country there is more double-dealing than in *Dallas*; more petty jealousy than in *Crossroads* – and more muck-spreading than in *The Archers*!' Or rather someone else did.

'The articles were entirely different to what we'd talked about,' Old insists. The Warwickshire secretary said, "I can't let any of these articles go through." I said, "If you say no, that's fine by me." A few phonecalls went back and forward and they kind of cobbled one together from some bits of it and gave it to me to read. It was okay, but bore no resemblance to what was printed.' Old was handed a £2,000 fine by the TCCB, plus a further £1,000 from Warwickshire, and banned from the opening Championship game of 1984, although no one at Yorkshire seemed to take the comments to heart. 'It is nowhere near as accurate as his bowling but far more hostile,' Burnet quipped. Old's former team-mates particularly enjoyed the instalment about being driven to drink. 'We were playing at Edgbaston and of course everyone was reading these newspapers so we were all taking the mickey,' Kevin Sharp smiles. 'Illy and Chris Old were both there and somebody handed Chilly a pint pot at nine o'clock in the morning because they said he looked like he needed a drink! I think he was a bit sheepish. It was quite amusing. He was just a top bloke and a good cricketer in the wrong place at the wrong time for someone like him, I'm guessing. It was a tough environment.'

Old had the last laugh in August 1984 when he became the first player to take ten wickets for and against Yorkshire, in a 191-run Warwickshire win. He also scored 52. 'If things had gone reasonably I would have loved to have stayed because with Graham Stevenson, Arnie, Paul Jarvis, Martyn Moxon, Bill Athey, there were some good youngsters coming through and I felt times were changing and we were going to get back to being at the top again,' he tells me. 'I felt even if I didn't play I could help in the future. I really did see my career finishing at Yorkshire and hopefully going on to be involved in the coaching side but it wasn't to be.'

Illingworth had won the power struggle. Whether or not he justified the decision to keep him on as captain in 1983 was a matter of interpretation but soon he too would be gone.

15

Champs and Chumps

EVEN at the age of 51, Raymond Illingworth was still a brilliant captain. In his first full season as skipper, he did what no Yorkshireman had for more than a decade, and led his county to a major trophy. Yorkshire being Yorkshire, he was sacked that winter.

While winning what was seen by some as a fairly trivial trophy, the team hit the depths in the most important county competition of all. That, plus another Geoffrey Boycott controversy, sparked a dramatic upheaval which changed the face of the club.

Illingworth's success at Leicestershire had been founded on limited-overs cricket, and he had an immediate impact on demoralised Yorkshire in that arena. The best they managed in the Sunday League under Chris Old in 1982 was a tie in his penultimate match, against Nottinghamshire. Illingworth put that right at the first opportunity. Two days before his 17th birthday Paul Jarvis took a hat-trick, all bowled, as Yorkshire won at Derby by 19 runs. It says everything about the shambles the new captain inherited that the *Bradford Telegraph and Argus* considered it noteworthy that, 'For the first time this season Yorkshire were a well-drilled unit with Illingworth leading, Boycott giving unselfish support and everyone else trying his utmost.'

In his next match Illingworth took 4-6 in eight overs as Middlesex were beaten at Hull. Winning three of his first four matches in the competition was a false dawn, four defeats and a no-result in the last five (four of them away) condemning Yorkshire to 16th, their lowest Sunday League position. Nevertheless, the initial momentum carried into the County Championship, where Yorkshire enjoyed three consecutive wins for the first time since 1978, beating Warwickshire, Nottinghamshire and Sussex. The pattern, however, continued in full, only winning once more all summer and losing the NatWest Trophy semi-final to Warwickshire at Edgbaston. There was cause for cautious optimism, but no more.

Illingworth, though, had proven that whatever his birth certificate said, he could still excel in professional cricket, even after three and a half seasons in retirement. 'His captaincy, his tactical nous and even his ability to bowl was remarkable,' says Martyn Moxon. According to Kevin Sharp, 'You always felt when he was captaining your team this guy knew what's going on here. There were some clever tactics.'

'He was tactically the most aware captain I ever played under,' Ashley Metcalfe adds. 'He knew the strengths and weaknesses of all the opposition players, where to bowl at batsmen and what you needed to be looking out for as a batsman. He was a great person to pick the brains of, and to watch how he controlled a game. I've always been pretty fortunate I've had him pretty close and I've been able to learn a lot from just speaking to him. I learnt a lot as a youngster, particularly on how to control a game and build pressure, and if we were batting listening to what targets we needed to set and the reasons behind it. He had a huge amount of expertise and was very talented in his own right, so he had the respect of every person in the changing room. That's not always the case with captains.' The *Telegraph and Argus* noted Illingworth 'was listened to attentively and even applauded' at the 1983 annual general meeting.

Perhaps the long spell on the sidelines improved his captaincy. 'He read the game really well and knew what was coming,' Metcalfe explains. 'Most people only get to that when they're retired. They say, "The game's a lot easier now I'm sat on the edge, I can see what's happening." It's 100 per cent right but Raymond was one of the few people who could do that on the field. Raymond's passion never left him. Somehow the sport finds a way of keeping the best people within it so it was no surprise for me that Raymond had a lifetime within cricket because he's one of the most talented individuals the game has ever had.'

Even without the usual flashpoints, the 1982/83 off-season was unsettling for Yorkshire. It began traumatically, 17-year-old Neil Lloyd dying of a neurological disease caused by a rare virus after taking ill in the stands at the Scarborough Festival. The left-hander from Ackworth had hit two second-team centuries against Lancashire that summer, and made his England Under-19 'Test' debut against West Indies at Hove. It came to a close with Sri Lanka offering Illingworth a two-year contract to be their manager, starting in September. He turned it down, but was already making plans for a new captain.

If Yorkshire were not in contention for silverware towards the end of the season Illingworth aimed to continue playing but hand the captaincy over. As it turned out, the county were in the hunt for a trophy and his preferred successor, Neil Hartley, was languishing in the second team. In announcing Hartley as vice-captain for 1983, cricket chairman Ronnie Burnet said if he failed, he hoped it would not be through 'sabotage' by other players. Instead, Hartley's form was to blame. Championship home games as captain against Northamptonshire and Nottinghamshire bookended a six-week spell in the second XI at his own request. A back injury which required surgery limited him to bowling six wicketless overs all season and he made just 261 runs from 19 first-class innings. Taking the vice-captaincy away was only fair.

When Yorkshire went top of the Sunday League in July, no one was getting carried away. With two matches remaining they were two points clear but the *Telegraph and Argus* cautioned, 'With Somerset also having two games in hand, Yorkshire cannot realistically hope to take the title.' Still, it had been a massive improvement. Limited-overs cricket is regularly portrayed as a young man's game, but often the old heads are its stars. An ever-present Illingworth topped the league's bowling averages and was its most economical bowler. He even won the toss in 11 of 14 games where play was possible. 'Illy was outstanding,' Moxon reflects. 'Him and Phil Carrick, the two spinners, played a big part in winning that competition.' Boycott was important too, though not so much with the bat – he was dropped at Cardiff in August after 64 runs from four games spread over 46 overs. Three times he opened the bowling, and the 42-year-old sometimes came back to use his nous in the crucial 'death' overs.

Not that it was all down to the veterans. Bill Athey came out to face one Michael Holding delivery against Derbyshire in the penultimate game, at Bradford Park Avenue, and had to be helped off after doubling up in pain, the legacy of a car crash the previous night. However, with Hartley as a runner he returned at 131/7 chasing 171 and hit 21 not out as Yorkshire won by two wickets. After Somerset surprisingly lost their penultimate match, at Worcestershire, they could only finish level on 46 points with Yorkshire. When play was abandoned at Essex at 3.30pm on 11 August, Illingworth had won his third Sunday League title by virtue of more away victories (5-3).

'It was a bit of an anti-climax because we didn't play on the day,' admits Kevin Sharp, 'but it was a good achievement because it had been the first trophy for a long time.' Two days later came confirmation Yorkshire had finished bottom of the Championship for the first time. They were fortunate other counties had not shared their enthusiasm for Illingworth's proposal to split the Championship into two divisions for 1984.

Poor weather handicapped Yorkshire from the start, and they were bottom in early June after drawing five badly weather-affected games at a time when there were no Championship points for draws. Boycott's 152 runs in 11 innings constituted his worst start to a season, hampered perhaps by the weather curtailing his preparations. With winless Yorkshire finishing bottom of the five-team Benson and Hedges Cup Group B, Illingworth soon decided to concentrate on the Sunday League, controversially resting Simon Dennis from July's Championship game at Sheffield where Kent made 424/5 declared to keep him fresh for a 40-over match which, thanks to rain, never happened.

As in 1975, the World Cup ought to have played into their hands – Yorkshire had no one at the tournament – but they were put to the sword by overseas players. A quarter of the half-centuries made against them in 1983 and 40 per cent of the five-wickets hauls came from overseas players. 'You were often at slip thinking it would be nice to stand another five yards back!' Sharp admits. 'Without these overseas bowlers sometimes we couldn't get nine, ten, jack out as quick, whereas the West Indian bowler would because the tail didn't fancy it. I can often recall being stood at slip when you'd been batting against Courtney Walsh, Curtly Ambrose, Malcolm Marshall, Michael Holding, Colin Croft or Imran Khan and you would think, "We're just lacking a bit of this."' The members had voted overwhelmingly against changing the Yorkshire-born policy in the April 1982 referendum, 4,493-537. A chink of compromise came in August 1983 when 17-year-old fast bowler Michael Smith, born to Yorkshire parents a mile outside the county in Darlington but brought up in Otley from the age of one, was told he could wear the White Rose if he proved himself good enough. He never did.

The weakness of their home-grown bowling held Yorkshire back in 1983. Boycott recovered from his slow start to pass 1,000 runs, as did David Bairstow and Jim Love, but *Wisden* noted their feeble attack 'made it difficult for Illingworth to gamble with challenging declarations'. David Warner concluded, 'Apart from Simon Dennis, who is an outstanding exception, the pacemen have lacked the heart for the battle and have too easily gone down with one injury or another.' Yorkshire lost the same number of three-day games (five) as champions Essex yet were never higher than 15th. The difference was they only won once, by seven wickets with just four balls to spare at Southampton in June. The last time that had happened to them was 1866 – and they only played three matches!

The Hampshire victory was immediately followed by four consecutive defeats, despite Phil Carrick taking 12-89 and Boycott carrying his bat in the first of them. Yorkshire had to win their final match at Chelmsford to have any chance of avoiding the wooden spoon, but neither Essex's John Lever, who took 7-78, nor the weather gave them a chance. That was the first time Sharp had doubts about Illingworth. 'I had an awful lot of respect for someone of his age to still be able to do what he did,' he says. 'That weekend he was batting against Norbert Phillip [a fast bowler who played nine Tests for West Indies between 1978 and 1979], who hit him on the head and you feared a bit for him, really. That was a time when you were thinking, "This is a bit too much." He didn't back down but this fella Norbert Phillip looked as if he was going to hurt him. That was it, his last game.'

Illingworth ought to have been able to bow out with his sore head held high having finally ended Yorkshire's trophy drought. To some, though, finishing bottom of the Championship was unforgivable. 'The victory in the Sunday "tap it and run" league does nothing to alleviate my grief,' E. Pickering wrote to the *Yorkshire Post* from Wellington, New Zealand. John Callaghan called it 'the equivalent of Laurence Olivier forgetting his lines as Hamlet before going off to win first prize in *Sale of the Century*'. Even the committee seemed lukewarm about the Sunday League trophy, with only Tony Cawdry and Dr John Turner in Chelmsford to see it presented. The players viewed it in a more positive – and pragmatic – light. 'Yorkshire had been starved of success for a long time. We weren't used to winning things, we were used to surviving a bit,' points out Sharp, their second-highest scorer in the competition. The balance sheet also benefited, with gate receipts up 78 per cent. 'A trophy's a trophy,' shrugs Martyn Moxon. 'Winning was very pleasing, from our point of view it was worth winning. But you look at the team we had and we should have been better than finishing where we did in the Championship. We vastly under-performed in that form of the game.'

Ashley Metcalfe, who made his Championship debut in 1983 but did not feature in the Sunday League until the following year, sees Yorkshire's one-day success as a missed opportunity. 'From the club's perspective, to win a trophy was huge in that era,' he argues. 'For somebody who was young and new into that environment it gave you the inspiration and confidence that you can win something with Yorkshire. At that stage there was a lot of negativity around and still a huge amount of expectation from the membership that we should be winning everything. Other counties had improved immensely and the regulations around overseas players hugely benefited other counties so to win something as 11 Yorkshiremen, all born and bred in the county, was just huge. That could have been the start of something really good but it needed to be seen through, the foundations had to change. Sadly the political manoeuvrings of individuals meant it wasn't. I think Yorkshire lost almost a decade at a really crucial time.' In 1984 they were back to finishing 16th.

Player discontent was growing in 1983, to the point where it could not be hidden. In July, 20-year-old fast bowler Nick

Taylor asked to be released. It prompted a row in the *Yorkshire Post*'s letters pages between former team-mates Illingworth and Ken Taylor, Nick's dad. Ken responded to the suggestion his son was unhappy at a lack of first-team opportunities by arguing his gripe was not getting the new ball in the second XI. Illingworth wrote back to say he had it seven times out of 12. Yorkshire refused Taylor's request and the next day he took a career-best 5-49 against Sussex. He left at the end of the season, joining Surrey.

If the loss of Taylor's potential was a disappointment, the rumours which emerged the day Yorkshire won the Sunday League that Bill Athey, their top scorer in the competition (he had the best average too), was thinking of leaving were far more troubling. He might have chuckled with Sharp at Illingworth and Boycott at Scarborough in 1981, but the interminable politics was stopping his enjoyment of the game. His antipathy towards Boycott was hinted at by Chris Old in May when he claimed the junior partner was always trying to outdo him. 'Boycott's attitude and the atmosphere he created had everything to do with my decision to leave Yorkshire,' Athey later revealed. 'In the dressing room with Boycott around, there was always a tense, highly-charged atmosphere. Spirit was always poor because it was never relaxed in there. Even after he lost the captaincy and Hamps [John Hampshire] took over, the very fact that Boycs was still there was a problem. Half of Yorkshire were vehemently on his side and the other half were vehemently against him.' In 1983 London-based Athey's unhappiness showed in his first-class cricket. If 1982 had been his best season for Yorkshire, making 1,278 Championship runs at 41.22, in 1983 – when another good year might have given him an excellent chance of being the next captain – he managed only 758, and no centuries. He dropped so many catches he was moved out of the slip cordon.

Yorkshire seemed complacent. On 4 October Ronnie Burnet commented, 'His present contract does not end until

March and I hope he will have a re-think.' The next day Athey agreed to join Gloucestershire. Inevitably he scored his first century for his new county on his maiden appearance against his old one. Athey made as many hundreds in his first two years at Gloucester as his previous eight with Yorkshire, and won 20 of 23 England caps there. His average jumped from 28 to 42. 'Bill Athey saw the light very quickly,' says Bryan Stott, then on Yorkshire's committee. 'It got so personal, particularly within the team. It must have been horrible to be part of the Yorkshire cricket team at that time. There was so much… you can nearly say hatred when you looked at people's faces and listened to what they had to say. You can't have it in a working environment. You need a mediator and we didn't have one.'

Moxon reflects, 'That period was very much about off-field battles rather than trying to win games on it. It was a total distraction and there was no real clear leadership on or off the field. It was just a bit of a shambles, it was not a co-ordinated club. There was no direction, it was very fractured, and there was a poor atmosphere around the place. The environment was poisonous and my experience now is that if that's the case, you haven't really got a chance. Any success was in spite of the conditions, not because of them.'

Old, then with Warwickshire, agrees. 'It was a strange time,' he says, '1970–80 was a very strange period and from 1979 to when I left at the end of 1982, that period became very political and there were a lot of people pulling in different directions. The guys that went out on the field weren't really considered, they were just the pawns. Between 1980 and 83, 84, possibly a year either side, was a very, very difficult time to play. It was difficult for senior players, so people just learning the game can't have enjoyed coming into some of the situations. There again, how often did they know what was happening? There were certainly things said to some people and not others. But you'd have a feeling.'

Northamptonshire captain Geoff Cook admits it was a tactic to exploit divisions in the dressing room and on the terraces. 'The older players were very resolute, that's what made them the players they were,' he tells me. 'They'd grown up in all of that ego-ridden environment but the young players were extremely vulnerable with one or two exceptions. People like [Colin] Johnson, Hartley, Bairstow, Phil Carrick to an extent although he had a great career, were continually on edge with the whole situation. Boycott was just eternally causing trouble and I just felt sorry for my contemporaries. You just felt people like Chris Old, Bairstow, Graham Stevenson and Phil Carrick were putting their thumbs in the dam while others enacted this drama behind the scenes.

'You would toy with the crowd and try to get them against their team, which they did very quickly. That was always worth a few runs or a wicket or two. The Yorkshire fans were so demanding of success. I played for Yorkshire Exiles against Yorkshire at the Scarborough Cricket Festival and we won for two or three successive years and the Yorkshire fans were on their players' backs. To a man in our dressing room we were saying, "Thank goodness we're in this dressing room and not theirs." They had no sympathy, no sensitivity for the team at all. I remember playing in the Tilcon Trophy when Yorkshire were in the middle of a plummet [in 1983]. Bairstow [a former Bradford City centre-forward] was batting. The ball hit his pad and went up in the air. He headed it and it landed on his stumps. Everyone else thought it was funny and if it had worked it would have been hilarious but the abuse he got, honestly, he should have walked off the other way! It was another Yorkshire wicket, another disgrace for Yorkshire. These two or three thousand people at the Harrogate Festival could have lynched him. It took a special player to keep playing through that.'

Cook's former Northamptonshire team-mate and fellow Yorkshireman Alan Walker draws parallels with football. 'It's like Liverpool Football Club – because you've got that history other sides are all out to prove themselves,' he says. 'It did weigh them down. Yorkshire's a little bit like a football crowd, isn't it? Currently it must be great to play there because they're right behind them but if it's not going so well they're on your back pretty quick. As a kid my dream was to play for Yorkshire, then you talk to people who did and you see the other side. I've looked back at the times I've been on the winning side there and they give them some unnecessary grief, really. Maybe they weren't tough enough characters to deal with the expectations. Maybe it's a bit like Nottingham Forest when managers come in and take all the pictures down because they wonder if the history holds them back.' As Yorkshire's 21st-century director of cricket, Moxon has successfully overcome that but admits, 'There's always been that pressure that you're not as good as the team of the 50s and 60s and they [the members] weren't shy in telling us that. That rankled with players, constantly being criticised.'

It was not just the players being worn down. Three weeks before the Sunday League triumph, as the Reformers put together yet another petition for his sacking, Illingworth announced he would retire from playing at the end of the season. 'I am sick and tired of all the aggro my family and I have had to take since I returned,' he told the *Scarborough Evening News*. 'If Yorkshire will pay me out of my contract [as manager, which ran until April 1985] I will leave now. I don't see why I should be playing first-class cricket at 51 to try to help Yorkshire cricket – and at the same time have to put up with a constant barrage of attacks from Boycott's supporters.' By the time of Chelmsford his mood had softened, offering to play on part-time, and at the end of the campaign his role as manager was watered down to spend less time with the team and cede authority to new captain Bairstow. In January Illingworth 'reluctantly' announced he would not play for Yorkshire again. 'I still think I could make a contribution in one-day cricket but I have taken enough of the shouting and bawling which went on last season and is likely to continue,' he said. The issue that finally snapped Illingworth's patience would ultimately end his association with the club completely, and prompt a revolution unlike anything seen there before or since.

On the opening morning of August's Championship game at Gloucestershire, Geoffrey Boycott was in an irascible mood. His first rebuke came before the match after twice giving young autograph-hunters the sharp end of his tongue. He made an unbeaten 140 after Illingworth won the toss, but the manner in which he did so would have implications far beyond anything anyone at Cheltenham that day could have imagined. He took 347 deliveries over his runs, slowing as he grew more accustomed to the conditions. He made 53 from Yorkshire's lunchtime 87/2, 95 out of 210/2 at tea, and had reached 120 by the 100-over cut-off for bonus points. After reaching three figures for the fourth time that season, he only scored three more boundaries. 'We had to spell it out to him stage by stage, "Look, Geoff, we need 30 runs off the next ten overs" – things like that,' Illingworth said. 'A player of his experience knew darned well what was wanted but he needed to be told so he would then have an excuse for making only 30 runs off the next ten overs... we knew that, having said 30, that was what he would get – 29 or 30... but not 31.'

It was, the *Telegraph and Argus* noted, 'extremely hot' at Cheltenham College, and the short boundaries, good batting pitch and fast outfield gave Yorkshire an ideal opportunity to claim much-needed maximum batting points for the first time that summer. Boycott had been batting for 22 overs when Sharp came to the crease and even though the left-hander had not scored a Championship century since his first, in June 1980, he beat his partner to the landmark. 'He ran me out!' Sharp laughs. 'He pushed one to midwicket and ran me out. I was about three yards short. I'm not sure he did it on purpose of course!' Illingworth was less sure. Sharp had just relayed a message from the balcony to Boycott. 'Illy had stood up and gestured to say make sure you get them,' he recalls. 'When I got out we only needed another 26 off seven or eight overs. I'd got 100 so I was kind of in a good mood. It probably hadn't registered that something was amiss until it actually got to it. I got showered and I just fully expected us to get those runs but I could hear things developing, people were saying, "Bloody hell, we haven't got any more runs off this over." We finished up with lads like Lovey [Jim Love] and Bairstow having to go in and play some shots straight away to try and get us up to 300 in 100 overs.'

Graham Stevenson, promoted to number five, made 11 before being caught by Chris Broad off the bowling of Phil Bainbridge with his side still six runs short. Yorkshire missed out by three and thoughts turned to the declaration. With 35 minutes left in the day, Illingworth sent out another message with 12th man Nick Taylor. 'Geoffrey's view probably would be that he didn't hear the instructions, didn't understand them or tried to carry them out, but the facts were people were losing their wickets at the other end to try to get maximum batting points and Geoffrey shall we say scored a minimum number of runs in a seven- or eight-over period,' explains Moxon, the first man out, for 27. 'It made it very difficult for Illy to have any control over discipline.' According to Taylor and Love, Boycott replied, 'Go and talk to the other man. I'll continue batting in my own way.' His own way involved scoring just six more and running Love out for 22 as Yorkshire reached 344/5 at the end of the day, and their innings. Boycott saw it as a 'misunderstanding', Illingworth a matter for the Peacekeepers.

Just as Sharp did not see much of the decisive inaction, he made sure he missed the aftermath. 'There was a set-to,' he says. 'There was some shouting and bawling going on and we all cleared out and left them to it! It all sounds a bit dodgy, doesn't it? It did appear as though something was amiss.' His response was much as it had been two years earlier, 'I can't honestly say all this affected my performance. You just think grown men carrying on in this way was more amusing than anything else.' Slow scoring was a feature of Yorkshire's season. Only Glamorgan's Championship runs came more slowly than Yorkshire's 46.07 per 100 balls in 1983, and Illingworth spoke to Athey about his pedestrian 39 against Somerset at Weston-super-Mare in the previous game. 'It was, I guess, a selfishness,' says Moxon. "If he's going to do it, I'm going to do it." It was childish, selfishness rather than working for the benefit of the team.' Ashley Metcalfe viewed it from a different perspective. 'I don't think people were trying to copy Boycs, I think it was a need to show they were scoring runs to keep their place,' he argues. 'If individuals could average 25–35 it might get them another year. At that time Yorkshire weren't looking to change the experienced players so they knew as long as they were performing at a level, they would be okay.'

Gloucestershire declared their first innings in arrears, yet won by five wickets to send Yorkshire bottom of the Championship. Boycott had not fielded on the third morning, ordered to rest by doctors because of a 'sleepless night'. It obviously did him good because when he batted again the *Scarborough Evening News* reported, 'Geoff Boycott led Yorkshire on a spree at Cheltenham today as they chased quick runs in order to set Gloucestershire a tempting target.' As in 1978, his post-go-slow innings was a demonstration of what he could do when he put his mind to it, hitting a six and 12 fours in a 200-minute 97. He was even more destructive in his next appearance, against Nottinghamshire at Bradford Park Avenue in the Championship. With Moxon involved in a car crash before the televised game, 19-year-old Metcalfe made his Championship debut and contributed 122 to a 248-run opening stand. Yorkshire supporter Neil Whitaker was there.

'Every time Boycs scored a boundary members were shouting, "Is that fast enough, Illy?"' he recalls. 'Every time

Metcalfe got ahead of Boycott, people were shouting out, "You'd better watch out, Boycs, or you'll be in front of the committee!" I would say about 75 per cent of the comments were light-hearted, but a percentage took umbrage. Athey, who was due to be the next man in, took a bit of a stand against the crowd when he heard something which riled him. He looked like he wanted to jump off the balcony and sort them out, but Illingworth calmed him down. The next time Boycs appeared on the field he got a standing ovation, and the next time Illingworth appeared his supporters gave him an ovation too but it wasn't as loud. There seemed to be more pro-Boycs than anti in the crowd. That was the first time I'd really noticed any of that animosity but I suppose you could sense it was coming because there had been some trouble two years previously at Scarborough. I wasn't at that match but it was on the ITN evening news. I remember commenting to my mother that it had even knocked Tony Benn off the main headline!'

Unlike Athey, Metcalfe was comfortable in his surroundings, and had an experienced cricketer helping him. Not Boycott, but opposition captain Clive Rice. 'Ricey kept telling Ashley what to do because Boycs was only interested in what he was doing. I think he was frightened that Ashley would get to 100 first, a young lad on his debut,' said Nottinghamshire's former Yorkshire bowler Mike Bore. 'Clive would say, "You're playing well, just keep going."' Metcalfe outdid even Moxon's debut, a sign Yorkshire were finally producing openers who could support and ultimately replace Boycott.

'At that time second-team cricket was a fantastic breeding ground,' Metcalfe tells me. 'Doug Padgett as coach was an exceptional leader. He had a really good style that could motivate and inspire. It didn't matter whether you were a batsman or a bowler, he managed to get the best out of good young people coming through. They'd been brought up in the right way and with the right experiences in second-team cricket to know what they had to achieve when they went up another grade. The other good thing was at that stage most counties had a second overseas player. Counties could have two per side but could only play one. You were playing against international cricketers even at second-team level so the gap wasn't as big as it perhaps is now. The biggest challenge was about personal confidence, not somebody bowling 20mph quicker than you were used to.

'It was a really strange year for me because the first half of the season I didn't get any runs. I was really lucky that Yorkshire persevered with me at second-team level. Midway through that year it changed and I started to score runs far more freely at club and second-team level. You always hope you get your opportunity when you're in good form. I'd come off the back of hundreds for my club on Saturday and Sunday, and in the week for the second team.'

Boycott had spent an hour and 45 minutes of the previous day putting his side of the Cheltenham story to Messrs Burnet, Sutcliffe and Trueman, who had also been written a letter by Illingworth which was, Yorkshire said, destroyed in Boycott's best interests and with his knowledge. With Illingworth missing because of fluid on the knee there was even speculation Boycott could captain Yorkshire at Bradford, but Neil Hartley was recalled instead.

Batting first after Nottinghamshire won the toss, Terry Brindle described Boycott's 'purposeful and sometimes violent march to 163'. Moxon put it more prosaically, 'It was two fingers to you, I can score as quickly as I want.' He was even more devastating in the second innings, making an unbeaten 141 in the draw. Ending day two 14 not out, he was on 117 at lunch on day three, hitting 20 fours and a six in his century. He was only the fourth Yorkshire batsman and the first in 51 years to score 100 in the first session of the final day of a first-class match, and the first to score centuries in both innings twice against the same opposition. 'I am of the belief that if Boycs had been playing today's game he still would have performed well and scored at four or five an over because that's what was demanded,' Metcalfe insists. 'He had the ability to do it, he just chose a style of play to get the best out of his career stats.' Yorkshire's belief he had put himself before the team at Cheltenham would have huge repercussions.

16

Revolution

A S AN opening batsmen in one of the club's most
successful eras, Bryan Stott experienced the joy of
having Yorkshire's cricketing public on his side. In
January 1984 he discovered how unpleasant it could be when
they turned against him.

'When we won the Championship in 1959 at Brighton
we drove up to Scarborough overnight for the next game,' he
recalls. 'It must have been two o'clock in the morning, maybe a
bit later before we got there, travelling two to a car. Hundreds
of members were still up, waiting for us, wanting to know
what had happened. They couldn't do enough for us even at
that time. When we got to the ground the following day it
was a hive of activity. People were absolutely in ecstasy as we
walked down a thick channel of supporters on to the square.
I can picture the scenes now – emotional, exhilarating, just
absolutely fantastic.

'Then I have a picture of me opening up our argument for
this damned special general meeting at Harrogate, and making
a complete balls of it. As soon as I started people in the front
were really, really letting go, shout, shout, shout. It was as near
hatred as you can get. I often think of those two pictures and

I bet a pound to a penny there were members at Harrogate who were shouting, swearing and really, really hating you who 25 years before would have been cheering away like mad at Scarborough. That's Yorkshire cricket. One minute you're as right as a bobbin and the next minute you're a load of rubbish – and they tell you!'

There was rebellion in the Yorkshire air in the winter of 1983/84 and when a national 364-day miners' strike kicked off in the pit village of Brampton Bierlow near Rotherham the county's cricket club was in the middle of a full-blown revolution. Unhappiness with the running of the club seeped out after Brian Close's 1970 sacking, and eight years later when Geoffrey Boycott was deposed as captain, yet the committee rode it out. In January 1984 the outrage was too great and those running Yorkshire County Cricket Club – since primary school teacher Mollie Staines's victory at the 1977 Dewsbury by-election they were no longer all men – were overthrown by a group of fiercely committed supporters who were better organised, harder working and more fanatical about their cause. Famous former cricketers like Ronnie Burnet, Bob Platt, Billy Sutcliffe and Fred Trueman were voted off the committee, replaced by what Close called 'all the nobodies of the Geoff Boycott fan club'.

Once more, the pace of Boycott's batting was at the heart of it. As in Yorkshire's previous landscape-changing go-slow, at Northamptonshire in 1978, the perpetrator was rewarded while someone else lost their job. Among the printers, postmen, preachers and petrol station proprietors of Members 84, as the Reform Group had been rebranded, their idol became a committee member while still a player. Yorkshire really had become Boycottshire.

'I don't think there will be a big hoo-ha about it,' was Burnet's spectacular misjudgement of how Boycott's Cheltenham performance would be viewed when the cricket committee met to discuss it six days later. Boycott's contract expired at the end of the season, and chairman Michael Crawford commented, 'I would hope that one would not take [a] decision on the evidence of one innings.'

Once the verdict was reached there were the now-traditional arguments over whether or not Boycott had been reprimanded. He claimed not, and that he had a letter from Don Brennan to that effect; Burnet and Ray Illingworth said he had been. Boycott denied having gone against his captain's instructions – not then, not ever – and Burnet spoke of 'confusion', but Yorkshire's statement read, 'We are satisfied that in this instance his batting was not in the best interests of the side and again he has been told that he must play the sort of innings the side needs irrespective of his own ambitions.' Terry Brindle interpreted it as Yorkshire having 'slapped Geoff Boycott across the wrist with an olive branch'. Burnet again stressed the matter would have no bearing on Boycott's long-term future, but a new contract was surely in the bag anyway.

Just 32 days before Cheltenham Boycott had been awarded a testimonial for 1984 but the formal decision on a contract was delayed because of Crawford's promise after agreeing terms with Boycott, John Hampshire and Chris Old during the 1980 season. 'It would clearly be illogical not to offer him a renewal in his testimonial year,' wrote Brindle. 'Unthinkable,' said David Warner. For all the conciliatory post-Cheltenham words, Yorkshire illogically did the unthinkable.

The cricket committee – Burnet, Brennan, Crawford, Illingworth, Stott, Trueman, his former new-ball partner Eric Burgin, Phil Sharpe, David Welch and Norman Yardley – unanimously recommended Boycott be released, Illingworth retained as manager and, as a sop that was never going to pacify the Reformers, they chose Boycott's former room-mate David Bairstow as the next captain. The general committee voted the decision – presented as a package – through 19-7. 'Michael Crawford said be very careful what you do because you may find you get a lot of repercussions,' Stott recalls. 'And sure enough we did – rightly so.' Committee member Julian Vallance can only laugh. 'He was going to go around with the collection bucket when not playing!' he points out. 'That made it an even braver decision – either braver or stupider! He wouldn't have been given a testimonial year in the expectation of being fired. He wasn't about to be fired. Illingworth had just got absolutely fed up with him. He could be a strong bugger too.'

It was, Stott admits, an act of desperation. 'You can't think what a stupid decision it was but unfortunately we didn't know which way to turn because whichever way we tried to suggest, it was always kicked out by Geoffrey's people,' he explains. 'Matthew Caswell ran rings around our legal people. You look back on it and think how on earth did we do that? We just got so frustrated. It got to be a battle with Geoffrey but we wanted to get Yorkshire back on track. It was always with the good of the county in mind. Individuals shouldn't have counted, but they did for more than 50 per cent of the members. I think they thought Geoffrey was carrying the fight, he was basically Yorkshire. The others, as far as the members were concerned, were not performing. But in a settled environment they would have settled into Test players. They might not have won the Championship but they would have been in the top half, not the bottom.'

Stott had joined the committee the previous year. 'You could see the players were struggling, the county was struggling, the performances were dreadful, the headlines were dreadful,' he says. 'Everything was falling apart. The future looked absolutely hopeless. How on earth could a cricket team perform with all this going off? It just wasn't fair on these lads. They were good cricketers, this was the annoying part. They were being overshadowed by all these ructions, people leaking things to the press, two people working for Geoffrey effectively, it was becoming a real problem. There was so much unnecessary bitterness. How they managed to play cricket and basically live together with such animosity and jealousy, I'll never know. There were bound to be one or two stirrers.

'I decided I could afford to spend time on the committee and when Harry McIlvenny retired I was elected for the Wharfedale district. There was a nucleus of former players on the committee. It was an effort, we thought, to bring the club back together because the team spirit in our side was absolutely out of this world. I'd worked with him [Boycott] – very well – when we batted against Lancashire [in 1963] and I honestly thought I had a chance of getting through to him.' Vallance insists the decision to sack Boycott was nothing personal. 'The difficulties were strictly cricketing-based,' he stresses. 'There was a feeling that some people had it in for Boycott – they didn't. There was no personal malice, to my knowledge anyway. It was just he was seen as too selfish a player for the good of the team.'

Boycott's presence was also a barrier to the development of Ashley Metcalfe and Martyn Moxon. The former did not make his second appearance until June 1984 because the latter came straight back into the side. 'One of the great things about the Yorkshire dressing room in that period was people like Raymond were immensely loyal,' Metcalfe explains. 'He'd said to Martyn, who wasn't fit for Bradford, that he would play in the following game at Scarborough. It would have been easy to say, "Actually Martyn, Ashley's done really well so we're going to play him again," but he didn't. He explained it to me and I was disappointed but I went to Scarborough as 12th man and was still part and parcel of it. I kind of thought that was something special. Not many people would have been as open and honest to explain the situation. Certainly coaches and managers since at Yorkshire would never have been.' The competition was tough for Moxon too, who did not play in more than half of Yorkshire's Championship matches in a season until Bill Athey's departure.

Whatever the thinking, releasing Boycott amounted to a declaration of war on the Reformers. 'I do not want to get involved in personal recriminations,' was Boycott's initial public response but his supporters were not going to take it lying down. 'They got on their high horses,' remarks Vallance. 'I don't think it came as a surprise. I think the committee decided to get on and do what it had to do and so what. A special general meeting wasn't thought of as a reason not to do anything.' Yorkshire commented, 'If 2.5 per cent of… members think that money spent convening a special general meeting is better spent on printing, postal and hall charges and professional fees then the general committee, while strongly disagreeing, will have to incur such expenditure.' Thirty members resigned that week and Bob Slicer predicted the final number following suit could approach 2,000. Peter Briggs urged them to resist tearing up their membership cards, realising they would have a part to play in the ensuing battle. 'The members will not allow matters to be left in this totally unsatisfactory way,' he warned. 'Continued despicable acts against Geoffrey Boycott have culminated in this last outrageous decision and those responsible have made our great club almost totally unmanageable.'

On 23 October around 400 people attended the meeting which saw Members 84 formed in place of the Yorkshire Cricket Supporters' Association. Briggs was back as chairman, Slicer the treasurer and Tony Vann the secretary after Sid Fielden refused because he was on the committee. The 240 signatures needed to force an SGM were gathered before it even started. 'There were meetings throughout the county,' Neil Whitaker recalls. 'I remember going to two at the Post House in Wakefield, the first one was the meeting when Members 84 were formed. They were very robust evenings. The language was very angry that things had gone wrong and the committee hadn't done anything about it. It was more the committee than Ray Illingworth they were angry with.'

The day after awarding his testimonial, Crawford sounded Fielden out about Boycott retiring at the end of 1984 but he seemed more inclined to try to revive his England career once his suspension expired in 1985. 'I think he would go on until he was 60 if he had the chance,' said Burnet. A *Yorkshire Post* poll found overwhelming supporting for Boycott being given one more year on the understanding he then left – 345 members and 824 supporters in favour, as opposed to just 44 and 39 saying no. A Radio Leeds phone vote produced 80 per cent support for Boycott. When the cricket committee acceded to the Reformers' request to reconsider, they were apparently given a written undertaking by Boycott that were he given one more season, it would be his last. Burnet claimed to have told the general committee, and said Peter Charles must have been asleep when he and other Reformers denied all knowledge. 'You don't go to sleep at Yorkshire committee meetings,' Charles responded. 'You are too frightened of being stabbed in the back.' As the battle lines hardened Members 84 changed their stance to argue how long Boycott played for Yorkshire should be decided by his ability, not arbitrary timelines.

The confusion was reflected on the *Yorkshire Post*'s front page. In 15 days its lead headline went from 'Boycott out' to 'Boycott not out?' then 'Boycott still out' when a second committee vote produced the same outcome. The cricket committee remained unanimous, and the only change in the general committee came because Tony Cawdry was back from his holiday to join Charles, Fielden, David Drabble, Reg Kirk, Jack Sokell, Dr John Turner and Tony Woodhouse in rejecting the move.

'You don't sack the top of the bill when the rest of the show is rubbish,' argued Slicer. Football manager Brian Clough, a friend of Boycott's, added, 'I don't know of any other club in history which finished bottom of the league, sacked its star player and left the manager in the job.' Ken McEwan, South African batsman for champions Essex, was the only player to better Boycott's seven centuries and 1,941 first-class runs in 1983, and sponsors Servowarm named him Yorkshire's player of the year. Arch-critic Burnet called Boycott's 112 not out in a two-day defeat to Derbyshire on a reported Sheffield pitch, 'The finest innings I have ever seen.' Fielden even took exception to that, as he felt it implied Boycott did not always play well for the team. Burnet later remarked, 'If Sid Fielden is demanding my resignation I take it as a great compliment because it shows I am doing my job reasonably well.'

It was not the number of runs Boycott scored but the manner which was an issue for Stott. 'When you're batting there's a lot of psychology in it,' argues the former opener. 'As a young colt, you take a lot of confidence from your partner, particularly if he's a good player. If you see a world-class player making hard work of county bowling, in your mind you're thinking if he's having problems, they must be bowling hand grenades. All Geoffrey had to do was make batting look easy because he was capable of it. Had he done that he would have instilled in his partners at the other end confidence but instead they had to take responsibility when they weren't mature enough. That's where I think Geoffrey failed in his approach to his cricket.' Metcalfe disagrees. 'Did I watch him and think, "Wow, he's our best player and if he's struggling, I'm going to struggle"? No,' he says. 'If Boycs wanted to defend a half-volley or a long hop, that was up to him. I wanted to try and hit it for four – sometimes I nicked it and got out.' Other more trivial charges were also levelled against Boycott – a couple of instances of bad language, one to a persistent journalist, and another for taking the meat out of his sandwiches at Edgbaston.

Yorkshire cricket had become so divided a day of reckoning was not only inevitable but necessary. 'Illy not Geoff' was daubed on the door of Scarborough Cricket Club's Trafalgar Square entrance and they decided not to take it down until the matter was resolved as there would only be more in its place. The *Daily Star* handed out 'I back Boycott' stickers. 'Yorkshire cricket has come to resemble one of those appalling domestic rows in which husband and wife beat and berate each other in public and in which those who seek to intervene… run the risk of being boxed on both ears,' read a sorrowful *Yorkshire Post* editorial.

With their support strongest in West and South Yorkshire, Members 84 favoured Bradford's Alhambra Theatre or Sheffield City Hall for a special general meeting. Slicer claimed the latter was prepared to host it for free, but Yorkshire opted for the 2,000-seater Harrogate Conference Centre. The Reformers threatened not to take part unless the Electoral Reform Society counted the proxy votes. After much debate it was decided they would be locked in a safe until 7am on the day of the SGM, when chartered accountants Spicer and Pegler would count them in the presence of a Members 84 solicitor, and be kept for another month to allow scrutiny. It showed the seriousness with which everyone was taking the issue, and the lack of trust – further undermined when Yorkshire published a letter from Briggs without permission casting doubt on the suggestion Members 84 were prepared to foot the £500–£600 Electoral Reform Society bill in return for equal space in election literature and two proxy voting forms per member. Yorkshire refused, 'As this is a vote on a resolution and not an election.'

That some committee representatives were doubling as leading figures in Members 84 caused the Revolution's first casualty. 'As you know I am dismayed by the conduct of Messrs Charles, Fielden and Kirk, who, while remaining members of the general committee refused to accept its majority decisions, democratically reached,' president Norman Yardley wrote in a resignation letter he asked to be made public. Kirk responded, 'We are surprised neither by Mr Yardley's letter nor by the club's decision to make it public. It seems to be a somewhat desperate ploy to attract postal voters to a thoroughly bad cause.'

Yardley's family believed the battles which followed took a toll on his health, and he refused to attend Yorkshire matches for the next couple of years. By now a campaign was well under way which many compared to a general election, except voters were probably far more exorcised by Boycott's future than trivialities like who ran the country. A key plank of the committee's manifesto – both sides published them – was, 'The damage to the morale of players is greatly underestimated by those who support Geoffrey Boycott, people who do not have all the background information and who are not as well informed as those who do take the decisions.' Typically, Trueman was blunter still, saying the Reformers 'wouldn't know a cricketer from a bar of soap'.

'First-class cricketers can be irritating when they say, "He shouldn't be on the committee, he's never played first-class." That's a silly line, isn't it?' says Vallance, who was on Trueman's side of the wider debate. 'I don't think they [Members 84] could find many old cricketers who wanted to work with them!' If the committee had far greater experience of playing first-class cricket – over 2,000 Yorkshire and 162 Test appearances – the Reformers watched much more. It was a problem the governing body acknowledged, both when appointing Illingworth as manager and in having a 'Peacekeeper' at every away game. In particular Bryan Stott, who ran his family's plumbing and heating business, was criticised for not seeing enough. 'I think that's a matter of what you're on the committee for,' Vallance argues. 'If you're on the cricket committee you need to watch some cricket, I don't think the chap who chairs finance needs to. You've also got to counter it with what age you want on the committee. I was working. Michael Crawford couldn't understand how I spent the time I did. You can't go and watch cricket for two minutes. It's different if you're retired but you don't want the committee full of retired people.' The Reformers were voracious watchers, often staying in the team hotel at away games, keeping them well informed not only of the issues on the terraces which made their way into Fielden's notebook, but also in the dressing room.

'One of the channels they used to influence people was the cricket societies,' explains Yorkshire cricket historian David Hall. 'The cricket society based at Headingley was a very strong source of support, and it was the same in South Yorkshire with the Sheffield Cricket Lovers' Society. They were hot-bases for bringing together fellow thinkers. Sidney was their voice-piece. He was quite articulate. He's a [Methodist lay] preacher so he's used to standing on the box, as it were.' The Boycott circus was a distraction from what the committee were trying to do, for Members 84 it *was* what they were trying to do. 'An active reform group is a blight,' comments Vallance. 'It's only a small management team at a cricket club, they're not big organisations with big kitties. [Assistant secretary] David Ryder and Joe Lister's days would have been invaded by the rumpus. It would have been very, very distracting, and the committee would have known that. Don't forget, they're doing it for nothing. You get very fed up with it.'

That attitude added to a picture of committee arrogance. As what he refers to as Yorkshire's 'chairman of public relations – failed!' since March, it was Vallance's job to change perceptions. An electrical retailer once tipped as a future club chairman – 'Aspiration is not the right word but I heard of it being suggested,' he tells me – Vallance had twice failed to get on to the cricket committee. He accepts the club did not communicate enough with its members. 'It's very difficult,' he argues. 'I tried to talk to the press quite a lot but the press were divided. David Warner understood the cricketing issues, he was a good man. He didn't always say we were right but he was always objective. Terry Brindle was very pro-Boycott and John Callaghan pretty pro-Boycott. John Callaghan was in no way malevolent, he just reported it as he saw it.'

While some committee members seemed content to simply stand on their reputations, the Reformers were far more willing to get their hands dirty. 'We were fired with enthusiasm,' Members 84 barrister Matthew Caswell explains. 'I was cheered on by the fact I was on the side of the rebels against the Establishment. Tony Vann would come here every day to take a dictation to give to the press. It took up an awful lot of my time. People thought I was getting money out of Geoffrey, but I didn't get a single penny. It didn't bother me.' Fellow member George Hepworth adds, 'We had a cause and we wanted to fight it to the end, and we did.'

Vann reckoned he spent 30 hours a week for five months canvassing for Leeds, while 37-year-old Bradford postman Dennis Pratchett delivered his 900 election addresses without stamps in his own time. Burnet, a banker with Hambros, signed a hand-written letter to his Harrogate constituents but his opponent, British Telecom engineer Roy Ickringill, did his best to speak to them all personally. 'I used to receive stuff from Members 84 with the times of meetings and things and when there was a meeting coming up which I didn't know the time of I got in touch with Mike Hellewell,' says Neil Whitaker. 'I didn't know him at that stage but before long I was canvassing for him.'

The Reformers did not just work harder, they played to different rules. A *Yorkshire Post* cartoon in October featured one committeeman saying to another, 'If you meet the Reform Group don't forget to wear a box!' At the end of it, Burnet reflected, 'Perhaps our campaign has been a little too gentlemanly.'

'They were,' Caswell agrees. 'For example, when we asked for a list of the members, so we could send out our statement, they gave us that. Mind you, people on our side were also gentlemen. Reg Kirk was as gentlemanly as anyone.' Vallance stresses, 'The rebels, if we can call them that, their views were sincerely held. By and large those that I knew were not malevolent, just mistaken. Some at least came to realise that after the event. They weren't malicious, they believed what they were saying and their members were fairly respectable.'

The committee hired a London agency to produce a glossy brochure. Although Boycott was a paid-up member he never received his, but was shown it. 'It is known that he [Boycott] has approached other counties to establish the basis on which he might play for them,' it alleged. It also pointed out Bob Appleyard, Frank Lowson and Barrie Leadbeater had been released before their benefits. The difference was, they had all retired, and Lister had told *The Sun* in October, 'I don't see how we could support his testimonial if he moved to another county.' Yorkshire argued they had resisted sacking Boycott many times, and their mail-out included a *Times* article highly critical of his attitude plus research from *Test Match Special* statistician Bill Frindall to show he was 'a match-saver rather than a match-winner'. Roy Wilkinson refuted that with his own figures.

The Reformers' leaflet argued, 'There was no discord in the dressing room, never any on the field of play… he never did, never said anything that justified the ending of his career with Yorkshire.' It added, 'The club is effectively preventing Boycott from playing first-class cricket next season. He could hardly participate in his testimonial in Yorkshire and play for another county even if he so wished.' The cricket committee was accused of over-reaching its powers, ignoring the general committee and withholding information from the Reformers, which it denied. Members 84 vowed to disband once Boycott got a new contract and all lawsuits were settled, and to take the cricket committee and post of manager with them. They would shelve their vote of no confidence in the committee if Boycott was given a one-year contract. Greater transparency was promised, and more investment in coaching, including a £500,000 cricket school.

'I think everyone felt our response was far more professional,' says Caswell. 'Everyone thought the rulers were professional people, they knew what they were doing, we did not because we were just ordinary people. In the newspapers, on the television and the radio we were running rings around them and showing them they were not as clever as they thought. We worked together more than they did. They were so haughty and arrogant they thought no one could challenge their authority but our tactics and our organisation were so much better.'

The turning point came when the 3 December special general meeting had to be postponed. Until then, the committee were expected to hold sway. At issue – again – was voter eligibility. The club sent ballot papers only to those who had paid subscriptions by 24 October, when Members 84 petitioned for the meeting.

'They were so shambolic the list wasn't up to date,' Caswell recalls. 'Some people had left, other people came in and were not mentioned, others died. In normal circumstances nobody would bother but because everyone in Yorkshire was alive to the fact we were in a big war, people started crying, "What about me?"' About 680 members had been disenfranchised. Two – David Thorpe of Huddersfield, and Kevin Birks from Leeds – issued a High Court writ. Thorpe had paid his membership fee on 13 November, Birks still had not. Yorkshire's rule 32 stated, 'A member shall not be entitled to vote at a meeting or election unless he has been a member for the last preceding six calendar months. Subject thereto a member may vote at a general meeting if he has paid his subscription for the calendar year immediately preceding.' Yorkshire's legal advice was to accept defeat because they had not given the defaulters sufficient notice. 'They took fright, they panicked,' says Caswell. 'They had a meeting at Headingley to call off the vote and start all over again.'

The Reformers tried to push on with the SGM regardless. 'A large proportion of members had already cast their vote, so if you started all over again, it would be like cheating,' Caswell reasons. 'They said there was no time to make a list of all the people who had been left out. I said, "Don't worry, give us a list and we will make sure that everyone gets their papers in time!" It indicated to everyone at worst they were cheating – which I'm sure they were not – at best that they were utterly incompetent.' The names and addresses of all members were listed in the club yearbook, vital information for Members 84.

Vice-chancellor Jim Blackett-Ord brought some much-needed common sense at the High Court in Leeds, ignoring Caswell's argument the proxy vote might hold sway and the meeting should be opened and only adjourned if not. Gerald Godfrey, QC for Lister and Crawford (against whom the writ was brought), called it 'a useless thunderbolt'. Yorkshire were ordered to set a new date first thing on Monday morning, but with 14 days' notice required and the subsequent Saturdays Christmas and New Year's Eve, it would be in January. The judge dismissed complaints this would incur massive extra cost, arguing the literature prepared for 3 December would still be valid, and told Yorkshire not to get fixated with their rule that SGMs had to be convened within 21 days of a request. The new date was 21 January and 503 members were struck off at the end of the year for non-payment.

Meanwhile, legendary former bowler Bob Appleyard worked with John Lister, chairman of ICI's Fibres division at Harrogate, to find a compromise. On Christmas Eve he proposed Boycott be given a final one-year contract on condition he bat down the order as part of a plan which also included raising money for the Reformers' proposed cricket school. The ludicrous idea of Boycott playing once on each of Yorkshire's six Championship home grounds, plus a Sunday League match at Hull, was also floated but given no truck by the Reformers.

'Ronnie Burnet took a few of us, including Appleyard, to a meeting to be umpired by John Lister as to whether the Appleyard compromise would work,' Vallance recalls. 'Burnet didn't think it would but he was prepared to have an independent arbiter. John Lister was regarded as a serious management guru who ran Harrogate ICI and was capable of making these decisions. I think Ronnie had said to Appleyard, "If you can persuade John Lister this is a good idea, then I'll support it." John Lister was not persuaded. As Appleyard closed the door to John Lister's office he said, "I've lost the battle but the war's still on!" I knew Bob well and he would not take no for an answer – about anything!' Compromise was not an option.

'Then we made our first big mistake,' Caswell tells me. 'Geoffrey said to me, "I've been a member of the club for so many years, paying my dues year after year, how about me standing for election in Wakefield?" I said, "If you want to stand for election, you stand." It's possible if I'd said, "No, it's stupid, not a good idea," he may have listened but on the other hand he may not have, being Geoffrey. I knew it would look as if he wanted control of the club but what I did not know was that the man he would be standing against, Dr Turner, was a very highly-respected member of the club and the community, and one of Geoffrey's supporters. It wasn't really honourable, that was probably a serious mistake. We didn't really give it much thought and he probably would have done it anyway.'

An MCC member, life member of Yorkshire, and Wakefield's committee representative since 1975, Dr Turner was Members 84 material. He had been president of Ackworth, the club Boycott joined aged ten, since 1977 and as a consultant cardiologist at Pontefract General Infirmary had treated his mother and been active in his benefit year. He had seen 18 Championship matches that summer (eight away), ten in the Sunday League (four away) and two NatWest Trophy ties, as well as watching five days of second-team cricket and five other matches featuring potential Yorkshire players. He voted against releasing Boycott both times in 1983 and sacking him as captain in 1978, and at one point considered joining the Reformers. The trouble was, unless he concocted a business address for another constituency, Boycott could only stand for the district he lived in.

Former police sergeant Russell Devy stood against Dr Turner in 1981, losing by 19 votes, and planned to do so again. 'It was me that proposed Boycott,' he told me before his death. 'It wasn't that Geoffrey asked me to stand down, he didn't. As it turned out, I'm pleased I didn't get through. I've no animosity. I didn't know Boycott particularly well at the time, I just knew his friend [Ackworth secretary] George Hepworth. From the very few dealings I've had with Geoff I always found him all right. I probably wanted to be more involved because I was retiring. I was interested in Yorkshire cricket and I had plenty of time to do the job. I don't know if I'd have been any good on the committee or not, but I'd have been for the supporters and the team. I used to get on well with the players because in those days they were nearly all local.'

Boycott announced he was standing in the *Daily Star* on 29 December. 'We needed money to circulate all the members with our side of the argument,' says Caswell. 'It was something like £2,200. I drafted a statement by Geoffrey which was published as a world exclusive, "All I want is to play cricket for Yorkshire, I'm a Yorkshireman." I drafted the whole lot here with Peter Briggs, who went along to the newspaper and got us £2,400. I'm sure he could have got more but that's all he wanted!'

In the article, illustrated by a photograph of him with a white rose in his lapel, Boycott insisted, 'The dispute is not entirely about me. There are other issues involved… Those issues would have had to be settled anyway, even if the question of my contract did not arise… But since the nomination paper had to be deposited with the club by the end of December, my decision [on whether to stand] had to be made while none of the issues [over his contract] had been resolved.' He added, 'I believe that I have a contribution to make as a member of the committee where decisions vital to the future of the club are made or ought to be made.' Dr Turner voiced his disappointment, Bob Slicer his reservations.

The Harris Research Centre conducted a poll asking Wakefield members who they would vote for and if they favoured Boycott as chairman and captain. Dr Turner seemed unfazed but the same was not true of his rival. 'Neither my opponent, Dr John Turner, nor I, is electioneering for the chairmanship of the club, and as for the captaincy I have said time and time again, and I repeat, that I am wholeheartedly behind David Bairstow,' said Boycott, who was campaigning for him to be given an unprecedented three-year term. Dr Turner was not the only Boycott supporter opposed by a Members 84 candidate. In Barnsley Mike Hellewell stood against Jack Sokell, honorary secretary of Wombwell Cricket Lovers, who had beaten him in 1980. 'When I was canvassing for Mike Hellewell it was about 75 per cent positive and the rest didn't want to vote against Jack Sokell, who had a good reputation in Barnsley and Wombwell,' Whitaker explains. 'After the result Mike Hellewell said even Geoff Boycott would have found it hard to stand against Jack Sokell. I'm not sure about that.'

In the week of the SGM Ronnie Burnet tried to up the ante by suggesting three players had not signed new contracts offered in October because they were waiting to see what happened with Boycott – the implication being if he did not leave, they would follow Bill Athey in doing so. The *Yorkshire Post* named them as Graham Stevenson, Arnie Sidebottom and Jim Love, but apologised the next day for suggesting that had come from Burnet. He would not have wanted them named because Stevenson and Sidebottom were well-known allies of Boycott's, playing winter cricket in South Africa.

The Reformers were blessed with some brilliant orators. Sid Fielden proposed the resolution that Boycott be given a new contract on the same terms as in 1983, seconded by Hellewell. Caswell put forward a vote of no confidence in the general committee, backed up by Peter Briggs, and Reg Kirk and Peter Charles presented the no confidence resolution in the cricket committee. Julian Vallance lined up Bryan Stott and Phil Sharpe, David Welch and Noel Stockdale, and Ronnie Burnet and Athol Carr to put the committee's case. 'That was a fair team,' he insists. 'Noel Stockdale was the chairman of Asda, he started it. He was a serious business guru with a very laid-back style and I got David Brook to sum up. We had some quasi-rehearsals, we decided who was going to say what. I don't know quite how you're meant to run an election, so maybe I was incompetent in that respect. Their speakers spoke with more passion. The passion ran highest on the objectors' side, it always does, and therefore they turned out and set the tone of the meeting. The people who are actively upset are more vocal than the people who are quietly satisfied. I think they were closer to the members than the committee was, which is a sad comment on the committee.'

An orange light went on when each speaker's time was up – eight minutes for the proposer, five for the seconder – and while most Reformers had completed their arguments, many a committeeman met with shouts of 'Sit down!' Stott was one. 'We were lost,' he concedes. 'We were outmanoeuvred. We thought the members would understand but we didn't realise the strength of feeling. They were really, really disgusted with us. I made an absolute mess of my speech, booed and heckled. The spectators were feet away, really, really shouting and bawling. Sid Fielden made an excellent speech on Geoffrey's behalf but the deciding one which really ridiculed us was Brian Walsh's. It makes you cringe now. He absolutely destroyed us in the most wonderful, beautiful language. It was a typical Brian Walsh speech – considered, accurate and delivered with a bit of passion. He really made us look absolutely stupid.'

Stott was booed and jeered when he claimed Boycott had cut out attacking cricket and his reference to 'continued verbal attacks' on John Hampshire, Illingworth and their families met with shouts of 'lies, lies!' Fielden spoke of 'injustice unparalleled in the history of our club', Hellewell of the 'iron fist of secrecy'. He added, 'Over my dead body will arguably the finest batsman in the world be sacked by this club.' Summing up, Walsh said, 'Giving a testimonial without a contract is like telling the condemned man he can order breakfast – except it won't be ready before the execution.' The vote went Boycott's way 4,115 to 3,109. 'I do not reproach the committee for mere failure, I reproach it for being indifferent to failure,' blasted Caswell as 3,609 expressed no confidence in them, to 3,578 supporters. Kirk called the cricket committee 'inefficient, apathetic, bigoted and both cruel and insensitive'. He was supported by 3,997, with 3,209 against.

Boycott was not in Harrogate. He had been invited to watch Manchester United v Southampton but decided to stay at home. In the evening he held two press conferences in Ossett because the room at the Post House Hotel was not big enough to accommodate everyone. He turned up 90 minutes late and spoke for less than two, confirming he would not stand down from March's committee elections.

The people had spoken but some did not feel compelled to listen. 'We are convinced we were right in our decision not to reinstate Boycott. Today's vote only demonstrates that the members do not yet know that it was the right decision,' argued Burnet, stressing with a straight face the resolutions were only 'advisory'. It was just bluster. Despite blizzards, and with Caswell threatening the appointment of a receiver, the general committee met at Headingley on Monday to resign *en masse*, leaving a ten-man caretaker committee and expanding March's election to every district seat.

The Reformers endorsed 21 candidates, leaving only moderate Bob Appleyard (an Ilkley resident who stood for Bradford on a business address) and Brian Close unchallenged. 'There is no way we would oppose a man of Close's stature and integrity,' argued Tony Vann, although two independents tried. Stott, Sokell, Phil Sharpe and Raymond Clegg were the only candidates to beat Reformers. Kirk (32 votes), Charles (16) and Sharpe (12) scraped re-election in Hull, Rotherham and York respectively, but 14 seats changed hands.

Close had the biggest margin of victory – 342, Ickringill the smallest, beating Burnet by four votes. Boycott claimed 203 votes to Dr Turner's 147, Billy Sutcliffe lost by 191 to Vann in Leeds, and the third Peacekeeper, Trueman, was defeated 129-65 by printer Peter Fretwell – or as he called him, 'Some bloke with a deaf aid from Keighley.' It was a humiliating defeat for one of the county's all-time greats. 'Many people admired Fred but he showed he didn't give a toss about the members,' Boycott explains. 'He could never grasp that he was acting for the members.' Bitter, Trueman threw out his Yorkshire kit and would only visit Headingley to commentate for *Test Match Special*. In August the Reformers tried to have his honorary life membership withdrawn after he referred to them in his *People* column as 'sewer rats'.

'Things have gone better than I dared to hope,' beamed Briggs, unable to stand because he lived in Manchester. 'It felt like the war had been won,' says Caswell. Boycott was back, stronger than ever.

17

Power Without Responsibility

THE Reformers' clear victory at the ballot box did not tend Yorkshire's in-fighting, it just changed the battles. The end of the Revolution switched the focus to a power struggle within the new committee. That Sidney Fielden and Brian Walsh were its chief losers would have far-reaching consequences. The biggest winner was an ordinary member of the public relations committee who played in the team but did not captain it. Geoffrey Boycott had far more power than ought to have come with his positions, and the next couple of years were spent struggling to rectify that.

On the night of their election landslide, the key figures of Members 84 assembled at Matthew Caswell's house to celebrate and plan. 'Ann [Wyatt, Boycott's girlfriend] came along with a case of champagne,' the barrister recalls. 'Very little was drunk because everyone else wanted beer! The agenda and everything about that first committee meeting was decided here, by me really.

'I always thought a big question was who would we have as the chairman? I thought the choice was between Reg Kirk of

Hull and Peter Charles from Rotherham. They were members of the old committee, so there would be some continuity, and it would add weight. The only alternative would have been Sidney Fielden but Sidney was a populist – a brilliant speaker very close to Geoffrey. I thought he would antagonise more people than he would please. I thought it should be Reg Kirk. He was a good man, imposing in stature, a very good speaker, a very cultured, intelligent man, blissfully poor – and he felt it! Even though he was a member of the old committee, nevertheless he felt he was not formally recognised in education and attainment. He spoke perfect French, he was very well-read, as straight as a die, and his own man. Afterwards he said the night we won the club was the happiest of his life.' Others were not in such a good mood. 'Sidney Fielden left disgruntled,' Caswell admits. 'He picked up the rest of the champagne and took it away, much to the disgust of my wife after all the beer drunk in the house.'

Walsh, who had done so much to swing the vote Members 84's way in Harrogate, also had ambitions to be Yorkshire's new chairman. 'As it had become obvious there was a possibility of winning Brian Walsh came to me and said, "Matthew, how do you think we are getting on?"' Caswell recalls. 'I said, "I think we have a good chance," so he became interested in joining us, which was important because he was a QC and a recorder, and what we lacked was social weight. All Brian wanted really was if we won he would be the most suitable person to lead the whole thing – as chairman, president, the lot – but we never had any intention at all to appoint Brian. We were using him as he was using us!'

Fielden and Charles had to settle for chairmanship of the public relations and finance sub-committees respectively; Walsh did not even get that. When the committee voted instead for Kirk, a former managing director of textiles company Craven and administrator of Wakefield's theatre trust, as general committee chairman Walsh was handed a place on Charles's finance committee. Within a year two of the snubbed trio had crossed the floor to oppose the Reformers.

Once Members 84 were defeated on their manifesto commitment to scrap the cricket committee, there was only one logical choice as its chairman. 'Brian Close had the knowledge and he could talk to any of the players,' explains David Hall, soon to be an important ally. 'He had all the nuances of leadership. He would sit on the balcony and say things about field placings I would never notice. He'd got a cricket brain which is well above average and would always ask people what they thought.' The Reformers encouraged Close to stand for the Bradford seat Don Brennan vacated through ill health because they saw him as an opponent of the old regime. But he soon turned on the new one.

Although an England selector from 1979 to 1981, it was still as true as ever that committees and Close did not mix. One of Yorkshire's finest captains was never going to be a patsy on a body extremely light on first-class playing experience. Close had Boycott's respect and a track record of handling him – he was perhaps the only Yorkshire captain who really had – but their relationship was fraught. 'When he got the sack as captain he didn't want to go,' says Boycott. 'Eventually it got to the stage where he said, "I'm going." When the members rose up for me I didn't do that so he was a bit peeved and miffed that they didn't get him back but they got me back. The members were rising up for him and quite rightly so because he was an excellent captain, but he said he'd go quietly and when he did he pulled the rug out from under his supporters because there was nothing to fight for any more. That was just a throw-away. He was always an admirer and yet a bit jealous.'

Divisions between Close and the pro-Boycott committee were evident from its first meeting when he raised objections to a current player serving. Close was under the impression that like the other sub-committee chairmen, he had a free hand to select his cricket committee as long as it contained at least two non-players. When Close asked for Phil Sharpe and Bob Appleyard as his ex-professionals, Roy Ickringill opposed the latter and Tony Vann – who had opened for Alwoodley in the Aire-Wharfe League – was instead voted on alongside Jack Sokell and Tony Woodhouse. 'Sometimes having played first-class cricket was used as a weapon against us because people would say it was jealousy,' says Bryan Stott. 'Nothing was further from the truth. The people that were on had no reason to be jealous of Geoffrey. What people didn't realise was that those old players were jolly good committeemen at getting things done.'

The obvious choice to serve under Close had refused. 'I didn't want to go on the cricket committee,' Boycott explains. 'I said, "You don't like me, you will vote against me, but you want me to accept collective responsibility? You want me to be a hostage to your views?" I had enough savvy and knowledge on cricket that I thought people would listen to me in the general committee. They wanted my name [on the cricket committee] but I knew I wouldn't be able to do anything because they would vote against me. There was obviously bitter feeling towards me, so that's not a recipe for working well. I had a duty to speak for my members and for Yorkshire cricket. I was happy to serve the club but you couldn't make me a hostage.' Instead he was handed a public relations brief.

Fielden recognised what a waste it was. 'I tried to get him to serve on the cricket committee because cricket was his strength, not PR,' he says. 'It was a nonsense him being on that committee with me. I said to him a man with his cricket experience should be on the cricket committee, not dealing with little things like pork pies and the state of the ladies' toilets, but he thought Brian Close would make him feel small. He seemed afraid of him.'

Given their animosity towards him it seemed inevitable once the Reformers controlled the club Raymond Illingworth would be the first up against the wall. The financial plight the Revolution exacerbated made that easier said than done. Illingworth had already relinquished the captaincy and seen his role as manager significantly diluted, no longer expected to attend every game. The total cost of the 1984 special general meeting was £27,925, including £13,306 legal costs, leaving Yorkshire with a surplus of £61,326 at a time when the Reformers had promised a £500,000 indoor school. Rather than sack him and pay up the final year of his contract, Fielden proposed Illingworth spend more time scouting and with the second team.

Before the elections Illingworth indicated it would not be an issue. 'If these people have got in charge of the club by then, they won't have to worry about sacking me – I will quit,' he said in February. After reflection with his accountant he used his remaining holiday time in his Spanish apartment waiting for the axe to fall. After six-and-a-half hours' debate, the committee obliged. The sacking was clumsily handled, with numerous missed phonecalls before Illingworth was told. He asked that it not be made public until he returned at the weekend, only to be told it already had. 'Yorkshire needs every cricketing brain it can get to recover,' commented Close. 'It's a terrible waste of ability and money.' Kirk argued it was necessary for 'the right foundation for harmony' but it was an expensive – and futile – way to try and achieve it.

If Illingworth's sacking was an act of mercy, Norman Shuttleworth's was brutal. Shuttleworth had been Yorkshire's acting chairman since January's SGM and, praised for his handling of the annual general meeting, he was seen as a contender to do the job full-time. A former Leeds and Hunslet cricketer in the anti-Boycott camp, he was chairman of Leeds Cricket Football and Athletic Company Ltd, which owned Headingley, and owed his position to a tradition of exchanging committee members with Yorkshire. 'I will never forget it,' says Stott. 'After the new committee had been voted on, the first item on the agenda [of the next meeting] was to do away with Leeds CFAC's position on the committee. Norman Shuttleworth, who was chairing that meeting, had to get up and leave his own committee room. It was his building but he was being voted off there and then. It was incredible, astounding.'

An ill-judged attempt to oust treasurer David Welch – also viewed as anti-Boycott – had failed at the AGM but he soon went of his own volition. Members 84 were unhappy Welch and John Temple were nominated to be co-opted on to the committee, something they opposed on principle. According to club rules those decisions and the agenda for March's AGM were made by the then-committee but Yorkshire's constitution had not been drawn up with a caretaker body in mind. Members 84 wanted the AGM adjourned so they could control the process but their misreading of the mood showed there were limits to their influence. There was slow hand-clapping when Caswell tried unsuccessfully to oppose Welch and Temple, voted on by big margins despite Boycott's opposition. Welch lasted just three weeks before resigning over the 'indefensible, totally disgusting and absurd' treatment of Shuttleworth. 'There is a caucus of closed minds running this committee,' he warned. Even in one meeting he had an impact, though, his speech important in winning the debate to keep the cricket committee. Peter Townend, a chartered accountant from Halifax and a friend of Caswell's, replaced him and Duncan Mutch became Yorkshire's solicitor.

The Reformers were determined to live up to their billing. 'The first thing I did was to draw up a new constitution,' says Caswell. 'Everyone had to be elected by the members, not co-opted. A lot of people opposed that because it was their way of being on the committee. Two or three influential people would pick their cronies. It widened the gap between the ordinary members and the top. We tried to make the club far more democratic and also had a concession for students to encourage young people. I looked at the lease [for Headingley] and was horrified. Yorkshire as a club owned nothing. All they had was the right to play cricket at Headingley. The agreement with LCAFC was a very one-sided lease tying Yorkshire for a long period without any break clauses. All the benefits of the merchandise and advertisements went to the rugby club. We forced the agreement to be rescinded and entered into a new one.'

Responsibility was shared out as for the first time all representatives appeared on one sub-committee. Attendance records were printed in Yorkshire's yearbook – Cawdry, Close, Ickringill, Vann, Woodhouse, Philip Akroyd and Peter Quinn were ever-presents in 1984, while Sharpe and Walsh had the worst records – and vice-presidents were no longer invited or received the relevant documents as a matter of course. Members could only vote at meetings and elections if their subscriptions had been paid and twice a year they received the new *White Rose Magazine* free. 'I think that period blew away so many cobwebs,' Caswell reflects. 'The people on our side were all sincere and devoted to cricket, as I was not. Someone like Reg Kirk, that was his life. They were saying we were trouble-makers – which we were in a sense! But I can assure you that once the ordinary people were on the committee I felt the club was healthier than under the old lot. It was all in the open and everyone was honestly interested in cricket and the club.'

There is an irony to Caswell talking about making Yorkshire more democratic as he held no position at the club. Born in Baghdad, he came to England as an 18-year-old student, studying first at King's College London, then Oxford University, before marrying a Yorkshirewoman – he took her surname and used the first name Matthew rather than Fuad – moving to the county and becoming a member of its cricket club. 'I never thought about standing for the committee,' he insists. 'First of all I'm not a Yorkshireman, not English by birth. I never had any ambition that way. I was very busy as a barrister. There was some suggestion about me becoming president, but I felt there would be quite a lot of objections because of my connections with Geoffrey and because I was an outsider.

'They [the Reformers] respected me because I was on their side, because I was a professional and because I was doing a good job for them. When they played in London they would invite me down with them, as if I was an honorary member of the committee. Once we won the election I said, "Right, I'm going back to my books," but they were still having difficulties so I could not wash my hands of the whole thing. It did not do me any good at the Bar. I think for a lot of us our involvement in the club harmed us professionally. Brian Walsh would be standing in the robing room in Leeds talking about Matthew and the club, and people were suggesting I was running the whole show. There was some truth in that. They listened to me, they respected my views but I never got anything out of it, nor did I suggest anything they would not have wanted to do anyway.'

Ashley Metcalfe's impressive debut had earned him a three-year contract shortly before the Revolution but the blood-letting left him feeling insecure. 'I was closer to Raymond than Boycs so it made you worry about the future,' he admits. 'The changes were really around prolonging Boycs's career. The new chairman and committee were puppets who supported Boycs. He still had a lot to offer but it made life difficult. I knew I was not in the safest of positions, although at no stage did I think the club would be divided as it was. In 1985 I was in Melbourne [playing for club side Ringwood] and Tony Vann, the cricket committee chairman, sent me a note just before Christmas to say my contract was due to expire at the end of the 1986 season and I wouldn't be re-signed. At that stage Boycs wanted to play on. I scored 1,800 runs that year [sharing the Cricket Writers' Young Cricketer of the Year award with Leicestershire's James Whitaker], so I made it impossible for them not to keep me on.'

Members 84 had promised to disband after the Revolution but whether they did or not was open to debate, as their links to Boycott had always been. 'I never got involved in the Reform Group,' he insists. 'Nobody saw me canvassing for the Reform Group. It was about me, but not of my making. It was a voluntary group and most of the people I never knew at that time. Peter Fretwell, I didn't even know he was a member but he got on the committee in place of Fred. I got to know him then and I asked why did he go up against Fred Trueman, a huge figure in Yorkshire? He said, "I said to my wife I thought it [Boycott's sacking] was wrong so she said I should put my name down against it. I was amazed when I got two-thirds of the vote!"

'They gave me a lot of support, which I'll always be grateful for. They thought what was happening was terrible and they rose up instinctively themselves. I wasn't involved. I've always believed that it's a members' club. To my dying day I will still believe it. Cricket was quite autocratic for a long time with the amateurs and the landed gentry running it. The people in charge were usually well off. The only safeguard was the members. It was one man – or one woman – one vote, and if they didn't like the way the club was being run they had the right to bring about a special meeting. It's not been used too often, but they did that when Brian Close was sacked, and they did it again in 1983. The members decided in their thousands to get me a contract and overturn the committee. It's like a vote of no confidence in the government – if you don't like what they're doing, you get them out.'

Boycott's claim he had nothing to do with Members 84 or its predecessors does not wash with everyone. Chris Old tells me that, during his captaincy, 'There seemed to be information going to them that wasn't in anybody else's realm'; Caswell claims, 'Everything was done with his knowledge and support.' There were accusations that in the committee room at least, he was actually directing operations. 'It is like a bloody puppet show,' an exasperated Close said. 'Every time anything is proposed, the heads turn towards Boycott; if he nods, up go the arms, if he doesn't, they stay down.' Despite Boycott's denials, Fielden and Bob Appleyard said much the same.

'That's exactly what happened,' claims Bryan Stott, although he goes on to paint a slightly more nuanced picture. 'Geoffrey thought things through and then other people put the things forward but that did eventually settle down. The real good committeemen that came in made their own minds up, even then. Of the original people on Geoffrey's ticket, there was a nucleus that became really good committeemen – who worked hard, had good ideas and became self-sufficient, very much Yorkshire-minded as distinct from Geoffrey-orientated.'

Caswell also thinks it is an exaggeration to paint Boycott as 'chairman of the club in everything but name', as Fielden claimed in 1985. 'Sidney may have said that but all Geoffrey was concerned about was himself,' he responds. 'All he wanted was to be secure as a player for Yorkshire. I don't think Geoffrey had any intention to be chairman or president. They all supported Geoffrey but behind that everyone had their own opinions. Reg Kirk was not fighting for Geoffrey. He resented the way the committee was being run and how they were looking down on people at the outer reaches of Yorkshire. Geoffrey was the symbol used by everyone but it was not the case that whatever Geoffrey wanted, everyone else followed. I may appear big-headed but I think they listened to me more than Geoffrey.'

Members 84 was never more than a loose coalition. In the run-up to the Craven elections, Fretwell stressed, 'I am endorsed by the Yorkshire Members 84 group, but I don't agree with everything they say.' Walsh was another keen to highlight his independence. The free-thinking shown by some elected on pro-Boycott tickets would be a constant source of frustration to the former leadership of Members 84, the perceived lack of it to their opponents. If some were easily led, it is hardly surprising. 'They'd never run any committee before,' Caswell points out. 'They never had any authority against anybody and suddenly they were in control of the club. They took fright wondering if they were good enough – Reg Kirk, most of all.'

Boycott did not claim to be independent but bound by his Wakefield members. 'My opponents on the committee couldn't grasp that they didn't have a divine right to tell the members what to do,' he argues. 'I made 100 hundreds for them, but I had no divine right to tell them what to do. It's a members' club, I've always understood that. I held my first meeting [as a committee candidate] at the Post House in Ossett, the same place where the Reform Group had their first meeting. Someone asked, "What happens if we don't agree with what you do?" I said, "If enough of you tell me you don't agree with me, I will vote against it. If enough of you want me to vote in a certain way it's my duty to do that, I promise you that." I didn't think of myself as God. I've strong views and I think I know my cricket, but I was there to represent the members of Wakefield. Some of the other people on the committee thought that because they were a solicitor or in the army they were different to the ordinary people. I didn't agree with that.'

Others suspected Boycott was the power behind the throne on the field too. 'I remember playing a three-day game at Headingley [in August 1985] when Bairstow was the captain,' former Northamptonshire skipper Geoff Cook tells me. 'We spun up and they were undecided what to do, you could tell. They won the toss and Bairstow just ran off the field – he didn't say anything. I'm shouting, "David, what's happening?" He said, "I've got to go and speak to Boycott!" How ill-mannered can you get? That was symptomatic of the overriding power these people had. They would burst through the traditions of the game, the integrity of the whole thing, good manners to the opposition – they would plough through that just to get their own way.'

Those that shared a dressing room with both, however, reject the idea 'Bluey' Bairstow was Boycott's poodle. 'They had a scrap in the dressing room at Bradford Park Avenue once,' Kevin Sharp recalls. 'It was a disagreement which finished up with a war of words and a few handbags but then they were all right. If you'd got something to say it was said, it wasn't swept under the carpet. If I felt I needed to say something, I said it, whether it went down well or not. I would say that, but others maybe might not.'

Former team-mate Mike Bore, then at Nottinghamshire, believed Bairstow would bow to no one in trying to do the right thing for his beloved Yorkshire. 'He could mix it around a bit,' he confirmed. 'He was only interested in the side being successful and people contributing to the team effort.' Northamptonshire's Alan Walker witnessed Bairstow's dressing-room feistiness. 'I remember playing Yorkshire at Luton and [Paul] Jarvis hadn't bowled well for some reason, or it might have been he didn't fancy [bowling from] one end,' he recalls. 'The changing rooms were very close and Bairstow absolutely bollocked him mercilessly, to the point of tears. I thought, "Shit, I've never heard anything like that!"' Ashley Metcalfe sums it up, 'Blue was captain on the field and within the changing room but off the field Boycs was massively influential, far more so than the captain.'

The incessant politics of Yorkshire cricket held no interest for Bairstow – he refused when asked to stand for election in Bradford during the Revolution – but that did not stop him being wrongly identified as being in one camp or another. He recalled overhearing one committee member saying, 'That's the little bastard who's causing all the trouble. Bairstow's the head of the Yorkshire Mafia.' The wicketkeeper wrote, 'The accusation stung, especially because I thought that I was doing my best to steer clear of all the politics.' Even Yorkshire's 1984 pre-season was scarred by it, the Huddersfield League having to carefully select a side to play them which did not contain anyone who objected to featuring in a testimonial match for Boycott. Most, though – Bairstow included – saw him as the unity candidate in a divided club.

It was easy to forget at times, but Yorkshire were a cricket club and for all the changes off it, there was frustratingly little progress on the field. From the day in 1970 when, having been given permission to sit his A Levels first thing in the morning, he marked his Yorkshire debut with five catches against Gloucestershire, Bairstow epitomised Yorkshire's cricket. 'David was such an explosive player and brilliant in the dressing room,' says Chris Old. 'He was everything you wanted out of a Yorkshire player.' England's doubts about his keeping up to the stumps helped his county. In announcing his appointment, the old committee had described him as 'ever-optimistic' but for all his popularity with team-mates and fans – Boycott and Members 84 included – and for all Terry Brindle described him as 'one of those Yorkshiremen to whom lose… always will be a four-letter word', he was no more able to coax success out of Yorkshire than Boycott, Hampshire or Old.

'What was Bluey like as a captain? Noisy!' chuckles Sharp. 'He led from the front. He was a red head, wasn't he? He shot from the hip, he was quite uncomplicated in many respects. He would pretty much just tell you to express yourselves, go and win the game. He probably didn't go overboard on tactics but he backed you. I liked him a lot. After he pinned me up against the dressing room wall in my first week my relationship with David just got stronger and stronger. He worked hard and played hard. He liked a pint, he played his cricket hard and he drove his cars hard. I remember one trip coming back from Taunton, bloody hell fire! We got back to Bradford from Taunton in three hours in his sports car!'

Metcalfe stresses there was more to Bairstow than tub-thumping. 'Blue was a good captain,' the former opener insists. 'After Raymond he would be the next best I played under. He had the respect of the players because he was a match-winner with the gloves and bat. He knew how to get individuals to play well. He might not have had the tactical nous that Raymond and people like Neil Hartley had but he could motivate. He did a decent job in a difficult period.'

Walker remembers that under Bairstow Yorkshire always ran on to the field but his captaincy was characterised by fast starts fizzling out. Yorkshire began 1984 with the *Bradford Telegraph and Argus* cautioning, 'A mid-table position may be the most the realists will be hoping for,' but for the first time since 1972, they started with a win. Bairstow had warned, 'I am not going to be a Brian Close overnight,' but victory over Somerset was all the sweeter because it came straight from the cricket chairman's playbook. Set 306 to win in 78 overs by Ian Botham, Boycott was dawdling when Phil Carrick persuaded his captain to move up the batting order and get the opener to speed up, as Close famously had in the 1965 Gillette Cup Final. Boycott made 60 and Bairstow 53 as Yorkshire won by three wickets with 11 balls to spare.

The next game saw an even more thrilling victory, clinched by Simon Dennis with two balls remaining against Nottinghamshire. Yorkshire even did well in the Benson and Hedges Cup, finishing second in Group A. Against Somerset at Middlesbrough in June Graham Stevenson broke a Sunday League record for the most sixes in an innings – ten – during his 29-ball 81 not out. Even Bairstow's call-up for three one-day internationals in May could not stop Yorkshire, Boycott overseeing back-to-back draws. They went into June's Benson and Hedges Cup semi-final as one of only two teams unbeaten in the Championship – and Leicestershire's run was about to end. So was Yorkshire's season.

Stevenson's 11 overs cost 70 runs as Warwickshire posted 276 in 55 overs in front of 15,000 at Headingley but he soon made amends, adding 71 in ten overs with Bairstow. 'In that vital penultimate over by [Gladstone] Small, Bairstow could hardly believe his eyes as he skimmed a shot to the cover boundary, where Paul Smith took an amazing catch around his ankles', the *Telegraph and Argus* reported. That over Stevenson was also caught on the perimeter. Yorkshire missed out on a first Lord's final in 12 years by three runs.

'Who would think I would hit a ball 50 or 60 yards never more than three feet high and that it would be caught by someone falling to his knees?' Bairstow asked afterwards. 'Or that Graham Stevenson would pick the tallest fielder on the ground in Bob Willis to give a catch to?' That Peter Parfitt named him man of the match was absolutely no consolation. 'It is probably the saddest moment of my life and certainly the saddest as Yorkshire's captain,' he said.

Martyn Moxon, who made 50, tells me Yorkshire's season 'could have been different if we'd won that game. It was a gut-wrenching defeat when we were so close to winning it.'

Metcalfe, who did not play, takes a harsher view. 'There were only four trophies you could win and the club needed something to keep moving forward,' he argues. 'But it was probably right we didn't because it showed there needed to be change. It would have just papered over the cracks.'

Yorkshire's campaign nosedived, as it would in 1985 and 1986. Their unbeaten start to the Championship ended when they were hammered in four consecutive matches, starting with an innings-and-153-run loss to Essex which was Yorkshire's heaviest at Headingley. More unwanted club records followed. Tim Robinson, Derek Randall, Graham Gooch, Keith Fletcher, Paul Romaines, Bill Athey, Hugh Morris, Mike Gatting, Phil Neale and Ian Butcher scored hundreds in seven consecutive games against Yorkshire, and September's defeat to Sussex was their tenth in a row in the Sunday League.

'We didn't do a whole heap of fitness in those days,' Moxon reflects. 'Whether we ran out of steam it was hard to tell but we certainly under-performed. There probably wasn't the focus for long enough. It's down to the senior players to set the tone. It wasn't a settled club so there wasn't that togetherness. If you think of what we're like now, there's that togetherness as a club on and off the field, a common goal, a common way of going about things, a true identity – this is what we're about, this is how we want to be seen, this is what we do. Things are all kind of joined up now where it was fractured then. There was no strong guidance or leadership from anybody.'

The low point came at Telford in July, where victory over Minor County Shropshire would set up a NatWest Trophy tie and possible revenge against Warwickshire. Yorkshire lost by 37 runs. 'We had a bad day at the office,' says Metcalfe, who made nought after former Liverpool goalkeeper Steve Orgizovic removed Moxon. 'It's rare that the whole team loses form at the same time. It came out of the blue. It did have an impact on the rest of the season, no question.'

Sharp, who later played for Shropshire, remembers the spinners did the damage. 'Malcom Nash was pro-ing for Shropshire and he bowled his overs for next to nothing [12-6-16-1] and the scoring rate was quite slow. Mushtaq Mohammad made 80 and bowled really well too [taking 3-26].' Boycott took 25 overs to score 27. 'He did take care,' says Sharp. 'He didn't play a lot of shots early on before he'd made sure he got himself in. You don't see that as much these days. That would have put a lot of pressure on the rest of the team but I can't really say his slow scoring rate affected me on a number of occasions.'

Bairstow was seething afterwards. 'We were beaten by a side of amateurs, which doesn't say a lot for the way we played as professionals,' he commented. 'We have gone from the heights of admiration by the Yorkshire public to the depths of despair in less than three weeks.' Unusually on an away ground, Boycott held a collection for his benefit which raised £200 and signed copies of his latest book in a tent. 'Not long after he was out Boycs was signing his book,' says Sharp. 'We were saying, "Where's Boycs?" I travelled home with Bluey and he was a bit quiet, I remember that. There was a big deal made about him signing his book while we were batting and of course Bluey didn't hold back. There would have been a few choice words!'

Boycott's slow scoring led to the usual post-mortem but now he and his supporters ran the committee, no action against him. Instead the upshot of a four-and-a-half-hour meeting was Bob Appleyard being co-opted on to the cricket committee to advise Yorkshire's bowlers.

Injuries also contributed to the collapse. Bairstow had been unable to play a full part in the first two Championship defeats, suffering heat rash against Essex and a hairline fracture of the skull at Middlesex. He was dogged by persistent back trouble all summer. Yorkshire did not have a full-time physiotherapist after Eric Brailsford joined Doncaster Rovers in April 1984 and their post-Revolution penny-pinching cost them. By the time their unbeaten run ended they were without the injured Sharp (broken finger), Stevenson (heel), Arnie Sidebottom (shins), Stuart Fletcher (sciatic nerve), Hartley – whose toe was broken in three places – and Moxon. The opener earned his first England call-up a month to the day after his county cap. A fractured rib left him unable to make his international debut at Lord's, that and the death of his father in the winter delaying it another two years. It would be typical of his luck with England, making a top score of 99 against New Zealand in 1987/88 when three runs scored off the bat were wrongly given as leg byes.

'The strongest 11 that Bluey could have picked was competitive,' Metcalfe argues. 'We just didn't have the depth of squad to replace key bowlers in particular, so it was always going to be tough to maintain our form throughout the season. It was no surprise that in the first half of the year we did well because people came in relaxed and injury-free from the winter and got into form but as each season went on the squad wasn't quite strong enough.' Released by Derbyshire, Steve Oldham had returned in 1984 as bowling coach but only two seamers sent down more Championship overs. Unsurprisingly, 14th-placed Yorkshire had the lowest bowling points tally in the league, unable to support six batsmen averaging over 35, four scoring more than 1,000 first-class runs. Committee member Tony Woodhouse felt, 'On some occasions the side had seemed to have some sort of death wish, particularly in the field where some of their efforts were frankly third-rate.'

Wisden acknowledged Yorkshire's bad luck but cautioned, 'It would be a mistake to dismiss their shortcomings on that basis, for there were times when they fell a long way short of acceptable standards. No real criticism can be laid against David Bairstow, who... showed a boundless enthusiasm.' Sponsors Servowarm named him their player of the season but it did not spare the wicketkeeper from an agonising and demoralising winter. For the previous six years, Yorkshire had picked a captain at the end of the season but in 1984 they dithered, as confused 'as a wobbling tightrope walker uncertain which way to fall' in the words of the *Yorkshire Post*'s David Hopps. 'In my day the captain was never appointed until the end of the year,' was Close's excuse but it did not wash with Bairstow, who found out via the television news. The frustration pours out of the postscript to *A Yorkshire Diary*, his account of the season. 'I was appalled to be in such a position,' he wrote. 'We can only wait and see what will happen over the next few months and whether or not people will go on stirring up the glowing embers of last winter's fire of discontent.'

A year on from 'probably the most important thing that's happened to me in my cricket career', Bairstow's reward for fighting the odds and his own body while trying desperately to stay out of club politics was to be left waiting to discover if he would be its latest victim.

18

Counter-Revolution

EVEN by Sidney Fielden's standards, it was an extraordinary thing to say. 'I have known Boycott for many years. I have been very close to him,' he told a press conference less than a year after the Revolution. 'We have shared times of joy and sorrow, moments of great elation, moments of extreme depression. He is a very great cricketer. I wish I had never met him.'

By January 1985, Yorkshire cricket's civil war was in a new phase. 'Peter Charles and I always discussed the matter,' says Members 84 barrister Matthew Caswell. 'We knew there would be a counter-revolution.' As with the Revolution, there were deeper issues but essentially it revolved around Geoffrey Boycott, who largely stayed out of it. Ostensibly the arguments were about the club's constitution, but chairman Reg Kirk argued, 'There was no reason to bludgeon through this set of rules other than a vindictive attempt to get rid of a 45-year-old cricketer.'

Five previous Yorkshire players had served on the committee, most notably for 12 years at the turn of the century when Lord Hawke captained them too, but Boycott was the first professional. As well as giving him a say in the future of his on-field boss, David Bairstow, he also had access to confidential information on his team-mates' contracts, wages and disciplinary records. His proposer, Russell Devy, had no concerns. 'There was nothing against it in the rules and actually he was a damned good committee member,' he told me. 'He's good at talking. He can hold his own with anybody.' When Devy put Boycott's name forward it was as an ex-Yorkshire player; and once his supporters won him a stay of execution, many hoped he would postpone his ambitions to serve on the ruling body. 'It turned the tide against us,' argues Caswell.

'I don't recall having any feelings either way, other than thinking this is a bloke who can get what he wants,' reflects Kevin Sharp. Then-team-mate Martyn Moxon says, 'I think it affected the senior players more.' But Ashley Metcalfe did feel unsettled. 'It divided the dressing room again,' he argues. 'People put individuals in certain camps and those in Boycs's camp were very secure. For those that weren't, life was far tougher. I was never, ever regarded as being in the Boycs camp and I wasn't from South Yorkshire [unlike Barnsley's Moxon]. There was a big influence of players from that area. All it did was make me want to work harder. I knew I was potentially less secure than other individuals but I was fortunate that I had a three-year contract [signed in 1983] and I felt I had those three years to prove myself.'

Boycott had argued a foot in both camps would be a good thing. 'I shall be a direct link between the team and the committee, which would strengthen the position of David Bairstow,' he claimed during his election campaign. 'I see no virtue in following the example of so many of our former players of leaving the county and returning as an elder statesman after an absence of some ten or 15 years by which time their ideas have been frozen as on the date when they last played for the county.'

The cricket chairman was dead against the idea, and as usual Brian Close was thinking outside of the box. At the end of the 1984 season the cricket committee's ex-players voted against a new one-year contract for Boycott but were outvoted by the non-players. With Phil Sharpe going home after the cricket committee meeting, the general committee rejected Close and Tony Cawdry's suggestion of a referendum and approved Boycott's contract 16-1 with four abstentions. Every other member of the squad had been given contracts until the end of 1986. 'A new Boycott contract means another year's delay in rebuilding Yorkshire cricket,' fumed Harrogate representative Ronnie Burnet, who had changed tune after the Revolution and supported Boycott staying on for his testimonial year but no longer.

Having wanted to release Boycott, Close now suggested him as captain. 'You might actually go down as someone who had contributed something to Yorkshire cricket rather than someone who just used his final years for batting practice while the rest of the team went to pot,' he told his old team-mate, arguing he should bat down the order and resign from the committee. None of that was acceptable to Boycott, who told him so in front of the committee.

'When he said I should run the whole show that was a bitter, angry remark,' Boycott says now. 'The captaincy was only really talked about when I was finishing. I was never offered it or unofficially spoken to about it. It was mooted, I think, in the committee but I wouldn't really have wanted to take David's job because I admired him as a cricketer. I actually thought it had gone, you can't bring back the past. David Bairstow was a fantastic lad, full of energy, vitality, a straight lad. I've never known anybody so enthusiastic. He would get nought and be disappointed about it and in five seconds he would be saying, "Come on, we can win this!" Even when he wasn't captain he was an absolutely fantastic character.'

There is no doubting Boycott's sincerity. 'David and Boycs got on really well,' says Moxon. 'Arnie [Sidebottom], Graham Stevenson and David Bairstow were the three players of that era who he thought could really play. I would suggest they were his favourites.' Nevertheless, the wicketkeeper's insecurity shines through in *A Yorkshire Diary,* his book about the 1984 season. Bairstow's frustrations with the Boycott circus are a regular theme. When the opener missed the Old Trafford Roses match to have a sinus operation – which he did not want made public until afterwards – his captain had to field questions about whether he had been dropped; it was the same when a hamstring strain kept him out at The Oval, leading to speculation about 'crisis talks'. When Close asked Boycott to prove his fitness with the second XI, Bairstow was annoyed some journalists attended that match rather than the first team's.

Throughout Bairstow stresses his friend has no interest in the captaincy, yet still keeps asking him about it. 'I am disturbed by these rumours,' reads his entry for 11/12 August. 'Any captain in his first year feels vulnerable, and under scrutiny the whole time.' A month earlier he wrote, 'I think he now fancies himself as manager rather than as captain. He once said to me, "With me as manager and you as captain we could do a [Brian] Clough and [Peter] Taylor for Yorkshire."' Boycott explains, 'David would not lie but it must have been a flippant, funny remark. Long before I finished playing I knew I was going to go into television if I got the chance because I wanted to be like Richie Benaud. Raymond [Illingworth] was the first person that ever put me forward as a manager. It was after I had retired and we were both working for the BBC. He'd written something in the *Daily Express* that England should have a manager and he put my name forward. I didn't see management as something I wanted to do.'

The cricket committee spent so long arguing over Boycott's new contract a decision on the captaincy had to be delayed, adding to Bairstow's frustration. As Moxon points out, 'If you feel you haven't got the 100 per cent backing of everybody at the club you haven't got the mandate really, have you? If a few results go wrong then you know there's going to be some knives in your back.' It was, says Metcalfe, par for the course. 'I think at that time the biggest issue was around everybody's futures so nobody could really worry about others too much,' he argues. 'It wasn't a pleasant environment.' Bairstow had not been appointed by Close and knew the cricket chairman shared his friend Illingworth's reservations about wicketkeeper-captains. Adding to his insecurity was a highly-rated youngster.

Steven Rhodes had been born to play for Yorkshire. Bradford-born batsman Billy Rhodes played for Nottinghamshire but when his wife was pregnant in 1964, he made sure she gave birth in Yorkshire. Steven was 17 at the time of his Sunday League debut, although bad weather meant he never got on the field. Bairstow's form and willingness to play through pain ensured four seasons later he had only appeared five times in all cricket. 'He was the best keeper we had at that time,' argues Metcalfe. 'Blue [Bairstow] could still have held a position within the team – he was a good batsman, a good fielder, and he even bowled a bit – but we needed a young Steven Rhodes as keeper to take us on. It was a tough job to be keeper, batter and captain.'

Bairstow claimed fewer first-class dismissals (46) in 1984 than any season in his career. In 1986 he would do worse still. 'It was an age thing,' Metcalfe believes. 'He was coming to the end of a really good career. Yorkshire missed an opportunity to give a little back. Rhodes and David Ripley [who left for Northamptonshire the previous winter] were exceptional keepers and I just wish Yorkshire could have got it right. It could have been a really good Yorkshire side for years to come but the political changes that cemented Boycs's career for a few more years allowed the senior players to cement their positions for much longer. It slowed Yorkshire's progress towards building a new, exciting, challenging team. It's just having that bit more vision. I'm not sure they quite had that once the Boycs group took over.'

In his biography of Boycott, Don Mosey describes the shuttle diplomacy, outlining the dates he says Close met separately with Boycott and Bairstow to discuss who should captain in 1985. The *Yorkshire Post, Bradford Telegraph and Argus* and *Northern Echo* were among the newspapers to carry reports about Boycott being offered the captaincy. On two separate occasions I asked Boycott about this and he is adamant, 'We never talked about it. Close never wanted me as captain. As far as he was concerned I'd been captain, and I'd been sacked.' Whatever the details, Boycott was no more willing to make himself a 'hostage' as captain than he had been to serve on the cricket committee. And Bairstow, having played one-day cricket for England that summer, was not prepared to stand aside as wicketkeeper.

With Close standing back, Bob Appleyard, Jack Sokell and Tony Woodhouse voted for Bairstow to be reappointed captain on condition it was as a specialist batsman. The general committee approved 11-10 but the crucial person did not. 'Not on your life,' Bairstow responded. When Tony Vann and Reg Kirk proposed him unconditionally, the second vote was 16-3 in favour with three abstentions. The captain had won a hollow victory. 'Almost inconceivably, circumstances may make Bairstow's task in 1985 as difficult as it was in April', the *Yorkshire Post*'s David Hopps concluded.

Yorkshire offered Rhodes a pay rise and Appleyard tried what he thought was an 11th-hour approach to Billy. But unbeknown to him, Kirk had reluctantly given Worcestershire permission to speak to the wicketkeeper. Rhodes moved to New Road and enjoyed a brilliant career featuring 11 Test caps, two Championships and two Sunday League titles. He did not leave until December 2017, when he was sacked as director of cricket for failing to tell the board about all-rounder Alex Hepburn's arrest on suspicion of rape in a timely fashion.

In the space of a year Yorkshire had gone from two highly-talented back-up keepers to none, but the bigger loss was

Close. He had gone to the initial committee meeting with a resignation letter in his pocket in case the cricket committee was ignored, and after postponing the decision on Bairstow was quoted as saying, 'I may not be the cricket chairman much longer and I do not want to saddle any new chairman with a captain he may not want.' Frustrated at constantly running up against brick walls, he kicked off a spate of resignations and inspired a new anti-Boycott movement.

'I hoped I could get people to see sense and find some common ground so that Yorkshire could put all their troubles behind them and get cracking again,' read Close's open resignation letter. 'One group has sat down and not been prepared to give an inch on anything I have suggested. They are serving the interests of one man and one man only.' Close had unsuccessfully attempted to dilute Boycott's influence by proposing secret ballots in committee. He concluded, 'I have been used by this Boycott-dominated committee.'

Phil Sharpe was next. 'During the last two months it has become apparent that the views of Brian Close and other cricketers are of little influence in the eyes of the general committee,' the England selector said, announcing his resignation the following day. 'We have two committees in one,' commented Appleyard, who after much thought stayed. The cricket committee carried on without Close and Sharpe, tipping the balance further in favour of non-players but even they were not all happy. A Reformer opposed to the dual role, Peter Fretwell told the press, 'I believe the character assassination of Boycott is nothing short of a disaster and I don't agree that he is a bad influence on the committee.' His resignation for speaking out was rejected. Hopps observed, 'The search for unity on the Yorkshire committee has long been a sick joke.'

On the day of Sharpe's departure another political group emerged, though its membership was largely secret apart from Capt Desmond Bailey – 'A strong opponent of Boycott as being unsuitable in a team, not on a personal level,' according to Julian Vallance – and Bob Platt, defeated in the 1984 elections for North Riding and Huddersfield respectively. Initially called Yorkshire Cricket Lovers, they quickly became Devotees because the name was already taken by a fundraising group for the club's beneficiaries. 'David Brook was the instigator,' their spokesman David Hall says. 'He was a Harrogate man who had a business selling cleaning materials. He cultivated the friendship of a number of ex-players, particularly the famous ones, and some of the members of the old committee who were dumped at the 1984 annual general meeting. The meetings used to take place in his office in Harrogate. Philip Sharpe, Bob Platt, Fred [Trueman] and David Brawn, a solicitor in Harrogate, were regular attenders.

'I got involved largely because of being friendly with Fred Trueman. I was the managing director of John Colliers, the menswear firm, and Fred did quite a lot of PR work for me after he retired. David Brook was quite conscious he didn't want any of the ex-players fronting up because they'd had their spats with Boycott and he thought if they brought someone in who was a businessman taking an objective view, it would look better. Quite falsely the pro-Boycott lobby thought we were just causing trouble but all of us involved were genuinely concerned with the welfare and long-term future of Yorkshire cricket. All that generation of players, or the vast majority, felt that a lot of Boycott's views and his followers were very self-centred. We weren't driven by malice but we felt what was happening wasn't for the good.' A 'progressive war of attrition' was promised.

Like the previous committee, the Devotees could not match the time the Reformers poured into their crusade. 'We used to meet fairly regularly and very often the communication was by telephone,' Hall explains. 'David Brook or somebody would ring me up and say, "Have you seen the comment about so-and-so?" We'd have a brief chat and agree to either respond or not. You could almost say they [the Reformers] were full-time on the job – I was running a national business! Sometimes it would get a bit embarrassing. I would be having a meeting and my secretary would come in and say she had the *Yorkshire Post* or somebody on the telephone. I used to go home and speak to David or write a press release. He was in business, I was in business and Philip Sharpe was a rep at the time [for a travel firm] so we used to have lunchtime meetings or occasionally in the evening. I can remember on one occasion speaking to Brian Walsh when he was fighting a case at Lewes Crown Court. To get to barristers, particularly when they're fighting serious cases, was not the easiest of exercises because they don't necessarily divulge their whereabouts – they don't want people turning up at the hotel in the evening.

'I used to get financial journalists ringing me up and asking fairly intense questions so I was used to dealing with the media. There was a bit of a tit-for-tat scenario where if one of the [Reform] group made a statement, the media would ring me up and ask if I would comment on it. Sometimes I made a point of not commenting because it got a bit almost childish. There was no point in just playing ping-pong. We tried to present a coherent alternative view without trying to score points.'

Close resigned from the cricket and general committees to step up the fight, not back down, and stood for re-election in Bradford. Less than a month after quitting he officially joined the Devotees and in December proposed a no confidence motion against the committee, seconded by Hall. Sidney Fielden spoke at the launch of his election campaign. 'Boycott couldn't take my friendship and admiration for Brian Close,' Fielden believes. 'Ever since I first met him he was someone I admired. Closey was a man's man and I was proud to have known him. He was one of my best friends but that didn't go down well with Boycott and his supporters.'

More discomforting for the Reformers was Fielden's opposition to Boycott's dual role. 'I thought it was wrong for Boycott to serve on the committee while he was still a player and I kept saying so,' he says. 'I said to him, "You can still keep playing and be our best batsman for another two or three years." I thought it was totally wrong for a man to be in a position of power like that. Bairstow said to me one day, "We don't know where we are with him."'

Boycott told the *Telegraph and Argus* that Fielden 'found it difficult to accept that I was on the same committee as he is and I spoke my own mind'. Caswell calls it 'a case of lovers falling out' and while not to be taken literally, it is not as overblown as it might seem. 'Ronnie Burnet used to claim that my only flaw was that I loved Boycott,' Fielden once said. 'I suppose I did, in the best sense. Even my wife used to say that I thought more of Boycott than I did of her.'

Fielden, Boycott and David Brawn were at Roy Ickringill's meeting of Harrogate members in November, where the former claimed Members 84 'have met regularly and sent out letters which are in poor taste'. Caswell responds, 'There was no more Members 84, there was the committee. Peter Briggs and George Hepworth stayed involved just as friends. I had very strong links with Geoffrey, Reg Kirk, Peter Charles, Peter Quinn, Tony Vann and Peter Briggs. We had contact in that sense but nothing official. Once the Revolution happened people were left to their own devices.' Like Ickringill, Boycott was heckled and when Brawn tried to ask about the dual role, he was told to attend Boycott's (as yet unscheduled) Wakefield meeting. Ickringill had asked Fielden to stay away from the meeting and the *Telegraph and Argus* observed, 'Mr Fielden's forthright answers clearly embarrassed Mr Ickringill.'

'I think it's telling that Walsh and Fielden changed their mind because no one changed their mind the other way,' comments former committeeman Julian Vallance. 'It's quite a brave thing to do when you've been leading a campaign. Fielden and Walsh were just blinded by his [Boycott's] batting ability, for me. He was a hero, Len [Hutton]'s successor. Many of the members were cricketers, though not all, and we all like heroes but this idol was being knocked off his pedestal and they didn't like that.' Hall adds, 'I was at that [1984 special general] meeting and there was no doubt about it, one of the influences in that changeover was Brian Walsh. He was the one on the day who really swayed it and at that time genuinely thought Boycott was a force for the good but I think he began to realise Boycott wasn't all that he made out to be.' Wharfedale representative Bryan Stott recalls, 'I can remember him rebuking Boycott when he was pontificating, saying, "You wouldn't be here today if it wasn't for me."'

Fielden faced most of the Reformers' ire. 'There was a lot of bitterness,' Caswell reflects. 'They hated Sidney and Geoffrey even now hates him. It was to the discredit of Geoffrey that in his books he referred to him as a "traitor" and "Judas".' The 'bitterness' seeped out in a smear campaign. 'I think the one dishonourable thing we did [not the last time he uses the phrase] was to circulate a letter implying more or less that he was behaving in a dishonourable manner,' Caswell admits. 'I wasn't the originator, but I should have stopped it.'

Phyllis Culpan was a 74-year-old Yorkshire member who had been a maths teacher, cricket coach and deputy headmistress of Skipton Girls' High School until retiring in 1963. 'Yorkshire and cricket are two of her great loves. But soaring away above both is her adulation of Geoffrey Boycott,' explained a 1979 *Yorkshire Post* profile. She had an oil painting of Boycott, and told the newspaper she would have cancelled her membership had he left in the winter of 1978/79. 'She used to stay at our home and use it as a base when she was watching Yorkshire and Boycott play at places like Chesterfield,' says Fielden.

Two days after Fielden addressed Yorkshire members in Harrogate, Culpan wrote a letter to Kirk which was forwarded anonymously to every committee member. 'In the autumn of 1981,' it read, 'Mr Fielden, who I had known as a Yorkshire member for two years, told me he would like to run for the Doncaster district representative… I offered him the cost of circularising all his members. I gave him £100 and he seemed very grateful. He had a massive vote in his favour. Realising that it would be an expensive job to do properly I have given him further financial assistance since. I cannot find the stub cheques for 1982 – probably destroyed – but in 1983 I gave him £100 on 24 June, £100 on 12 July and, to his wife Maureen – a joint account – £250 on 31 August. In 1984, on 11 July, I paid him £200.' She added, 'I was working on a way to help them further financially when the *Yorkshire Post* revealed Fielden's open attack [on Boycott].'

Fielden is upset by the inference he was motivated by money, denying another money-related allegation made to me. 'It was very hurtful for me and could have been professionally too for a detective sergeant,' he points out. 'I was once called in by my chief superintendent who wanted to know how much I was being paid by Yorkshire's committee. I had to explain to him that you didn't get paid to serve on Yorkshire's committee.

'Cricket was my hobby. When I give talks and things people will often say, "What's your fee?" and I say, "I don't have a fee, I only take donations." They end up elsewhere. Phyllis Culpan once left my wife a small amount of money under her pillow one day because it was her birthday – it was £20 or something like that to get a new dress or something – and they magnified that out of all proportion too.'

Although Fielden had done nothing wrong the letter added to the pressure on him, prompting his press conference remark. 'I was quiet until at the end when a journalist asked how I was getting on with Boycott,' he tells me. 'That was when I said I wished I had never met him. The phrase went around the world. Bob Platt was on holiday in Spain and he saw it. Some people said I should do something about it but how could I? I said it.' After a three-hour meeting the committee decided not to identify Mike Hellewell and Peter Briggs as the source of the leak, though it became known later. They were censured but escaped expulsion. Fielden survived a vote of no confidence to cling on as PR chairman until the AGM. 'Why should I resign when they plan to sack me anyway?' he reasoned.

Boycott's dual role was only one of the Devotees' concerns. Sponsorship was down 22 per cent for 1984, profits more than £7,000. They told members Illingworth's sacking cost Yorkshire £25,000 and a car; a £40,000 computer system had been considered without alternative quotes, and more than £33,000 invested in a new club shop without putting it out to franchise. Membership was, however, up for the first time since 1977. The Devotees argued the credit for some achievements claimed by the committee belonged elsewhere – the 1984 Second XI Championship success was down to Ray Illingworth and Doug Padgett's groundwork, Fielden responsible for improved PR, enhanced playing contracts agreed by their predecessors, and improvements to the sightscreens forced on them by the TCCB. The Devotees' nine-page letter to members – backed up by newspaper adverts – pleaded, 'I ask you to return YCCC to sanity and sound management.' Kirk, who refused to debate with Close and Hall on Yorkshire Television's flagship news programme *Calendar*, argued, 'Any members who support a motion of no confidence are really expressing a lack of confidence in their own judgement as more than half of the present committee were [first] elected last March.'

The Devotees believed their opponents were riding roughshod over Yorkshire's traditions. 'One of the things that irritated Fred more than anything was their attitude to the Yorkshire rose with its 11 petals, one for each player,' Hall explains. 'That was designed by Hawke and the only people allowed to use it were first XI capped players. When it was adopted by Yorkshire as the club emblem, Fred was beyond himself. He used to entertain me occasionally at his house for dinner and if you got him on the subject, it was just like lighting a touchpaper!'

When Boycott sold one of his Yorkshire sweaters for £100 to raise money for his testimonial, Trueman told a meeting of Yorkshire members in Skipton, 'If I saw any of you in a Yorkshire cap there is a fair chance I would knock it off your head because you are not bloody well entitled to wear it. You don't sell or give away things like that.' With the club struggling financially, the Reformers had no such qualms. 'I argued and argued for the best part of half-an-hour-plus to stop them using the players' rose on all the merchandise,' Stott reveals. 'It was the only recognition we players had got and here's Geoffrey, a Yorkshire player, wanting to sell it. It would have made thousands of people the same as Yorkshire capped players. I managed after a fight to persuade them to put "Yorkshire County Cricket Club" underneath. At least there was a differential between the players' blazer, cap and ties.'

David Brawn, seconded by Platt, put a resolution to the 1985 annual general meeting to stop players serving on the committee, though it would not apply to Boycott until his three-year term expired. 'We did something dishonourable in that we flooded the agenda with other resolutions to protect Geoffrey,' Caswell admits. 'We kept saying, "Geoffrey, Geoffrey, give up, resign from the committee and we guarantee you will be protected." But Geoffrey had a paranoid touch.'

The 31 resolutions debated everything from the size of the committee to publishing the minutes of meetings, the Yorkshire-born players policy and even the use of obscene language. Most, though, concerned the club's constitution and if the proposal to set up a sub-committee to look into it was passed, 18 would be redundant. It prompted the usual pettiness, the Devotees proposing amendments, only for Peter Briggs to submit seven himself. When an emergency general committee meeting unanimously refused to hear the Devotees' amendments, they launched a High Court injunction. That afternoon, as new president Lord Mountgarret headed to London to discuss his options with counsel, they backed down.

'How can we players begin to prepare properly for a new season with all this going on?' Bairstow complained.

Only Mountgarret's skilful manoeuvring prevented another £5,000 SGM. Yorkshire's presidency had been vacant since Norman Yardley's resignation until the 17th Viscount Mountgarret, Richard Henry Piers Butler, heir to the earldoms of Ormonde and Ossery, was unearthed in the autumn of 1984. 'The tradition was that you had Lord Hawke and other lords at the top,' Caswell explains. 'So the question was, if the peasants had taken control of the castle, could we have someone with a certain weight?' The previous regime's choice, Sir Leonard Hutton, opposed the Reformers. They favoured Huddersfield-born Lord Hanson, founder of multi-national industrial management group the Hanson Trust, and a life member. When Boycott approached him, Hanson declined because he spent half his year living in the United States.

Mountgarret was a 47-year-old Old Etonian and former Irish Guard who owned Hardcastle Moor in North Yorkshire. Rumour had it he owed his new post to listing cricket among his hobbies in *Who's Who*. 'Roy Ickringill said, "How about having Mountgarret as the president, he's very rich and has a large estate?"' Caswell recalls. 'Roy may have looked him up in *Who's Who*, I don't know. I knew nothing about him other than he was a viscount. I had a solicitor from Harrogate who instructed me and played golf with him quite frequently. He sounded him out and Mountgarret said he would be honoured.'

Opinions on the new man varied. 'Richard Mountgarret did a super job,' says Stott. 'He called a spade a spade to everybody and handled it well in his own particular way.' Caswell regarded him as 'a bumbling fool', adding, 'That was another big mistake. Anyone else would be better but he was a viscount and a rich man and that impressed a lot of people.' Members 84 supporter Neil Whitaker tells me, 'He didn't think much of the members. He thought they only had rights, not privileges.'

Introduced by Kirk as 'Viscount Mountbatten', Mountgarret was an unknown quantity when it came to Yorkshire's politics but started well, elected by 90 per cent of proxy voters and praised by the press for his handling of the 1985 AGM. 'He was an unusual character in many ways but he tried very hard to be a mediator,' says Hall. 'He was an ex-Guards officer and he knew a few things about how to try and talk reason into people. I think he was a quietening influence.' The *Northern Echo* wrote of the AGM, 'The most encouraging part of another grim day in Yorkshire's history was the magnificent handling of the meeting by the new president.' Mountgarret quoted Churchill as he appealed for unity, and banged the table with a cricket bat for quiet.

Kirk's proposal that all further rule changes be considered by a special sub-committee was passed by 148 votes, but counsel sided with Walsh against Caswell and Duncan Mutch, and advised the Devotees' resolutions had the right to be heard at an SGM. Mountgarret suggested a referendum, admitting, 'It is a common- sense approach but it is legally wrong. If one member considers this route is wrong, they can challenge it in the courts and the committee would have no choice but to reschedule the special meeting.' When nobody did he triumphantly declared, 'We have seen a welding together of two warring factions.' In Boycott's absence the general committee decided the dual role was wrong in principle and the members agreed, 2,595 voting to abolish it, with 560 in favour and 83 abstentions.

The seven-hour AGM suggested Yorkshire's members were almost equally split between support, opposition and apathy towards the committee. Close's vote of no confidence was narrowly defeated – it had a majority among the proxy voters who replied before the Devotees' High Court climbdown – but around a third of the membership did not take part. Instead, the main act of defiance came when the committee refused to re-nominate John Temple, which Ken

Harvey lambasted as 'based on meanness, spitefulness and vindictiveness'. The matter was referred back to the committee to rethink, and Temple re-elected 2,352-320 in April's postal vote, which also passed a motion requiring ten per cent support to call an SGM.

The Devotees had endorsed 21 committeemen or potential election candidates – including Tony Cawdry, Fielden and Walsh who enjoyed Members 84's support in the Revolution – but not all were grateful. Jack Sokell did not want to be part of any 'faction', while as chairman of its committee Russell Hutchinson worried about the impact on Phil Carrick's benefit. Geoff Cope, interested in standing for Leeds if Close's no confidence motion forced fresh elections, said, 'I support the Devotees in some of the things they say, but on the other hand, people such as Tony Vann of the present committee have been kind enough to suggest I could do a good job.' Tim Reed also turned down their support. The Devotee-endorsed quintet of Cawdry, Sharpe, Stott, Walsh and Raymond Clegg were returned unopposed, Close back with a reduced majority, Kirk an increased one. Peter Fretwell defeated Wharfedale farmer and Devotee Anthony Roberts, and Reed beat Tim Jarvis by two votes in Sheffield, producing a committee of 12 Boycott supporters, eight anti and three moderates.

The Reformers made the most of their advantage when selecting the sub-committees. With Sharpe and Reed on holiday and Appleyard coaching, Vann was voted cricket chairman 9-8 over Close. Stott calls it a 'fairly childish' decision, and along with Close, Appleyard and Sharpe refused to serve under him. With Peter Quinn chosen as PR chairman at Fielden's expense – 'What Boycott wants, Boycott gets,' commented the latter – and Peter Charles (finance) and David Drabble (grounds/membership) re-elected, all the sub-committees were in the hands of Reformers for the first time, although Mutch was dispensed with as legal adviser. Kirk was voted back in as chairman, defeating Walsh 11-8. A three-man selection committee of captain, cricket chairman and senior professional was set up – meaning Boycott and his ally Vann could outvote Bairstow. 'David Bairstow is captain of Yorkshire in name only', the *Telegraph and Argus* concluded.

Although in the minority, Stott felt it became a good committee. 'There was a real period of settling down,' he tells me. 'Some of the new committeemen [in 1984] weren't worthy of being on and they went by the wayside but there were two or three who have turned out to be really superb committeemen who've worked very, very hard for the club. They certainly modified their opinions.

'For quite a long time there was us and them – not an equal balance, but certainly a split committee between Geoffrey's followers who were quite convinced in their own opinions, and the traditional people like we were – but we were working together and getting things done. There were individuals from each side prepared to leak things to the press, which is disastrous, but when it settled down it worked very well. Geoffrey played his part and matured. It was a good time to be on the committee, in all honesty. Things were being achieved which are paying dividends even now. Some good people came on to the committee who wouldn't normally have stood.'

An indoor school run by John Hampshire was set up in Sheffield and, inspired by a trip to see Australia's, Appleyard was the driving force behind an academy which continues to keep not just Yorkshire but England's first team well stocked. Making the most of Yorkshire-born talent was essential, and the post-Revolution committee was particularly conscious of it. A 'tentative' approach was made in late 1984 to bring Chris Old back from Warwickshire, and there was interest in Neil Mallender until Yorkshire discovered he had signed a new contract with Northamptonshire. Peter Hartley, released in 1981, returned after three matches for Warwickshire, one against his home county. Even Derbyshire's 42-year-old all-rounder Barry Wood was considered, 20 years after leaving.

Despite his re-election, Kirk was anything but secure. 'Reg Kirk was under pressure from two directions,' explains Caswell. 'Mountgarret wanted more control of the club and Brian Walsh all the time was making snide remarks. Reg Kirk really went to pieces. He would come here moaning to me, "I'm 65, I can't put up with this anymore." We told him he must soldier on or one of the others would get in.' Kirk was damaged when in December 1984 he did not oppose the TCCB's decision to take away Headingley's automatic right to stage a Test match every year, something it had done since 1961. But a controversy involving Viv Richards was the breaking point for his relationship with the hands-on president.

On the second day of Yorkshire's NatWest quarter-final against Somerset in July 1985, Richards appeared to edge Chris Shaw behind. The West Indies batsman was ten not out from a score of 87/4. Richards put his bat under his arm, removed a glove and headed to the pavilion but when umpire John Jameson did not react, captain Ian Botham called him back to make 87 not out in a four-wicket win. Shaw, an apprentice electrician, believed Richards had nicked the ball, but he insisted, 'It is just one of my mannerisms when I have had a lucky escape.' The *Yorkshire Post* and *Telegraph and Argus* pointed out he had done the same when Steve Oldham pretended to celebrate a 'crowd catch' which dropped just in front of him the previous day.

Far more serious was Botham's claim the Headingley crowd racially abused his team-mate. Yorkshire had previous. In July 1984 there had been reports of 'National Front-type salutes', shouts of 'Sieg Heil!' and bananas and oranges thrown at Gloucestershire's David Lawrence and John Shepherd during a Sunday League match at Scarborough. It led to the bar being closed until 4.30pm for the next game (costing the hosts around £1,000), apologies from Bairstow and Fielden, and a plea in the 1985 yearbook to treat the pair 'with particular warmth when they visit our grounds in future years'. Ray

Illingworth asked for stricter controls on the Scarborough bar after Yorkshire's players were abused in 1982, and in 1983 the *Telegraph and Argus* reported during Kent's visit, 'Scores of drunken hooligans kept invading the ground, staggering around and fighting. Several dropped their trousers on the field, much to the embarrassment of families.' There had also been crowd trouble during Sunday League matches at Scarborough and Chesterfield in 1984.

On this occasion, however, Richards had not made a complaint and umpire John Holder, a fellow West Indian, claimed not to have heard any abuse. Kirk and Mountgarret – already at odds over the chairman's opposition to the rules revision the president was championing – disagreed over how the incident should be dealt with. Kirk refused Somerset's letter of apology because he wanted one from Botham, and unilaterally demanded TCCB action. Somerset chief executive Tony Brown insisted, 'While we have regretted Botham making these remarks we believe that they were well-founded for we have conclusive evidence from several independent and fair-minded people.'

Mountgarret preferred to handle things man-to-man with Somerset president Colin Atkinson and when he learnt Kirk had taken matters into his own hands, he urged him to resign. When Kirk refused, Walsh and Stott put forward a censure motion. Legal threats headed it off, but not a vote of no confidence. With Kirk at a wedding and ally David Drabble on holiday, Peter Townend chaired the meeting but it was argued a stand-in could not have the casting vote. Mountgarret did not vote either. 'I do not think I should use my vote on a personal issue,' he said. It saved Kirk, tying the result 11-11, but Somerset's apology was unanimously accepted and the TCCB asked to take no further action. Peter Quinn's proposal to better define the responsibilities of chairman and president – the latter now heading a new management committee – was rejected, so the struggle went on.

When Kirk tried to put off new dual role rules for another year, David Warner wrote, 'The gulf is now so wide between the county club's top two officials that it would seem impossible for them to remain in office together much longer.' Mountgarret's view was, 'If Mr Kirk cannot accept majority decisions then he has no course but to resign.' On New Year's Eve he did, replaced by Walsh. 'I have been disgusted with the personal attacks directed against me,' Kirk said. Initially he vowed to stay on as Hull representative to campaign against the new constitution, but admitted to defeat on that too – this time to bronchitis.

The Reformers also finally lost Peter Fretwell, twice talked out of resigning in the summer. 'I am no longer prepared to endure the distrust and hypocrisy which is present at every sub-committee and general meeting,' he said. 'So many meetings are dominated by personal abuse. They are ten per cent constructive and 90 per cent vindictive.' Bob Platt returned as Huddersfield representative and Mountgarret supporter Gary Denton replaced Kirk in Hull. The Reformers' grip on the committee was loosening.

19

Finally, Boycott is Out

BY February 1986, Geoffrey Boycott had been to the brink of leaving Yorkshire so many times few were taking anything for granted when the annual general meeting overwhelmingly decided to end his dual role at the end of the season. Boycott had always said if he had to choose, he would sacrifice his off-field role, but the matter would be taken out of his hands. His playing career ended without him saying goodbye, yet he still managed to inspire an argument on his final day.

The 45-year-old was becoming more vulnerable to injury but when fit he was still Yorkshire's best batsman. Even so, with Phil Carrick vice-captain for 1986 he was feeling insecure. 'Towards the end of that season I thought Brian Close and people were going to sack me,' he tells me. 'I felt people like Closey and Stotty were waiting to get their own back because they grew up with Raymond [Illingworth].' Even Boycott's bodyguards were wearying of the fight. 'I think by 1985, 1986 a lot of people just felt they'd spent enough time supporting Boycott and didn't want anything more to do with all the trouble,' comments Members 84 supporter Neil Whitaker. Not all, though, had given up. When Lord Mountgarret said in

January 1986, 'I think we have an extremely workable agenda for the annual meeting, unless someone fires an Exocet missile,' two Boycott supporters took up the challenge.

Tony St Quintin, a 35-year-old maths teacher at Benjamin Goff School in Leeds, and Rev Nicholas Plant, vicar of Armley with New Wortley, proposed an alternative set of rules be debated at the AGM which conspicuously ignored the dual role to focus on streamlining the committee. When the vicar was persuaded to withdraw his support, Peter Charles, Roy Ickringill, Reg Kirk and Peter Quinn jointly seconded the rules but president and acting chairman Mountgarret deemed they had been submitted too late. An emergency general committee meeting voted 11-6 to ask the quartet to resign and when they refused, adjourned and reconvened as a sub-committee supporting the new constitution, effectively kicking them out. 'It was contrary to the interests of the committee to discuss the legal situation in their presence,' Mountgarret argued. Quinn had little choice but to resign as PR chairman, Sidney Fielden returning. 'We are faced with a naked dictatorship,' Ickringill warned.

When the resolution to end Boycott's dual role was put to members at Sheffield City Hall, it was seconded by Reform Group stalwart Tony Vann. 'I had seen how the issue was tearing the club apart and I thought, on balance, that it was just not right that a player could be in both the dressing room and the committee room,' he said. Russell Devy tried desperately to hold back the tide, proposing any Yorkshire member on 31 December be exempt. 'If you join something under the existing rules and later on they change, you should be allowed to stay on,' he was still arguing 28 years later. The game was up, though. While Boycott holidayed in Jamaica, his dual role was ended by 3,370 votes to 310. 'The political troubles are now behind us, and the future must be considered rosier,' proclaimed Mountgarret.

Brian Close was back as cricket chairman after seeing off pro-Boycott Peter Baren at an election for the third year running, and had Vann, Bob Appleyard, Phil Sharpe, Bryan Stott, and Tony Woodhouse, who defeated David Hall in Leeds, under him. The selection committee was scrapped. Not that the fighting was over – 1,011 proxy voters rejected Halifax member Tom Naylor's motion that Yorkshire should focus on cricket, not politics!

Whether it was his powers waning or the security of being on the committee, Boycott cut an even more negative figure at the crease in his final years. Vann had told the 1985 pre-season lunch, 'We should be more impressed with a rapid, match-winning 70 under pressure than with a five-hour century on a shirt front,' but *Wisden* claimed, 'His words fell on deaf ears.' In Boycott's first post-Revolution season his 1,567 first-class runs came from 1,187 overs. 'This negative attitude will kill county cricket,' fumed Worcestershire's Kapil Dev at Harrogate in June 1985 after Boycott – who had taken 91 overs making a first-innings century – showed no inclination to chase the 271 in 59 overs Yorkshire had been set for victory. He took nine overs to get off the mark before crawling to 64 not out against an attack depleted by John Inchmore's injury. Yorkshire's senior players felt their target was 20 or 30 too many, David Warner thought it 'reasonable'. David Bairstow alone tried his damnedest to reach it.

The next game, against Leicestershire at Bradford Park Avenue, was even worse. Boycott could not shoulder much blame this time, facing only nine overs during which time he played one scoring shot. His opening partner Martyn Moxon made 33 in 49 overs and it took 61 for Yorkshire's scoring rate to creep above two an over. The match was drawn because although Bairstow hit a century before lunch on day three, his team only had time to take six wickets. *Wisden* called Boycott's 261-delivery century against Nottinghamshire at Scarborough 'dreadfully slow'. When he made seven off the final morning's first 45 balls the *Bradford Telegraph and Argus* noted, 'David Bairstow came out of the dressing room and glared at the pavilion clock.' Boycott got the runs he needed to equal Herbert Sutcliffe's 149 first-class centuries before accelerating, by which time any chance of victory had been passed up.

There were still moments of brilliance, though – 184 in a 351-run opening stand in the return match against Worcestershire, five days after the last, and at Edgbaston in August becoming only the seventh batsman and the first since the war to score 100 centuries for his county, five minutes before the game was called a draw in fading light. Bairstow was 49 not out, needing one in his next innings to reach 1,000 runs for the third time in five seasons. Boycott finished third in the County Championship averages behind Ian Botham and Graham Gooch.

Yorkshire went bottom of the Championship when, in Bairstow's words, 'We played like a bunch of twerps' against Surrey at Sheffield, with five of ten capped players injured. The three capped seamers, Arnie Sidebottom, Graham Stevenson and Simon Dennis, bowled just 328 overs between them in all competitions. Aged 31, and with his three-year ban for touring South Africa expired, Sidebottom was driving between matches at Bristol and Maidstone when he heard on the radio he had been called up for what would be his only Test appearance. Sidebottom injured his big left toe at Trent Bridge and broke down after 18 overs.

Yorkshire's attempts to address their bowling deficiencies met a tragic end. Johnny Wardle had rebuilt his relationship with the club by working with Geoff Cope after his 1972 suspension but three days after being appointed bowling coach in February 1985 the 62-year-old was admitted to hospital complaining of dizziness. He had a brain tumour which, despite surgery, killed him in July.

The White Rose finished 11th in the Championship with only three wins but were in the Sunday League title race until losing a rain-affected third-last game at Glamorgan, finishing as one of four teams level on points in sixth. Despite his team's struggles and a four-match ban – suspended for two years – for protesting to umpires Don Osler and David Constant about the Trent Bridge pitch in July, Bairstow was unanimously reappointed for 1986 – recognition, perhaps, that he did not have much to work with, at least in bowling terms. Servowarm, whose sponsorship was up for renewal at the end of the year, had sympathy. 'Each year there seem to be disagreements within the Yorkshire committee,' said operations director Syd Starkie when he presented Bairstow with their player of the year award. 'It really is time the committee got their act together, creating an atmosphere that gives the players some confidence.'

The most notable bright spot was Richard Blakey, who added 223 with Moxon for the second wicket against Somerset in May. 'At 18 years and four months, Blakey looked like becoming the second-youngest Yorkshire player to hit a century but at 90 he was bowled by a fine off-break from Vic Marks,' Warner reported. Despite never having done so even for the second team, Blakey took the wicketkeeping gloves on his debut when Bairstow was injured. He would eventually replace him permanently but at the end of Blakey's maiden season *Wisden* called him 'the most likely successor to Boycott in due course'.

Yorkshire were again quickly out of the blocks in 1986, winning six of their first seven games in all competitions. They went second in the Championship after beating Middlesex in mid-June but only won once more that year. The *Yorkshire Post* partly blamed the absence of a manager. 'Perhaps there was an element of fatigue,' comments Kevin Sharp. 'We didn't have the [bowling] pace. Paul Jarvis was the one who had pace but he was young and perhaps he got over-bowled.' A back injury prevented Jarvis playing in the Championship after 5 August and at the end of the month a furious Bairstow was denied Chris Shaw's services because Brian Close decided it was more important he played in the final of the Under-25 competition.

Boycott was also becoming more susceptible to injury. He had missed the start of the 1985 season with back and wrist injuries. Later that summer he sat out two matches with a hamstring injury and fractured his left thumb in the final Sunday League game. He pulled his hamstring at home to Leicestershire in 1986, although gritted his teeth to make a 267-ball century, then broke his left wrist when making 135 not out against Surrey a fortnight later, causing him to miss the next nine Championship games. Although his appetite for runs was as strong as ever, Boycott batted just 17 times for Yorkshire's first team in 1986.

He was not greatly missed. Yorkshire took more Championship batting points than any other county. Despite losing Bill Athey at the end of 1983 and Richard Lumb retiring 12 months later, they had an embarrassment of top-order riches. Moxon won his first England cap in 1986, two years later than planned, and Ashley Metcalfe his Yorkshire one in what was his best season. The pair posted the country's highest opening stand of the year at Old Trafford. Blakey hit over 1,000 Second XI Championship runs and made an unbeaten century for England Young Cricketers against Sri Lanka at Headingley, but even with Boycott limited to 12 Championship outings (he featured only twice in the Sunday League in his final two seasons), *Wisden* argued that the youngster's 'limited appearances raised a question mark over the selection policy'. The *Yorkshire Post*'s review of the season gushed, 'The county possesses the best crop of youngsters for a generation, in terms of ability but even more strikingly in attitude. They are all ready to learn.'

Boycott amassed 4,002 Championship runs in three years as committeeman/player but again in his final season it was the pace which was the problem. It took him 59 overs to make 60 against a Derbyshire attack led by Michael Holding at Sheffield. 'Boycott is a world-class batsman and while he cannot be expected to blaze away at top Test bowlers in the opening overs he should be able to take more runs from the other end,' Warner commented. In his next innings Boycott made 74 out of 120 before lunch against Gloucestershire at Harrogate, only to follow it with 69 from 228 deliveries against Middlesex at Lord's, including one run in its final half-hour. He was heavily criticised, but Boycott top-scored in each innings as Yorkshire won by 69.

Once his wrist healed, Boycott was made to prove his fitness, scoring 121 against Warwickshire in the Second XI Championship at Edgbaston on the back of 81 for Brian Close's XI against New Zealand. Chris Old also played, and the 100th Scarborough Festival would be a first-class curtain call for all three. Boycott returned to Yorkshire's first team for the festival – and season's – finale, a Championship match against Northamptonshire. Moxon made way, despite being only 18 short of 1,000 first-class runs for a third consecutive summer. Boycott needed 69. Since establishing himself in the side in 1963, he had never missed the benchmark. The *Northern Echo*'s preview was headlined 'Boycott's final fling?' but nowhere in the copy did it suggest this would be his last appearance. The *Scarborough Evening News* did not even mention the possibility of one of cricket's great careers ending in their town. After all the false alarms, journalists were wary of drawing a line under Boycott. 'I don't remember anybody saying he was playing because it was going to be his last game,' Moxon tells me.

Northamptonshire bowler Alan Walker was looking forward to his trip to the seaside. 'Maybe because I'm a Yorkshireman it was always a big game for me because I wanted to do all right, but Scarborough was a fantastic place to play too,' he says. 'When you walk back on a night the whole place comes alive for cricket. You'll see the same people in the same pubs at the same times, stopping in the same guesthouses. My uncle and people from my village, Emley, go there every year, religiously. I think it's brilliant. It's a throwback to old-fashioned cricket.' It would be a memorable match for Walker.

Boycott had batted solidly for three hours 20 minutes to make 61 not out when Jim Love, yet to score, edged David Capel to third man. 'I'd bowled at him a little bit and never looked like getting him out,' Walker admits. 'He played me as if I was bowling it backwards! I was quite a good fielder so I don't know what I was doing at third man – maybe I was bowling at the other [Trafalgar Square] end. Jim Love nicked it between gully and slips and I remember him calling two. I've run round to my left, picked it up and pinged it in straight over the top. Boycott had touched down and gone back for a second run and as Jim Love's turned he's probably seen I've got the ball and sent him back. He was stranded two or three yards out. It was a good throw actually – even in Boycott's autobiography it says so. It's upsetting at the time for them but it's not a drama. I didn't really get any stick from the fans behind me because I think the attitude at that stage was that he'd get what was needed in the second innings. It's only subsequently it's become more of a talking point.'

Moxon recalls, 'Myself and Neil Hartley [also dropped] had gone to the pub up the road for lunch and word came round that "Love's run him out!"' Ashley Metcalfe had completely forgotten the incident. 'Boycs run out? That was unusual wasn't it! I should definitely have remembered that,' he laughs. Love went on to make his first Championship century for more than two years as Yorkshire declared at the end of day one on 352/7.

On day two, Bairstow fractured the forefinger first broken seven weeks earlier and was in hospital when, in front of an unusually large number of committeemen in town for a function that evening, Phil Carrick led Yorkshire to what David Hopps called, 'One of their most inspired hours of the season.' From 74/0 off 12 overs, Northamptonshire were bowled out for 197, their last seven wickets falling for 44. Shaw claimed a then-career-best 5-38. Back from hospital, Bairstow spoke to Boycott on the boundary to ask if he should enforce the follow-on, and was told to push for victory. The prospects were very good. A Stuart Fletcher delivery had chipped a bone in Geoff Cook's right index finger, and the visitors came out for the second innings with two makeshift openers. 'I think Wayne Larkins had just gone for a bit of a walk so it was, "Shit, where's Wayne?" and someone else had to open,' Walker explains. What followed summed up Yorkshire at that time, according to Metcalfe. 'We bowled a side out on a good pitch, but couldn't do it twice,' he points out.

'We batted poorly in the first innings and then in the second we did show some fight which culminated in David Ripley's first first-class hundred,' Walker recalls. 'Rips signed on when I signed on and got capped on the same day. He played really, really well. We avoided an innings defeat and just after tea, I think, he had the chance to get his maiden first-class hundred and the crowd were getting restless.' The Leeds-born wicketkeeper, who turned 20 the following day, had been released by Yorkshire in 1983 without making an appearance. Ripley had only made one first-class 50, against Surrey in 1984, but his patient batting had secured a draw and now the crowd wanted to see Boycott reach his landmark.

'We were batting on,' says captain Cook, who came in at nine to help Ripley to three figures. 'There was absolutely no reason, other than Boycott getting 1,000 runs, for us to declare. The whole mass of people in front of the pavilion, every ball we faced they were turning around and abusing us like you've never heard abuse in your life. It got nasty. They really felt we should declare. There was no thought in my mind about that whatsoever. First of all there was Ripley getting to his first hundred, and by the time he did there was nothing left in the game anyway. What was the point?' Ripley defied his home county for 293 minutes. 'They batted, batted and batted,' recalls Metcalfe – 'Probably in spite,' says Kevin Sharp.

'I've always been a watcher so I always sit in front of the dressing room at Scarborough,' says Walker, Northamptonshire's number 11 that day. 'Even when we go back there now, people sit in certain places just for gossip, to be part of it. It makes me laugh because I've never been a bat thrower, I don't enjoy it, but sometimes someone will get out at Scarborough – not in this particular match – and there'll be a few expletives and it'll be, "Ooh, ooh!" Don't sit there if you don't want to hear all that! I think they choose their spots to catch that sort of thing happening, but when it happens they seem amazed by it.

'In that game they started muttering, and then it increased to hearing people say we should declare and by the end they were turning around and shouting, "Declare! Declare!" because they wanted to see Geoffrey get his 1,000. They were pissed off by the end. I could see if you'd been there why you'd want it but there was just nothing in it for us. What was the point in going out there for – well, it probably would have been 20 overs with Boycs batting?! He has actually said there was no reason for us to declare. It would almost have looked as though, "Well, it's over to you to get your runs." I'm not sure he would have wanted that anyway, although he would have got them.'

Cook adds, 'Being captain in an environment like that, it was very wearing. It should have been a relief that the end of the season was coming but instead you thought, "Oh my word, here we go again!" We were amazed when a game against Yorkshire took place without any controversy. That sea of people at Scarborough, we just toyed with them. We were probably a little bit unprofessional but we just stoked up their ire.' The *Yorkshire Post* argued, 'The onus was on Yorkshire, having enforced the follow-on, to bowl out Northamptonshire,' and with Simon Dennis unable to bowl on the final day because of a back strain, they were incapable.

At 5.21pm, Northamptonshire declared on 422/8. The game was due to finish at 6pm, but Championship rules allowed the captains to call a halt during the last 40 minutes if they decided there was no chance of either side winning. With a 5,000 crowd inside North Marine Road, many were hoping Yorkshire – or rather Boycott – would come out for one last bat. 'I suppose the worst thing for them would have been if we'd got bowled out again and he had not got a chance to bat but they probably assumed the best case scenario was we'd get a bit in front, and he'd hit the winning run to get his 1,000 runs again,' says Walker.

'It was the arrogance of the whole environment really,' Cook comments. 'I didn't know it was his last game. It was a sad game to go out from his point of view but in a way that summed up his whole career. It was shrouded in mystery, shrouded in controversy, shrouded in people making decisions that he was the centre of, and they really shouldn't have had to.' Sharp was 42 short of 1,000 runs, but as usual he was laid back about it. 'I can vaguely remember it,' he tells me. 'I was probably under the influence of alcohol at Scarborough! It wouldn't have been a big issue for me. I'm guessing I would have thought, "They've done this because of Boycs." I wasn't particularly a big stats person, I just did my best.'

Boycott's Yorkshire career ended as his England career had – with nobody quite sure it was over. 'The only time I realised was when the game had finished,' Metcalfe says. 'He didn't take his pads off, he was sat in the changing room for an absolute age. I reckon it must have been well over an hour before he moved or did anything. Everybody else had got showered and changed. I remember thinking to myself, "I wonder if this is going to be his last game?" It just looked odd.' Metcalfe's memory is actually playing tricks. 'I wasn't padded up,' Boycott says when I put this to him. It is somehow right, though, that Metcalfe remembers Boycott the batsman, ready to go out and score more runs. 'I knew as I walked off the field my career had ended because I looked up at the clock to see what time it was and Bluey [Bairstow] checked with the umpires,' Boycott explains.

It was no more than gut instinct. Even with his 46th birthday a month away, he still wanted to keep playing, and Yorkshire had not yet decided if they would offer him the chance. Boycott's was not the only career in the balance. The *Telegraph and Argus* speculated his friends Graham Stevenson and Arnie Sidebottom could be released. Stevenson made 20 first-class appearances in 1983, then 14, four and two in the subsequent seasons. He joined Northamptonshire for 1987, and played once. Sidebottom too was injury-prone, playing nine times in each of the last two summers. He survived.

When the cricket committee met to decide the players' fate at 2pm on 23 September, there was speculation Boycott could be made captain. 'If Boycott were to win the role, when his whole future is again uncertain, it would confirm him as the Great Survivor,' wrote Hopps. Yorkshire were well blessed with openers but there was a school of thought he should lead from the middle order, passing his knowledge on to Moxon, Metcalfe and Blakey. If it seemed logical, it was unlikely to work. 'After he retired I learnt far more from him and he became far more open,' says Metcalfe. 'There were a couple of periods in my career when I struggled for runs and I spent some time with Boycs. It wasn't around technical issues, just the way you applied yourself and concentrated, and how you thought about the game. I learnt more in a couple of hours talking to him than I had in four seasons playing with him. Once he finished his own career he offered far more.'

The cricket committee voted 4-1 to release Boycott. A general committee amendment proposing a new contract was defeated 12-9, and when the retained list was put to them, they supported it 18-3. Boycott's 24-year Yorkshire career was over. 'Unlike last time when the general committee was overthrown and Boycott reinstated, there seemed no way back,' the *Yorkshire Post*'s front page concluded. According to committeeman Bryan Stott, 'It was just the obvious next step. It had run its course. Had we not been blinkered in 1983, and made the sensible decision to say, "Have one more year," who knows what would have happened?' Chairman Brian Walsh produced some suitable rhetoric. 'Boycott has been one of the world's great batsmen, a colossus of the stage,' he told the media. 'But the future lies with the young and we're confident they are going to grab it by the scruff of the neck.'

'The committee had probably had enough of it all and we'd had a decent season,' Sharp reflects. 'As far as Geoff was concerned, he never went away because he was still on the committee. Bizarre, isn't it, when you think about it, but that's Yorkshire cricket. So it wasn't a big deal. I didn't really have any great emotion about it. A lot of what did happen just washed over me. Great players come to an end. He was 45 years old – how long can you play for? We had some good young players and if we'd had an overseas player we would have been quite a formidable outfit.' For Metcalfe, though, 'It was actually quite surprising when it did come out because I thought he would keep playing for a couple of years at least, but actually when I look back it probably wasn't a surprise. The time was good for the club but Boycs didn't see himself as not contributing or as not still being the best player. I thought at that stage he still had enough power to dictate when and how he was going to finish.'

When asked if he had considered Boycott as captain, Brian Close, who retired from county cricket aged 46, commented, 'Quite honestly the thought had never entered my head.' A decision on who would be was deferred until November, however. Bairstow had looked increasingly forlorn in 1986 and the pressure seemed to be taking its toll on his wicketkeeping. As usual when Yorkshire wanted to change captain, alternatives were thin on the ground. Neil Hartley had averaged 27 that season, nudging his career figure up to a paltry 25, and had scored more slowly even than Boycott. Vice-captain Carrick was seventh in Yorkshire's seasonal bowling averages, and had held talks with Derbyshire, worried he too might be shown the door.

'There was a bit of speculation about me taking over,' Geoff Cook tells me. 'One or two people from the Yorkshire newspapers rang up. I sat down one night on my own having a beer and I thought, "If there are any legs in this, do I want it?" The next morning when they rang, I said, "I honestly, unequivocally, have no interest in it." It was a bit of an ego boost, but it wasn't even a labour of love, it was a masochistic commitment. I was never envious of Yorkshire's players, I've got to say. Maybe that was a weakness on my behalf, not wanting to take on the ultimate challenge, but the whole environment I never found particularly enjoyable. There were really good cricketers who maybe didn't fulfil their potential because of the burdens of expectation, the burdens of history, the external burdens. When you're involved in Yorkshire cricket everything's magnified.'

With Cook emphatically out of the running, Carrick replaced Bairstow as Yorkshire's sixth captain in nine seasons. 'His effort could not be faulted,' Close said of Bairstow. 'But having to look after everything affected his form behind the stumps and this was something we could not afford.' Bairstow and Carrick went back nearly 20 years, team-mates for Yorkshire Schools in 1967, as their fathers had been at Laisterdyke. The cricket committee recommended Carrick 5-1 but the general committee were more sceptical, seven of 19 opposing.

There was still a potential twist in the Boycott story. Glamorgan and Derbyshire showed an interest – 'They contacted me, I didn't contact them,' he stresses. The Welsh county signed Alan Butcher instead, but Derbyshire – prepared to risk supporter backlash – verbally offered a two-year contract. Yorkshire's new rules had only banned Yorkshire players serving on the committee, and set a precedent that changes could not be retrospective. Dr John Turner had recovered from illness to fight the Wakefield election in early 1987, but there was the possibility Boycott could spend the next two seasons playing for a rival while helping make decisions at Yorkshire.

The morning he made up his mind, the *Yorkshire Post* asserted, 'Boycott looks certain to sign for Derbyshire next month.' Instead, on the day the decision was made for Championship matches to be spread over four days from 1988 – a format better suited to Boycott's patient batting – he declined. A glorious career was effectively, if not officially, over. 'It is not easy to imagine a season without him,' wrote *Wisden* editor Graeme Wright. 'I have a feeling he will be back, for Yorkshire even.' He was not. Boycott never played again, not even in a charity match.

'Some committee members, and particularly the president, have tried to stir up potential opposition to me serving on the committee if I played for another county,' he explained. 'Some of them have such an unhealthy obsession with Geoffrey Boycott that they spend their time trying to get me out of the club. Yorkshire come first and I have put my career on one side so that I can go on helping the county.' In Australia when the votes were cast, Boycott was re-elected Wakefield's representative. Claiming to be too busy writing his autobiography – out of TCCB jurisdiction now his playing days were over – Boycott was not seen at a committee meeting between November 1986 and November 1987, to the frustration of even his supporters. 'Why does he stay on the committee if he has no desire or interest in other aspects of the operations?' John Callaghan asked in the *Yorkshire Evening Post*.

Boycott was still causing arguments among Yorkshire fans but the end of his playing career effectively marked the conclusion of the War of the White Roses. As usual, Walsh had chosen the right word. Boycott retired a colossus, Yorkshire's third-highest run-scorer of all time, their only world-class player for nearly two decades, an ultra-reliable run machine with the charisma to make some supporters more fanatical about him than the county he epitomised and dominated; a lightning rod for controversy and conflict, whether he meant to be or not. Of all the millions of words said and written about the most traumatic period in Yorkshire's history, perhaps the saddest come from Bryan Stott. 'Geoffrey was a good player,' he tells me. 'I just wish he'd played for somebody else. We'd have still been able to see him play for England, he'd have still got 100 tons and all that. It's a pity.'

Postscript

GEOFFREY BOYCOTT had been retired for little more than half a year before Yorkshire were lifting silverware at Lord's.

With the scores level in a thrilling 1987 Benson and Hedges Cup Final, Jim Love kept out Winston Davis' final-ball yorker to win the trophy by virtue of having lost one wicket fewer than Northamptonshire.

New captain Phil Carrick had claimed the first prize available to him and there was an air of optimism around the club not seen for a dozen years, perhaps longer.

'Phil made a really big effort to try and hold the club together and get some unity,' explains Martyn Moxon, who put on 97 for the first wicket with Ashley Metcalfe. 'We had some young players in the team – Paul Jarvis, Richard Blakey, Ashley, Stuart Fletcher. There was fresh blood around the place and we played really well in that Benson and Hedges [competition].

'It was a brilliant day at Lord's and everyone will always remember that. It was a great game of cricket, perfect weather, it went to the last ball. It was just a day to remember.'

Huddersfield-born Alan Walker was on the losing side that day. 'Lord's seemed to be full of Yorkshire people,' he recalls. 'When they were on top it must have been brilliant.'

Having finally tasted success after a largely barren decade and a half when the club revolved around one man, some drew the inevitable conclusion. 'We couldn't have done this with Boycott in the team,' claimed cricket chairman Brian Close.

Earlier in the competition Yorkshire-born cricket journalist Don Mosey had noted 'a Yorkshire team transformed from the hang-dog, bickering, demoralised bunch of previous years into a side with a spring in its collective step, a glint in the eye'.

The club's problems ran deeper than just one man, however.

'Initially I think it just carried on without Boycott,' David Hall, the Devotee who became a vice-president of the club and director of its museum, says.

'After we won the final we hardly won a game, I think we just ran out of steam,' recalls batsman Kevin Sharp as the then-title challengers repeated the pattern of the past three seasons. 'The pitch got flatter. We really fancied our chances in the Championship but we couldn't get wickets at Headingley after that and because we were at the top people didn't want to lose to us.'

As Metcalfe points out: 'It was an ageing squad and we didn't have the depth of the other counties, who all had overseas players.'

Once again Yorkshire's season collapsed midway through and they finished eighth – their last top-half finish until 1995. David Byas succeeding Moxon as captain the following year gave the side a tougher edge, and in 2001 they ended Yorkshire's 33-year wait for the County Championship trophy they had hogged for so long.

In 2000 the Championship had split into two divisions, and with Byas shunted aside after the title win in the quest for younger blood – he retired, then signed for Lancashire – the champions were relegated in 2002, the 50-over Cheltenham and Gloucester Trophy picked up on the way even less of a consolation than the 1983 Sunday League had been. A second relegation followed in 2011, the year Lancashire celebrated their first title outright since 1934, but it had a cathartic effect. Executive chairman Colin Graves forced through a restructuring of the coaching staff which saw Sharp lose his job as batting coach and Australian Jason Gillespie installed as head coach.

Yorkshire won promotion from Division Two in 2012, and claimed Division One titles in 2014 and 2015. Director of cricket Moxon had at last been able to reap what he had sown, having left his coaching role at Yorkshire the winter before their drought-ending 2001 title, and Durham in the months prior to their maiden trophy as a first-class county.

During his playing days, fast bowler Gillespie had been one of many to benefit from the overdue decision to drop the county's Yorkshire-only stance in November 1990. 'There was a commendable sense of pride among Yorkshire members but we were fighting a losing battle really,' Hall reflects.

Two years after pressure from then-captain Carrick and his players had come to nothing, the committee voted 18-1 to allow youngsters who had grown up in the county to represent Yorkshire even if they had been born elsewhere. The first to join was a 16-year-old born in Manchester but brought up in Sheffield from the age of eight. Michael Vaughan would not only represent Yorkshire with distinction, but lead England to a first Ashes series win in 18 years. Once that initial obstacle was removed, full parity with their rivals quickly followed thanks to the appointment of another hands-on president.

Lord Mountgarret had been moved aside in January 1990 amid concerns he was too active in the role. But the death of his successor, Sir Leonard Hutton, before the year was out saw the appointment of another man unwilling to be just a ceremonial figurehead. Former police chief constable Sir Lawrence Byford ignored the objections of some supporters and former and current players – including the likes of Michael Parkinson, Fred Trueman and Paul Jarvis – and persuaded the general committee that an overseas player was a cricketing and financial necessity.

Knowing what the answer would be, he did not stop to ask the wider membership. The initial proposal had been for one overseas player to supplement a squad of Yorkshire-born (or raised) players, but Boycott and Tony Vann successfully pushed for an open-door policy. Almost immediately Australia fast bowler Craig McDermott signed a three-year contract but when groin surgery prevented him taking it up, the honour of being Yorkshire's first overseas player fell instead to India batsman Sachin Tendulkar in a 1992 Benson and Hedges Cup group match against Kent at Headingley.

The performances of Yorkshire's overseas players have ranged from the legendary to the ordinary, but the infusion of new ideas has arguably been more important than anything provided on the field. The three titles Yorkshire have won in the 21st Century have come under the direction of Australian coaches, with Wayne Clark overseeing the first.

Despite that, the 2015 Championship success had a very home-grown feel. The county's three overseas players – Cheteshwar Pujara, Aaron Finch and Glenn Maxwell – played bit-part roles and the vast majority of the team came through the academy Bob Appleyard had been such a driving force behind setting up in 1989, with Mike Bore its head coach.

Yorkshire's outstanding performer in 2015 was a wicketkeeper named Bairstow, who passed 1,000 Championship runs for the season despite international duties limiting him to nine appearances. Jonny is the youngest son of David, who committed suicide in 1998, while Arnie Sidebottom's son Ryan was the old head in the bowling attack.

The world's best batsman was again a Yorkshireman, although in an era of central contracts the only appearance Sheffield's Joe Root made in 2015 came in a Twenty20 Cup defeat, making emulating Boycott and taking on the captaincy impossible for as long as he remains an international cricketer.

In 2017 he became England's full-time Test captain having only led Yorkshire in three Championship matches.

The vast majority of the Englishmen in the 2015 squad would have qualified to play for Yorkshire before 1990, although like future Ashes-winning captain Vaughan, exciting young batsman Jack Leaning had been born elsewhere (in his case in Bristol to Yorkshire parents) but learnt his cricket in the county (in York). Leading wicket-taker Jack Brooks was born in Oxford and had been signed from Northamptonshire, the side Yorkshire paid a transfer fee to sign England all-rounder David Willey from in the winter of 2015/16.

Pushed out of the first team partly by Vaughan's emergence, Metcalfe joined Nottinghamshire in 1996 – 'I left to see if the grass was any greener and was it? No' – and is now chief executive of British Weightlifting, based in an office just down the road from Yorkshire's Headingley headquarters. Chris Old finished his playing career with Northumberland before retiring to Cornwall. He used to own a fish and chip shop there, but now works for Sainsbury's. Sharp joined up with an old team-mate as batting and second XI coach at Worcestershire. 'When I left Yorkshire as a coach [then-director of cricket] Steve Rhodes was the first person I wrote to because if I could have had any choice as to where I'd go, it would be Worcester,' he tells me. Sharp worked his way up to head coach in 2018, and is part of the England set-up too – recognition in part of his work with Root and Jonny Bairstow at Headingley.

Since retiring from the legal profession, Matthew Caswell has drawn on his Iraqi heritage, completing a doctorate in Arabic and writing a number of books. 'I stopped being a member once there was a counter-revolution,' he tells me, pointing out of his living room window towards Roundhay Park. 'I was much more likely to watch the local club here than Yorkshire.' Ted Lester retired as Yorkshire's scorer in 1988 and died in March 2015, six days after his former team-mate

Appleyard and three months before Russell Devy. Mike Bore died in May 2017.

Those who had been calling for a smaller committee finally won the argument in 1993, when the 23 district representatives became 12. The county was split into four parts, each with three representatives. The new rules stipulated only one per district could be a former Yorkshire player. 'That made the decision for us,' says Bryan Stott. 'Bob [Appleyard] and I just automatically stood down and left Brian [Close] there, rightly so, as the colossus he was.'

Boycott supported the reorganisation, but it cost him his place on the committee he had served for ten years, finishing fourth in the West district poll behind Philip Akroyd, Tony Cawdry and former player Bob Platt.

In December 2002, the banks demanded action with Yorkshire's debts – not helped by the legal battles of the 1970s and 80s – now in danger of becoming unmanageable at around £6m. The committee was abolished and replaced by a management board dubbed the 'Gang of Four' – Colin Graves, Robin Smith, Brian Bouttell and former spinner Geoff Cope. In 2017 Yorkshire's debt had risen to around £24m, potentially rising to £40m to fund Headingley's new main stand. They are fortunate almost half is owed to a trust set up by Graves, now chairman of the England and Wales Cricket Board.

In 2005 the club made a conscious effort to strengthen bonds with its ex-players by forming the Yorkshire County Cricket Club Players' Association, with Stott its first chairman and Cope the secretary. The following year they went a step further, introducing a policy whereby the presidency was held by illustrious ex-players for a maximum of two annual terms. Appleyard was the first, followed by Close, former England manager and chairman of selectors Ray Illingworth, and Boycott. Before his death in 2014, Phil Sharpe had been earmarked to succeed Dickie Bird. Instead that honour fell to John Hampshire, but he was in poor health and it got the better of him a couple of weeks before he was due for re-election in March 2017. He was succeeded by Richard Hutton.

Boycott was embarking on a career as a forthright media pundit when he finally joined Yorkshire's cricket committee in 1992, and was given honorary life membership the following year.

In 2006 he joined the club's board and proposed Fred Trueman as president, having finally reconciled his differences with the fast bowler. Boycott had sent Trueman a 70th birthday card in 2001, but it was the news Boycott had been diagnosed with throat cancer the following year which brought the feud to an end.

'I'm quite friendly with Geoffrey now,' says Hall, another who opposed him in the 1980s. 'But there's no doubt about it, the turning point in his life was when he had cancer. Fred, who had been very anti for many years, became very sympathetic and would speak to him regularly on the telephone [every Sunday at 1pm] during the time he was in remission. Their relationship was mended in the latter years, as was mine. I now have quite a good relationship with him.'

Boycott survived his illness but in 2006 lung cancer claimed the pipe-smoking Trueman. Sidney Fielden, who had also unsuccessfully nominated him for the presidency, read psalm 23 at the funeral.

Sadly, some hostilities remained, and Appleyard and Richard Hutton objected to Boycott's nomination as president. In response to Hutton's letter to Graves, Boycott wrote to his long-time critic, 'Your bitterness, resentment and jealousy appears to know no bounds'.

Boycott was voted in by 1,115 votes to 109, a level of acceptance that would never have been possible even at the peak of his popularity as a Yorkshire player. Hutton was made a vice-president, an honour also granted to one-time rebels Fielden, Tony Vann and Roy Wilkinson. 'I think he [Boycott] always wanted to be the president,' Lester told me. Boycott and his wife Rachel proved energetic fundraisers during his two-year presidency, bringing in over £120,000.

Close also succumbed to cancer, but typically only after a prolonged fight and not before seeing Yorkshire finally restored to the pedestal he helped keep them on. He passed away four days after Andrew Gale emulated him in leading the White Rose to back-to-back Championships. Gale was unable to complete the hat-trick as Close did in 1968. To date no captain, no county, has since.

Close captained Yorkshire's academy side into his 60s and his fearlessness left an indelible mark on Gale, who gave up the captaincy to succeed Gillespie as head coach in November 2016. 'I want to play my cricket just like him', Gale had written in a tribute. It highlighted the important links between the past and present at Yorkshire.

Boycott may have failed to win re-election to the board in Easter 2016 but, like Close, his influence on the club will outlast him. Honouring Yorkshire's many glory days is an important ingredient in the greatness of the club but remembering the bad times is necessary too.

For as long as there is a Yorkshire County Cricket Club there will be Yorkshiremen passionately arguing about it, but the War of the White Roses is definitely a thing of the past.

It is vital its lessons are never forgotten.

Select Bibliography

Books

John Arlott, *Fred: Portrait of a Fast Bowler,* Eyre and Spottiswoode, 1971

David Bairstow with Derek Hodgson, *A Yorkshire Diary,* Sidwick and Jackson, 1984

Dickie Bird, *My Autobiography,* Hodder and Stoughton, 1997

Henry Blofeld, *The Packer Affair,* Readers Union, 1978

Derrick Boothroyd, *Half a Century of Yorkshire Cricket*, Kennedy Brothers Publishing, 1981

Geoffrey Boycott, *Put to the Test,* Arthur Barker, 1979

Geoffrey Boycott, *Opening Up,* Arthur Barker, 1980

Geoffrey Boycott, *In the Fast Lane: West Indies Tour 1981,* Arthur Barker, 1981

Geoffrey Boycott, *Boycott the Autobiography,* Macmillan, 1987

Geoffrey Boycott, *Boycott on Cricket,* Partridge Press, 1990

Geoffrey Boycott, *The Corridor of Certainty: My Life Beyond Cricket,* Simon and Schuster, 2014

John Callaghan, *Boycott, a Cricketing Legend,* Pelham Books, 1982

Stephen Chalke and Derek Hodgson, *No Coward Soul: The Remarkable Story of Bob Appleyard,* Fairfield, 2003

Brian Close, *I Don't Bruise Easily,* Macdonald and Jane's Publishers, 1978

Andrew Collomosse, *Magnificent Seven: Yorkshire's Champions of the Championship Years*, Great Northern Books, June 2010

Paul Donnelley, *Cricket On This Day*, Pitch Publishing, 2009

Grenville Firth, *Yorkshire's Cricketing Legends: Yorkshire-born Test Cricketers*, Breedon Books, 2009

Guy Fraser-Sampson, *Cricket at the Crossroads: Class, Colour and Controversy from 1967 to 1977*, Elliott and Thompson, 2011

John Hampshire, *Family Argument: My 20 Years in Yorkshire Cricket*, George Allen and Unwin, 1983

Alan Hill, *Brian Close: Cricket's Lionheart*, Methuen, 2003

Derek Hodgson, *The Official History of Yorkshire County Cricket Club*, Crowood Press, 1989

David Hopps, *A Century of Great Cricket Quotes*, Robson Books, 2006

Martin Howe, *Norman Yardley: Yorkshire's Gentleman Cricketer*, ACS Publications 2015

Ray Illingworth, *Yorkshire and Back: The Autobiography of Ray Illingworth*, Queen Anne Press, 1980

Ray Illingworth, *Ray Illingworth the Tempestuous Years 1979–1983*, Sidwick and Jackson, 1987

Christopher Martin-Jenkins, *Wisden Book of County Cricket, 1873–1980*, Queen Anne Press, 1981

Leo McKinstry, *Boycott: A Cricketing Hero*, Collins Willow, 2005

Robert Mills, *Field of Dreams: Headingley 1890–2001*, Great Northern, 2001

John Morgan and David Joy, *Trueman's Tales: Fiery Fred, Yorkshire's Cricketing Giant*, Great Northern, 2007

Don Mosey, *Boycott*, Penguin, 1986

Don Mosey, *We Don't Play for Fun: A Story of Yorkshire Cricket*, Methuen, 1988

John Stern and Marcus Williams (eds), *The Essential Wisden: An Anthology of Wisden Cricketers' Almanack*, Bloomsbury, 2013

Fred Trueman, *Ball of Fire: An Autobiography*, Granada, 1977

Fred Trueman, *As It Was: The Memoirs of Fred Trueman,* Macmillan, 2004

David Warner, *The Sweetest Rose: 150 Years of Yorkshire County Cricket Club 1863–2013,* Great Northern, 2012

Chris Waters, *Fred Trueman – The Authorised Biography,* Aurum, 2011

John Woodcock, *The Times One Hundred Greatest Cricketers,* Macmillan, 1998

Anthony Woodhouse, *The History of Yorkshire County Cricket Club,* Christopher Helm, 1989

Peter Wynne-Thomas and Peter Arnold, *Cricket in Conflict,* Newnes Books, 1984

Newspapers, Periodicals and Annuals (various editions)
Bradford Telegraph and Argus/Sports Extra/Yorkshire Sports
The Cricketer
Daily Mirror
Daily Star
Daily Telegraph
The Guardian
Harrogate Herald and Advertiser
Northern Echo
The People/Sunday People
Scarborough Evening News/Mercury
The Sun
Sunday Mirror
Sunday Telegraph
The Times
York Evening Press
Yorkshire Evening Post
Yorkshire County Cricket Club Yearbook
Yorkshire Post
Wisden Cricketers' Almanack

Videos/DVDs

The Official History of Yorkshire County Cricket Club, Watershed
   Pictures, 1991

*Yorkshire's Cricketing Legends: Perfectionist Player to President
   Geoffrey Boycott,* Leeds Metropolitan University, 2013

Websites

Cricket Archive

Cricinfo

The Guardian

Wikipedia

Yorkshire County Cricket Club

Index